A big thank you to my amazing wife, Allison, for helping edit this book.

Also, thank you to Allison, my dad (Larry), mom (Beth), brother (James), and sister-in-law (Lacy) for all the love, support, and feedback throughout this journey.

Preface

Meatheads expecting this book to focus solely on sports will be let down; historians expecting a politically correct, hoity-toity writing style can take a hike; readers expecting an enlightening masterpiece for the ages can probably shut the book now.

Go ahead and save yourself some time. I'll wait.

Contents

Introduction

Oh, you're still here? All right, let's do this!

As an overzealous college freshman looking to unleash my creative mind on the world, I had this crazy idea to marry my interests in sports and history by comparing U.S. presidents to athletes. The backwardness of the idea made so much sense in my head that I was determined to merge these two worlds as the foundation for a graduate-level thesis or dissertation. That is, until I ran my idea by a history professor who looked at me like I was an abomination; or worse, as if I told her that I still believed Christopher Columbus discovered America.

What new, ground breaking information was I going to unearth in this fictitious playground? How would my hypothetical sports-history hybrid contribute to the broader society? It was made clear that I would need to re-think my idea if it were going to withstand the scrutiny of intense academic judgement. Universities apparently prefer their degrees to be earned off of serious research that contributes to academia. You know, unless you're a celebrity who brings copious amounts of cash and cachet to a school; or if you're Kermit the Frog because, of course, he also has a Ph.D.

Rather than spending half a decade trying to fit this square peg into a round hole, I decided to stick it to the institutional fat cats of higher education and double down (literally), spending roughly a decade cobbling every bit of this book together. While it has been a long and winding road, this ridiculous marriage between sports and history has now been brought together in holy matrimony. More importantly, its union has birthed a number of important, philosophical questions that are sure to stand the test of time alongside those posed by Socrates, Aristotle, Kanye West and the rest.

For example, have you ever wondered which president would be better suited to run a two-minute drill? Or which one would have relished (and succeeded) in locking down a LeBron James iso? Was Abraham Lincoln actually the GOAT? Would John Tyler have survived in the age of social media? And, as most of you are probably wondering, who the hell was John Tyler?

Of course you haven't thought about these questions because it's a ridiculous premise. Luckily for you, though, I've already spent far more time analyzing how presidents would fit inside a sports ecosystem than I like to admit. I've broken down each president to examine how their personalities, skill sets, and accomplishments in office would manifest themselves within athletics.

Just as professional sports are littered with plenty more Jonathan Benders and Jim Sorgis than Michael Jordans and John Elways, there are more James Garfields and Chester Arthurs than there are George Washingtons and Abraham

Lincolns. That is to say, there are far more average players and presidents than transcendent ones.

Just as every professional athlete has served a role on their team and been judged against fellow athletes, so have presidents who are judged against their fellow politicians. Right or wrong, we have an insatiable desire to see how someone stacks up against their competition. Examining each president will not only allow us to unpack who they were as politicians and humans, but also how their sports journeys would have been shaped.

Besides, meaninglessly comparing one person's success or failure to another's is the pillar of any hokey political or sports talk show, article, or message board debate. Especially when we get to critique professionals who are immensely more talented at their jobs than 99 percent of us are at our own jobs. So why not cross-pollinate the two areas and see what monstrous abomination we can unleash on the world?

1

George Washington (1789-1797)

Simply put: Washington was a straight-up baller. Granted, that might not be the first word that comes to mind when thinking of the nation's first president, but that doesn't make it any less true. *So what* if James Naismith was a century away from inventing a game called "basketball" and *so what* if the term "baller" was an additional century away from its origination. Without a doubt, Washington was *the* baller of his time.

He was a bona fide superstar. But to simply say Washington was a superstar and end the discussion doesn't do him justice—and wouldn't make for much of a chapter, either. There have been a number of superstar athletes capable of competing with Washington. But Washington was the first of his kind in so many regards, revered by his countrymen and universally respected. He wasn't just the star player. He was the star player, the team's head coach, and its general manager.

Growing up in a moderate, slave-owning, planter family, Washington ascended to the presidency unanimously after his success as a general and commander in chief of the Army during the Revolutionary War. He is still the only unanimously-elected president in the country's history.

Washington was an unbelievable supervisor of personalities as he helped unify and effectively manage a "who's who" of political celebrities and egos that included John Adams, Thomas Jefferson, Alexander Hamilton, Henry Knox, and Edmund Randolph. Despite its stark contrast in personalities, the nation's first president managed to keep this talented but strong-headed group of statesmen from splintering in a way that would have been detrimental to the country's survival.

Washington's cabinet assembly formed a super team that put the likes of the Miami Heat's "Big Three" of LeBron James, Dwayne Wade, and Chris Bosh to shame. It makes that trio look like the Jonas Brothers next to the Beatles or make the Golden State Warriors' former quartet of Kevin Durant, Steph Curry, Klay Thompson, and Draymond Green look like One Direction by comparison.

Wait, I probably went too far there. One Direction was definitely more talented than the Warriors…

An abnormally athletic man for his time, Washington was considered by many to be an action hero. He stood an imposing 6'2" at a time when the average male height was 5'6", depending on which source you believe. That height advantage relative to his peers would have given him a distinct advantage on the court.

A team sport would have been imperative for Washington because he wouldn't have been as great of a president—and, thus, an athlete—if he didn't have other men to lead, inspire, and unify. Not to mention the fact that Washington flatly refused the title of "king" when it was offered to him because he was dedicated to securing the stability of the American Republic rather than securing his own self-aggrandizement. That rules out any individual sports.

While Washington was known to have an occasional temper, he was by no means hot-headed or overly emotional. Washington knew how to keep his cool and, despite some feistiness, did not exert the level of anger or aggression that accompanies sports like football or hockey. Yes, he could have been a team's field general and commanded the quarterback position; after all, he was literally a field general in America's fight for independence.

He could even have been a great baseball player. Washington would have resembled a dream shortstop. A two-way player, oozing with the ideal leadership qualities to command the infield, while working well with his teammates to create a cohesive and resolute squad. He was known to encourage his soldiers to exercise and play games when not on duty. Not only did Washington participate and play catch, sometimes throwing for hours at a time, but he also partook in "wicket," similar to today's version of cricket.

Most likely sport: Basketball

However, the fact is a superstar in basketball has more power and influence on a game than a superstar in any other sport, and you could count on one hand the number of people who have had more influence on the country than Washington.

Playing as a traditional "three" would allow the dynamic Washington to contribute in more facets as he possessed one of the best all-around games of any president in history. Washington would have been able to do it all on the court. From offense, defense, and leadership to ball handling, court vision, and an ability to make those around him better, Washington would have dominated the NBA.

Best Comparison: Larry Bird

As one of the greatest players of all time, Larry Legend shares a lot in common with Washington. Not only were they great competitors in their occupation, but they shared similar personalities, as well.

Despite their ability to come up big in big moments, neither man sought the spotlight. In fact, both were very hesitant about it at first. To say neither Washington nor Bird embraced the attention immediately would be an understatement. Similar to how Washington had no desire to enter the world of politics as a brand-new nation's leader, when Larry Bird was 18 years old and ready for college, he dropped out of Indiana University and stepped away from a Bob Knight scholarship because he was too overwhelmed by the situation. After a year off and three years of college at the much smaller Indiana State University, Bird entered the NBA and took the league by storm, proving himself anything but overwhelmed. He had entered the professional ranks at a time when the fledgling league desperately needed help boosting its fanbase and viewership.

Bird helped catapult the NBA to new heights with his rugged demeanor, sharp shooting, and flair for the dramatic. And his rivalry with Magic Johnson revitalized the league, helping it evolve into the billion-dollar industry it is today. The stories of Bird telling opponents how many points he was going to score on a given night or where he was going to take, and make, his game-winning shot are legendary.

In that same vein, Britain was Washington's Lakers. And Washington's entire presidency took place in the final two minutes of the fourth quarter. With the game, and an entire country on the line, Washington helped lead America to victory in the Revolutionary War. He balked at becoming a king, and even a third term as president, in favor of returning the power to the people. He helped ratify the U.S. Constitution and the Bill of Rights.

Perhaps his biggest accomplishment as president was that he never faltered in the clutch. Under unrelenting pressure to keep America from crumbling, Washington succeeded admirably. One ill-timed turnover and the United States of America likely never exists. But it didn't happen. Washington defeated Britain, helping create a new nation by working relentlessly and outsmarting his opponent.

From one champion to another, Washington and Bird are clear-cut Hall of Famers who have earned their reputations as two of the greatest of all time.

Trading Card Stats

George Washington	Name	Larry Bird
•Father of Our Country •The Old Fox •Mr. President	**Nickname**	•Larry Legend •The Hick from French Lick
•1789-1797	**Experience**	•1979-1992
•57	**Age Entering the League**	•22
•6’2”/175	**HT/WT**	•6’9”/220
•First Term: None •Second Term: Federalist	**Team**	•Boston Celtics
•French and Indian War participant •Revolutionary War •Whiskey Rebellion •Jay Treaty •Pinckney Treaty	**Stats**	•24.3 points, 10 rebounds and 6.3 assists per game •3-time NBA champion •2-time NBA Finals MVP •3-time league MVP •12-time All-Star •Olympic gold medalist
•Billiards •Cards •Fox hunting •Walking •Horse riding •Swordsmanship	**Hobbies**	•Wine enthusiast with his own line
•“My movements to the chair of government will be accompanied by feelings not unlike those of a culprit who is going to the place of his execution.”	**Quote**	•“I want all of you to know I am winning this thing. I’m just looking around to see who’s gonna finish up second.”
•Liked gambling and was the largest American distiller of alcohol in 1778	**Interesting**	•Bird would tell his opponents what he was about to do on the court just to prove that nobody could stop him
•Yes	**Hall of Fame**	•Yes

2

John Adams (1797-1801)

Just because you're one of the most qualified people ever for a job doesn't mean you'll succeed once there. Just ask Adams.

He is regarded as one of the smartest, most well-prepared men to make his way into the White House. Unfortunately for Adams, his production didn't live up to the talent.

Adams was born in Massachusetts as a direct descendant of Puritan colonists, and he began studying law at Harvard when he turned 16 years old. Adams is still widely viewed as one of the most intellectually gifted presidents to ever lead the United States. As a statesman, diplomat, and political philosopher, Adams excelled. He was a successful practitioner of the law, standing for what he believed to be right even in the face of criticism and hostility.

When the Boston Massacre occurred in 1770, Adams was one of the only lawyers in the colonies willing to defend the eight accused British soldiers amid rising tensions. He did so understanding that the soldiers had been provoked by an angry mob and deserved a fair trial. Adams exhibited a high level of courage and morality as a lawyer by defending the British soldiers, despite being a leading purveyor of the American Revolution, which he helped launch by being part of a group that wrote the Declaration of Independence. He then played a key role in negotiating the Treaty of Paris, which brought an end to the war in 1783.

The nation's second president was considerably well rounded. However, Adams was insecure and often made decisions based on his own opinions, which created enemies in both political parties with his *screw you* attitude. This began to occur with more regularity once he was president.

Adams is the first and only president to maintain his predecessor's cabinet upon entering office. There was no precedent for handling a previous president's cabinet at the time, so Adams kept Washington's crew intact. This turned out to be a huge mistake as Adams did not get along well with Thomas Jefferson or Alexander Hamilton and each actively tried to impede Adams.

Adams may ultimately have been better off playing an individual sport because of the tension with teammates. In that scenario, he could have displayed his brilliance and been free of the burdens that come with needing to be a willing and reliable teammate.

Most likely sport: Football

Adams' talent, though, was so evident and overwhelming that he would have gravitated to a sport that had a larger societal impact, more spotlight, and played out on a bigger stage. Adams possessed so much talent that he would still have been good in a team sport, but it would have been more difficult to navigate. He consistently proved his toughness and forcefulness, not to mention an irritability, which makes him a great contender for a contact sport. He also showed a feisty resolve in his unwillingness to bend on his principles.

At 5'7" and 150 pounds, Adams wouldn't exactly strike fear in the heart of the opposition based on stature alone. However, his stocky physique and bravery would have made him a very formidable football player.

Adams wasn't fit to be the leader of the team, but he possessed so much skill that he needed to be involved in every play. As a result, Adams would have made a very good running back.

Best Comparison: Ricky Williams

On the surface, Adams seemed like a presidential prodigy. He could have been the Mozart of music. The Picasso of painting. The Taylor Swift of victimization.

Instead, his stubbornness as a leader held him back. As did a personality that wasn't completely compatible with his era's political climate.

Similarly, Ricky Williams appeared to possess the talent that would have made him one of the greatest running backs of all time. Williams burst onto the scene as a star at the University of Texas by becoming a two-time All-American and a Heisman winner. The New Orleans Saints traded eight draft picks to move up in the 1999 draft and acquire Williams in a deal with the team formerly known as the Washington Racial Slurs. (Side note: the Cincinnati Bengals rejected a similar offer from the Saints—one that would have yielded nine draft picks, including three first-rounders—in order to draft Akili Smith. Yeah, Akili Smith…Bengals gonna Bengal.)

Williams spent three productive years with the Saints before being traded to the Miami Dolphins. As a Dolphin, Williams began to blossom into one of the league's top rushers. However, his enigmatic personality began to clash with the structured rigidity of the NFL when he failed a third drug test for substance abuse in 2004 and was likely to face a suspension. At that point, Williams decided he was no longer willing to acquiesce to the NFL's hypocrisy that spoon-fed its players painkillers with no regard for long-term consequences. At the same time, they would not allow players to smoke weed as a method for dealing with physical pain. So, Williams retired.

He would return for the 2005 season after a year off before being suspended for the entire 2006 season due to another failed drug test. Williams then returned to the field in 2007, ultimately retiring in 2012 with more than 10,000 rushing yards on his resume.

Like Adams, Williams became a world traveler, a smoker, a voracious reader, and also struggled with mental illness. Adams was believed to have been manic-depressive, suffering from extreme highs and lows. Williams, on the other hand, suffered from a very public bout of social-anxiety disorder.

They also shared a common cause by fighting for what they believed in. Adams fought Jefferson (philosophical reasons) and Hamilton (personal reasons) in an attempt to stay true to his vision of the American Republic, while Williams fought the perception that the NFL was doing all it could to protect its players from the dangers of enacting mini-car collisions on every single snap. To this day, Williams is still fighting on behalf of NFL players to make recreational marijuana use permissible in the NFL—a cause that has garnered a lot of support as it becomes legal in more states each year.

While neither Adams nor Williams will go down as Hall of Famers, both will be remembered as very good players, even if their professional talent wasn't fully realized.

Trading Card Stats

John Adams	Name	Ricky Williams
•His Rotundity •Colossus of Independence •Duke of Braintree	**Nickname**	•Little Earl •Texas Tornado
•1797-1801	**Experience**	•1999-2003 •2005-2011
•61	**Age Entering the League**	•22
•5'7"/150	**HT/WT**	•5'10"/226
•Federalist	**Team**	•New Orleans Saints •Miami Dolphins •Baltimore Ravens
•Declaration of Independence •XYZ Affair •Alien and Sedition Act	**Stats**	•10,009 rushing yards •74 total touchdowns •1-time Pro Bowl selection •1-time All-Pro selection
•Walking (up to five miles a day) •Reading •Smoking •Fishing •Sailing •Swimming •Swordsmanship	**Hobbies**	•Reading •Smoking •Yoga •Tai chi •Photography
•"No man who ever held the office of president would congratulate a friend on obtaining it."	**Quote**	•"It was embarrassing. He smoked me under the bus. Bad. I was crawling off the bus." -On smoking with Willie Nelson
•Personally defended the British soldiers involved with the Boston Massacre while in court	**Interesting**	•Has appeared on *The Celebrity Apprentice*
•No	**Hall of Fame**	•No

3

Thomas Jefferson (1801-1809)

It's simply human nature to be hypocritical. But even the biggest of hypocrites (Hello, Steve Jobs! Hello, NFL owners!) would respectfully tip their hat to Jefferson. One of the best, yet most conflicting, presidents this nation has seen. His contradictions were blatant, even bordering on dumbfounding.

Jefferson tried toning down the previous regime's aristocratic aura in many ways, but his personal hypocrisies always lingered. One of which was to receive foreign dignitaries into his home while wearing pajamas, which he countered by living lavishly in his Monticello mansion. Another example of his was publicly advocating for the abolition of slavery. This included a fiery condemnation of slavery in the Declaration of Independence rough draft, a take that was too hot for his peers to touch, but he countered that by owning hundreds of slaves throughout his lifetime.

Jefferson was a forward-thinking humanist and someone who held Native Americans in low regard. He was a proponent of small, state-run governments but often acted in the interest of the federal government.

There is no shortage of confounding actions and feelings when it comes to Jefferson's presidency. Although his actions did not often align with his words, Jefferson's brilliant intellect still made him a political force with which to be reckoned.

The country's third president began his political career after being elected to the Virginia House of Burgesses in 1768. Next, Jefferson was elected to the Second Continental Congress in 1775. A year later, he was drafting the Declaration of Independence.

From there, Jefferson climbed the political ladder as he moved from Virginia governor to minister of France, and then from secretary of state to vice president. As president of the United States, Jefferson was far from perfect with his policy development and implementation. For example, the Embargo Act of 1807 was meant to hurt the European economy by shutting down American ports to foreign trade in an attempt to prove how valuable the U.S. economy was to its foreign counterparts. All it wound up doing, though, was hurting American commerce and playing a role in the 1807 economic depression.

But what Jefferson lacked in policy, he made up for with his vision and leadership. Jefferson was one of the few politicians at the time who understood the importance of western America. For example, the Louisiana Purchase provided the United States with 828,000 square miles of land at a cost of roughly $15 million, equal to roughly three cents per acre. Jefferson also led the charge for western expansion, commissioning Lewis and Clark to explore the newly acquired territory.

Most likely sport: Basketball

His talent and ability to outthink the opposition would have contributed largely to his success in sports, enabling him to be a multi-sport star. As a pitcher, he likely would have outsmarted hitters with a well-crafted game plan and pinpoint accuracy to manipulate the hitter into looking for a breaking ball off the plate before freezing them with a fastball right down the middle.

However, the sport Jefferson would have undoubtedly thrived at would have been basketball. On the court, Jefferson would have used his calculating nature and impeccable timing to slowly wear down his opponents. He would have outworked them with his maniacal approach. Much like Washington before him, Jefferson's height and athletic build at the time would have also suited him well for a sport like basketball.

Jefferson would have been a combo guard, capable of running the offense for his teammates or himself but wanting the ball in his hands regardless. He also would have wanted complete, decision-making autonomy, able to do as he saw fit on any given play.

Best Comparison: Kobe Bryant

More than simply being an asshole and an occasional ball hog on the court, Kobe Bean was also meticulous and studious. A person who was willing to outwork anyone in the name of winning. He and Jefferson share many similar traits in that sense.

In addition to having immense natural talent, both men were willing to put in the work necessary to make themselves great. Kobe was well known for having some of the best footwork in the game. It was a facet of the game he worked on for decades.

Like Kobe, who studied tap dance after winning the 2000 NBA Finals, Jefferson was also adept with his footwork. He studied dance for six months as a teenager, spending hours on end developing a love for the craft that would last a lifetime. Jefferson became singularly focused on honing his talent in a way that few people outside of Kobe could understand.

Kobe was obsessed with this singular-focus mentality. From the time he turned pro at age 17, the Mamba dedicated his life to the game. It was what helped him achieve the success he did in the NBA.

The Lakers star played all 20 of his seasons with the same organization en route to winning two Olympic gold medals, one MVP, and five championships. It helped him become one of the greatest and most beloved basketball players of all time. As far as his fans were concerned, the man could do no wrong on the court—whether it was his salty attitude toward teammates or his unrelenting need to hoist up shots seemingly every time he touched the ball, Lakers fans just loved watching Kobe be Kobe.

The love and adoration for Kobe was plainly evident on January 26, 2020, when he was tragically killed in a helicopter accident along with his daughter, Gianna, six other passengers, and the pilot. Poor flying conditions led to a loss of control of the helicopter, resulting in the descent and demise of all on board. In the wake of his death, a global outpouring of support was seen and felt in a way that transcended sports. Kobe's life, and his story, had left an indelible mark on fans and admirers around the world.

His story was not without tumult, however, as the Lower Merion, Pennsylvania, native was charged with rape in 2003 after an encounter with a front desk worker at a hotel in Eagle, Colorado. Though Bryant admitted to having sex with the woman and committing adultery, he staunchly denied the rape accusation. The charge was dropped in 2004, more than a year after the incident came to light.

Similar to Bryant, Jefferson had to battle his own scandalous immoralities. Jefferson is known to have had an affair with at least one married woman and tried with another. Even better known, though, was his sexual relationship with Sally Hemings, who was one of his slaves. Although no records exist to legitimately accuse Jefferson of rape, one can safely assume that Hemings had little choice in ultimately giving birth to an alleged six children fathered by Jefferson. Either way, the scandal still sticks with Jefferson's legacy as much as it will with Kobe's.

Whether that alters your personal view of the two men is completely understandable. Regardless of how they might be viewed personally, their professional prowess cannot be denied. What they did on the court and in the office is largely unparalleled. Both guys are worthy of the Hall of Fame.

Trading Card Stats

Thomas Jefferson	Name	Kobe Bryant
•Sage of Monticello •Philosopher of Democracy	Nickname	•Black Mamba
•1801-1809	Experience	•1996-2016
•57	Age Entering the League	•18
•6’2”/174	HT/WT	•6’6”/212
•Democratic-Republican	Team	•Los Angeles Lakers
•Declaration of Independence •Louisiana Purchase •Founder of Library of Congress	Stats	•25 points, 5.2 rebounds and 4.7 assists per game •5-time NBA champion •2-time NBA Finals MVP •1-time league MVP •15-time All-Star •Olympic gold medalist
•Architecture •Botany •Animal husbandry •Meteorology •Mechanical engineering •Reading	Hobbies	•Swimming •Soccer •Film making
•“I wish to see this beverage (beer) become common instead of the whiskey, which kills one-third of our citizens and ruins their families.”	Quote	•“Smush Parker was the worst. He shouldn’t have been in the NBA but we were too cheap to pay for a point guard…I was shooting 45 times a game (in 2007). What was I supposed to do? Pass it into Chris Mihm and Kwame Brown?”
•Often greeted ambassadors in his pajamas	Interesting	•Spoke fluent Spanish and Italian
•Yes	Hall of Fame	•Yes

4

James Madison (1809-1817)

One could argue that James Madison's most likely sport and position would have been as a horse jockey. At 5'4" and 100 pounds, Madison's stature was meek. In addition to Madison's feeble physique, he was also the sickliest of presidents who suffered from a variety of maladies including depression, dysentery, hemorrhoids, and attacks that resembled epilepsy. But for as weak as Madison appeared physically, he was a mental giant who commanded respect.

Like his fellow founding fathers, Madison played a significant role in setting the country's course. He began his governmental duties by serving as a delegate to the Virginia Convention in 1776 and 1777. Three years later, at age 29, Madison would become the youngest member in the Continental Congress.

Madison became known as the "Father of the Constitution" as one of the more ardent supporters of a strong, centralized government. Although many voices contributed to the drafting and crafting of the Constitution, Madison has since been considered the superstar of this Constitutional team.

Madison is also largely responsible for our understanding of what happened at the Constitutional Convention in 1787, where state delegates congregated to decide how exactly America was going to be governed. He was the most copious note taker at the convention. It is largely thanks to Madison that we know so much about what transpired inside those conventional walls, which did not allow press coverage.

As if his contributions weren't already significant enough, Madison also introduced the Bill of Rights. This additional legislature guaranteed certain personal freedoms and limited the government's power in various proceedings. It also cemented Madison as a brilliant mind and a political force.

As president, Madison led calmly but firmly. While cautious in his decision making, he held steadfast once a decision had been made. One of Madison's more controversial decisions was the initiation of the War of 1812. The war, which lasted three years, pitted British and American forces against each other. British resentment began when America had chosen to remain neutral during the Napoleonic Wars between Britain and France. Unhappy with America's attempt to abstain from international politics, Britain began to provoke America through tactics like supplying Native Americans weapons for the purpose of raiding Americans on the frontier. This led to a war that was largely unsuccessful for American forces.

The battle did, however, produce several memorable moments that now live in American lore. There was the burning down of the White House in August 1814, which was successfully accomplished by British forces. In an attempt to protect the nation's capital, Madison had accompanied his troops into battle before being forced to flee the area. A month later, Francis Scott Key famously penned what would become known as "The Star-Spangled Banner," which has become the country's most revered (and potentially racist) national anthem.

It also provided the world with Andrew Jackson's coming out party. Late in 1814, peace talks between the U.S. and British forces had already begun, but word had yet to reach America. In a surprising upset, Jackson led American forces to a huge victory at the Battle of New Orleans. Announcement of a peace agreement reached U.S. shores not long after the battle and left Americans feeling confident and victorious about a war in which their victories were few and far between. American faith in Madison and the strength of its still new nation had been restored and saved the fourth president from a potentially disastrous legacy.

Most likely sport: Baseball

While Madison's size would have pigeonholed him into very particular sports and positions at an early age, football and hockey would simply be too dangerous for the injury-prone Madison. His size, docile demeanor, and well-rounded skill set would have made him ripe for baseball.

As a player of smaller size, Madison would have been pegged for a middle infield role where he would have served admirably.

Best Comparison: Nomar Garciaparra

Just as Madison was one of the country's founding fathers who helped usher in the Era of Good Feelings in the United States, you could say Nomar was one of the founding fathers who ushered in the current group of modern-day shortstops. Along with Alex Rodriguez and Derek Jeter, Garciaparra entered the majors in the mid-1990s and became an instant star as a slick-fielding defender with a potent bat.

Garciaparra was on his way to becoming a potential Hall of Famer before injuries derailed him. Perhaps best known for his intricate pre-pitch ritual at the plate, Garciaparra would adjust and then re-adjust his batting gloves, mesmerizing audiences with the fluidity of his superstition much as he did with his on-field play. He became a superstar and a Boston icon.

Like Madison, though, Garciaparra had issues with his health. He suffered from numerous injuries, including ankle and Achilles problems, as well as a surgically-repaired wrist and groin. Garciaparra accumulated a 41 Wins Above Replacement (WAR) from age 23-29, placing him in the top-50 position players of all time. He just wasn't able to sustain that excellence during the second half of his career.

Neither was Madison, who took the United States to war against Great Britain despite having relatively few resources. This second war for independence was fought to open maritime trade and prevent impressment of American soldiers.

Despite some good in-game adjustments, Madison was unable to achieve either of those tasks when the Treaty of Ghent was signed and brought an end to the fighting. In fact, he was lucky that a couple well-timed victories salvaged the perception of this largely unsuccessful war.

Beyond their injury-prone natures, Madison and Garciaparra also shared a number of similar personality traits. In addition to having great study habits and being very alert, both men were known for being extremely quiet and reserved during their careers.

Garciaparra was often referred to as "No-Comment Nomar" during his playing days because of how little he spoke. He preferred to let his play do the talking. Madison, meanwhile, was so notorious for his reticent nature that the wife of one Virginia delegate to the Continental Congress called Madison, "the most unsociable creature in existence." Madison even refused to speak up for himself during his bid for a second term. The sitting president refused to run a formal campaign or make any speeches and barely made any comments on his way to re-election.

If we were judging their success on a lifetime body of work and cultural impact, Madison and Garciaparra would both have Hall of Fame plaques. Unfortunately for them, solely judging their presidential and MLB achievements leave them stuck in the Hall of Very Good.

Trading Card Stats

James Madison	Name	Nomar Garciaparra
•Father of the Constitution	Nickname	•Nomah
•1809-1817	Experience	•1996-2009
•57	Age Entering the League	•22
•5'4"/100	HT/WT	•6'0"/165
•Democratic-Republican	Team	•Boston Red Sox •Chicago Cubs •Los Angeles Dodgers •Oakland Athletics
•U.S. Constitution •Bill of Rights •War of 1812	Stats	•.313 batting average •.882 OPS •6-time All-Star •AL Rookie of the Year •NL Comeback Player of the Year
•Walking •Horseback riding •Chess •Reading	Hobbies	•Soccer
•"Nothing more than a change of mind." -Uttered just before he died	Quote	•"My idol was Bugs Bunny, because I saw a cartoon of him playing ball—the one where he plays every position himself with nobody else on the field but him. Now that I think of it, Bugs is still my idol."
•One of only two presidents to accompany troops into battle while in office (Abraham Lincoln being the other)	Interesting	•Nomar's dad used to give him a quarter for every hit he recorded as a kid while applying a 50-cent fine for every strikeout
•No	Hall of Fame	•No

5

James Monroe (1817-1825)

Can you imagine a time when the political climate was so amicable that there was no outcry to replace the incumbent's political party in the Oval Office because no opposing political faction could muster a complaint about the party in power? Yeah, me neither. Sounds like the kind of fake news a dictatorial regime would spout to mask political oppression. Or like Harvey Weinstein asking for potted plants because he wanted to accent the room's drab appearance.

Except it was true. No, not the part about Weinstein's plants. That guy is just a scumbag and a criminal.

But there actually was a time when political strife was virtually nonexistent. It was known as the Era of Good Feelings and was led by James Monroe.

The last of the Founding Fathers to be president, Monroe was a war veteran who served in the American Revolution as part of Washington's army. He also fought in the First Seminole War. After that, Monroe carved out a space in politics.

Monroe's various political roles included minister to France, Virginia governor, special envoy to help with the Louisiana Purchase, secretary of state, and secretary of war. With each successive role, Monroe used his warm, endearing personality to gain popularity.

Thanks to that likability and his prior success in war, Monroe won all but three states in the 1816 election, easily securing the fifth presidential nomination. Monroe largely ignored traditional party lines while in office; instead choosing to try and find the best person for each job. This, along with the recent War of 1812 triumph, propelled the country into an era of unity and optimism.

The country was so politically united during the time that Monroe ran unopposed in his 1820 bid for re-election. Monroe received all but one vote, from New Hampshire Governor William Plumer, which preserved Washington as the only president to ever be elected unanimously. It is still not completely certain whether Plumer did this to preserve Washington as the lone unanimous selection or because of his genuine disdain for Monroe, whom he believed to be incompetent and unnecessarily extravagant. Regardless, Monroe's second term carried on much like his first.

During Monroe's tenure, the biggest domestic issue he tackled was the Missouri Compromise. This compromise brought Maine into the Union as a free state and Missouri as a slave state, while declaring that any new states added as part of the existing Louisiana Territory north of the parallel 36°30' latitude line would be free states. This effectively simmered the slavery issue that began bubbling and kicked the proverbial, divisive can of slavery down the road.

In terms of foreign affairs, Monroe demilitarized the Great Lakes region with Great Britain thanks to the Rush-Bagot Agreement. He also acquired Florida and Oregon, while Spain got Texas, through the Adams-Onis Treaty.

Most likely sport: Football

Monroe governed in a low-key and reserved fashion. He was honest, patient, hands-off in his approach, and refused to do anything that might overstep his constitutional authority. He was well-respected by almost everyone, although he was never deemed to be the true leader of his party with Jefferson and Madison still around.

As a result, he was not the superstar persona that would make him *the man* on his team. He was a steady player who respected the game and brought a high level of consistency to work every day. Monroe was non-confrontational but possessed a quiet toughness, which would have allowed him to excel in the NFL.

As an athlete, Monroe had good size and even better instincts. He was not a good inspirational leader who could galvanize the team via oration. However, he had talented, and reliable, hands as evidenced by his skillful writing. Monroe's traits best translate to being a wide receiver.

Best Comparison: Henry Ellard

Monroe may not be one of the most popular presidents in history, but he served in his role admirably. The same could be said for Henry Ellard.

While Ellard may not be particularly well remembered, he was a force during his days with the Los Angeles Rams and his short stint with the Washington Racial Slurs. Ellard's career spanned much of the 1980s and '90s as he amassed a slew of receiving stats that placed him in the upper-echelon as far as receivers go.

Ellard began his NFL career with the Rams in 1983 after playing four years at Fresno State. It didn't take long for Ellard to establish himself as a reliable source of production on the outside. From 1984-1997, there was only one season in which he didn't lead his team in receptions.

Ellard currently ranks 33rd all-time in receptions despite playing in an era where passing was much less prevalent than it is now. To add context, if you look only at players who started their careers prior to 1990, Ellard would rank 8th all-time in pass catching.

He also played with a crew of quarterbacks that would make Andre Johnson cringe. Ellard's starting quarterbacks during his heyday with the Rams included Vince Ferragamo, Jeff Kemp, Dieter Brock, (a washed up) Steve Bartkowski, Steve Dils, and Jim Everett. Not the most stellar quarterbacking contingent.

Like Monroe, Ellard was a prized jewel during his prime for those who were paying attention. Ellard just lacked the same reflection, refraction, and dispersion of his predecessors Steve Largent and Art Monk as Monroe did with Jefferson and Madison.

Ellard, though, didn't complain about the lack of passing talent during his playing days. He stayed quiet and played hard, becoming more and more underrated as time has passed.

All the same is true for Monroe. While he didn't make big waves as a president, his ability to prevent any real discord during his eight years in office is largely underappreciated.

As for their Hall of Fame chances, Monroe and Ellard are the type of people for whom you could make a very compelling case. Unfortunately, they don't have the requisite accomplishments on their resumes to separate themselves from the rest of the pack. Although neither man is worthy of the Hall of Fame, they come a lot closer than one might think.

Trading Card Stats

James Monroe	Name	Henry Ellard
•Last Cocked Hat	**Nickname**	•Grasshopper •Hop
•1817-1825	**Experience**	•1983-1998
•58	**Age Entering the League**	•22
•6'0"/189	**HT/WT**	•5'11"/180
•Democratic-Republican	**Team**	•Los Angeles Rams •Washington Redskins •New England Patriots
•American Revolution •First Seminole War •Acquired more land for American expansion	**Stats**	•814 receptions •13,777 receiving yards •65 receiving touchdowns •3-time Pro Bowl selection •2-time All-Pro selection
•Horseback riding •Hunting	**Hobbies**	•Track and field •Model planes
•"Mrs. Monroe hath added a daughter to our society who, tho' noisy, contributes greatly to its amusement."	**Quote**	•"I never got that opportunity to play with a Hall-of-Fame quarterback, so who knows what might have happened if I had that opportunity?"
•Monroe stopped a sword fight at the White House between two foreign dignitaries by jumping in the middle with his own sword drawn	**Interesting**	•Set a world record in the triple jump for men 55 years and older at 13.36 meters
•No	**Hall of Fame**	•No

6

John Quincy Adams (1825-1829)

Just because you're one of the most qualified people for a job doesn't mean you'll succeed once there. Just ask Adams.

Oh, wait. I made this same claim about the elder Adams, didn't I? Oh well. You know the saying: like father, like son.

The younger Adams may not have been quite as destined for stardom in the run up to his presidency, but if dad was a first overall draft pick then son was a first-round draft pick. The problem was none of the fans really wanted to draft Adams at the slot in which he was selected.

But there was no denying that JQA was a rising political star in the early 19th century as Adams had one of the more successful pre-presidential careers ever seen. It included stints as both a state and U.S. senator and also four separate roles as minister to another country—the Netherlands, Prussia, Russia, and Great Britain. Serving as secretary of state, though, was where he shined brightest.

As secretary of state, Adams established the Convention of 1818 (setting the U.S.-Canadian border out to the Rockies), concluded the Adams-Onis Treaty (removing Spain from Florida and Oregon, giving the U.S. claim to those territories), and helped formalize the Monroe Doctrine. By that point, Adams was becoming well known nationally for his own success rather than for being the son of the second president.

The 1824 presidential election saw Adams faced against Andrew Jackson, William Crawford, and Henry Clay. To win the election, one of the candidates needed to amass 131 electoral votes. Jackson received 99 votes, Adams had 84, Crawford collected 41, and Clay brought up the rear with 37. By rule, the vote would be decided in the House of Representatives as each state picked among the three highest vote-getting candidates. Adams won support from 13 of the 24 states, making him the winner much to Jackson's disdain.

Jackson had won the popular vote but lost the election when Congress chose Adams, thanks in large part to Clay's support. Having finished last in voting, Clay decided to throw his support behind Adams, which is largely believed to be the reason Adams ultimately secured the 1824 bid. When the newly appointed president selected Clay as his secretary of state, Jackson and his cronies were enraged. Though lacking in evidence, the Jacksonites cried collusion and swore to make Adams' tenure miserable.

They succeeded.

The younger Adams' presidency was marred by ineffectiveness at the hands of embittered, partisan politics.

While Adams had a solid vision for his presidency, he lacked the ability to unify others in government to go along with him. One of his visions was for internal improvement across the country. He proposed the construction of roads and canals, a national university, and an astronomical observatory. Congress shut him down, however, as the constitutionality of such a plan was immediately questioned. The argument over federal rights vs. states' rights once again became an issue and Adams was forced to settle for one road and one canal.

Such was the case for Adams throughout his presidency. He either settled for small victories or was blocked completely by political opposition, making Adams' tenure not nearly as successful as one would have thought given his background.

Most likely sport: Football

In sports, as in politics, Adams would have followed suit with his father and played football. While ambitious, Adams didn't want to toot his own horn and steal the spotlight from his team. He was brought up around the game thanks to the elder Adams and would have been a natural at the sport.

Adams was at his best when using his brain. He was incredibly intelligent as his fluency in seven languages would prove. Though Adams could be a bit arrogant and stubborn at times, that intellect, coupled with his raw talent, would have led him to be a quarterback.

Best Comparison: Jay Cutler

Adams' skill and natural gifts could not be denied. From afar, he fit the presidential mold about as well as one could hope. He would have been the ideal franchise quarterback for a team in the same way Jay Cutler was.

Scientists in a lab could not have manufactured a quarterback's arm any better than the one already hinged to Cutler's right shoulder. Born in Santa Claus, Indiana, (yes, I said Santa Claus, Indiana) Cutler played four years of football at Vanderbilt University. While there, he earned SEC Offensive Player of the Year honors and was selected in the first round of the 2006 NFL draft.

Cutler spent his first three seasons with the Denver Broncos where his arrogance, reserved nature, and lack of charisma drew the ire of teammates and fans.

In many ways, this resembled the personality of Adams. It's fair to say he wasn't exactly a man of the people. He once insisted on dining separately from his fellow Americans while the delegation negotiated the Treaty of Ghent. His lack of interpersonal skills was apparent just as they were for Cutler.

After the quarterback's third season in Denver, the team hired first time Head Coach Josh McDaniels (speaking of arrogant and lacking charisma) who promptly butted heads with Cutler, ultimately leading to the quarterback being traded to the Chicago Bears.

Unfortunately for Cutler, his tenure in Chicago wasn't any better as his gunslinger mentality led to consistently inconsistent play. Twice, Cutler led the league in interceptions, falling into the habit of trusting his big arm too much and throwing into double or triple coverages. His body language and perceived indifference to anything and everything continued to rub teammates and fans the wrong way. Although the gifs and memes they produced became a bit of a low-level phenomenon among social media sports dorks.

After eight seasons with the Bears, Cutler was cut. He briefly announced his retirement but came back to play one more uneventful season with the Miami Dolphins in which he had 10 million reasons to do so.

Despite the immense talent, Cutler never lived up to the initial billing. He had periodic moments of success but could never overcome the inconsistency. Much like Adams, his austere nature and combative relationship with peers made his professional life difficult.

Though neither of the two men were busts, they entered their professions with such high hopes that they were surely viewed as disappointments. As a result, neither man is Hall of Fame worthy.

Trading Card Stats

John Quincy Adams	Name	Jay Cutler
•Accidental President •Old Man Eloquent	Nickname	•Smokin' Jay
•1825-1829	Experience	•2006-2017
•57	Age Entering the League	•23
•5'7"/174	HT/WT	•6'3"/225
•Democratic-Republican	Team	•Denver Broncos •Chicago Bears •Miami Dolphins
•Negotiated Treaty of Ghent •Tariff of Abominations	Stats	•35,133 passing yards •27 touchdowns •160 interceptions •1-time Pro Bowl selection
•Billiards •Reading •Writing •Observing nature •Domesticating wild plants •Theater •Swimming	Hobbies	•Basketball •Hunting •Volunteering with charities
•"The four most miserable years of my life were my four years in the presidency."	Quote	•"Uh...no." -Response to being asked if he was sorry for cussing out his head coach
•Accidentally shot himself in the face while showing his son how to load a gun	Interesting	•Cutler was approached by a fan in a bathroom bar who allegedly told Cutler he was a big fan to which Cutler leaned his head back, rolled his eyes, and yelled, "DON'T CAAARREEE!!!"
•No	Hall of Fame	•No

7

Andrew Jackson (1829-1837)

Dumb ass? Probably. Bad ass? Definitely.

Most people who enjoy shooting other human beings as a sort of recreational pursuit are deemed manic. Or deranged. Or a serial killer.

One was called "president."

While most presidents use their spare time to read or play games, Jackson found life to be more fulfilling when it involved fighting. The man known as "Old Hickory" earned his nickname for standing as tough as old hickory wood on the battlefield. But this was just as evident in his personal life where he allegedly participated in more than 100 duels during his lifetime. The most famous of which occurred when Jackson dueled a man named Charles Dickinson.

Jackson's foe fired his shot first, striking him in the chest. Rather than falling in a heap of agony, Jackson stood firm. With one hand, he worked to stop the blood flowing out of his body. With the other hand, he tightly clasped the gun and returned fire. Dickinson was struck below the ribs by what turned out to be a fatal blow.

Such was the life of Jackson whose rise to prominence came via his war prowess. Jackson joined the American Revolution when he was 13 years old. He was even captured by the British and forced to march 40 miles to a prisoner-of-war camp where he spent two weeks held captive until a prisoner exchange set him free.

From that point, Jackson spent time bouncing back and forth between politics and war. On the political side, he served as a U.S. representative, a U.S. senator, and a Justice of the Tennessee Supreme Court. In addition to the American Revolution, his war resume included the War of 1812 and the First Seminole War as he rose to the rank of major general of the United States Army.

After losing to Adams in the 1824 election, Jackson spent the next four years trying to make his life miserable. By 1828, Jackson would supplant Adams for the nation's highest office, where he would serve two terms.

As president, Jackson was a bit of a mixed bag, utilizing some deft strategy along with brutish bullying. In terms of policy, Jackson supported internal, national improvements. He opened trade with the British West Indies. Disputes were quashed and treaties or trade opportunities were created with the Kingdom of Naples, Denmark, Columbia, Mexico, Siam, and the Turks.

Jackson also got France to pay for damages caused to American ships during the Napoleonic Wars by threatening war against them. In the end, Jackson never did go to war with a foreign country despite his ruthless approach.

Domestically, Jackson was even more ruthless in his handling of Native Americans. He implemented the Indian Removal Act of 1830, which ignored a Supreme Court ruling stating Georgia had no right to govern Native Americans. Jackson ignored this ruling and authorized the forced removal of 15,000 Cherokees from Georgia to present-day Oklahoma in what has become known as the Trail of Tears. One out of every four people died during that trek.

Most likely sport: Hockey

It's not surprising that Jackson's rough and tough demeanor would push him to a contact sport. And with a propensity for physical violence, hockey would have been the perfect fit.

Jackson had some underrated political skills such as courage and the ability to motivate others that would have allowed him to go on the offensive. That skill, combined with a willingness to drop the gloves and fight at any moment, would have allowed him to slot in well as a right winger.

Best Comparison: Dave Williams

It's hard to fathom Jackson playing something other than hockey, and his feisty personality is a perfect fit with Dave Williams.

Jackson's success as an athlete would have relied on his ability to intimidate others through brute force. He was the type of person you either loved or hated. He was passionate, fiery, and with a hint of crazy that you didn't want to cross.

If he was on your team, it was advantageous because he was fiercely loyal and took shit from no one. But if he was on the other team, he was a boorish asshole. At the end of the day, though, Jackson would have been a goon. Just like Williams.

The 14-year veteran forward was notorious for being a tough guy. Williams is the all-time leader in penalty minutes, and it isn't even close. The next player on the list is more than 400 minutes shy of his record.

Both Jackson and Williams were willing to fight it out with anyone—peer or bystander. Jackson once leveled a tax evader with a block of wood while he was the Tennessee prosecutor. Williams, on the other hand, went into the stands in 1982 as a member of the Vancouver Canucks and attacked a fan who had thrown ice at him.

You could see Jackson doing the same thing over even less. Mere words could have prompted Jackson to start climbing walls and confronting paying customers.

For both men, the fighting was often done as a matter of demanding someone else's respect as much as it was about exerting their power and anger. And in both cases, their hot-headed, drawn-to-fisticuffs nature masked an underlying level of skill each guy possessed.

Jackson tactfully handled foreign policy and improved America's standing in the world without much remembrance of it. In Williams' case, he was capable of helping out occasionally on offense and even put together one All-Star campaign.

But the two men will always be remembered more for their brash demeanors and sharp tongues. And they both took control of situations as they saw fit, regardless of what others thought. In 1818, Jackson invaded Florida despite orders from President Monroe not to do so. The invasion wrestled Florida's control away from Spain and put it in the hands of Jackson who subsequently spent months as the military governor of Florida.

Likewise, Williams has taken action into his own hands on multiple occasions. He once grabbed a female reporter and threw her out of the locker room because he didn't believe women should have been allowed inside. In another instance, Williams wanted to make a citizen's arrest after a driver tossed litter outside their window. Williams supposedly confronted the man and chased down the car for so long that the driver went to the police station for help.

While their personalities may have been as rough as sandpaper, as professionals, they were solid performers. However, neither merits Hall of Fame consideration.

Trading Card Stats

Andrew Jackson	Name	Dave Williams
•Old Hickory •Sharp Knife •King Andrew the First	**Nickname**	•Tiger
•1829-1837	**Experience**	•1974-1988
•61	**Age Entering the League**	•20
•6'0"/140	**HT/WT**	•5'11"/190
•Democrat	**Team**	•Toronto Maple Leafs •Vancouver Canucks •Detroit Red Wings •Los Angeles Kings •Hartford Whalers
•Indian Removal Act of 1830 •Ended the Second Bank of the U.S. •Opened trade with the British West Indies	**Stats**	•241 goals •272 assists •3,966 penalty minutes •1-time All-Star
•Raising gamecocks •Cockfighting •Reading •Shooting people •Breeding and racing horses	**Hobbies**	•Hunting •Fishing •A gun fanatic
•"If you have a job in your department that can't be done by a Democrat, then abolish the job."	**Quote**	•"The Penguins are done like dinner."
•A well-known dueler, Jackson is rumored to have participated in more than 100 duels during his lifetime	**Interesting**	•NHL's all-time leader in penalty minutes
•No	**Hall of Fame**	•No

8

Martin Van Buren (1837-1841)

The Little Magician was an apt nickname for Martin Van Buren. The eighth president was a master of behind-the-scenes, political maneuvering in his ascent to the White House. Oh, yeah, and he was little! At 5'6" Van Buren is tied for the second shortest president behind Madison.

In a way, Van Buren was the first in a new wave of presidents. He was the first president to be born after the Declaration of Independence and as an American citizen. Van Buren grew up relatively poor, delivering produce and helping at his father's tavern after school.

Perhaps because of this, Van Buren gave off an aristocratic aura as he aged. He dressed in fancy clothes, threw lavish parties, and detested large crowds—all of which made him seem pretentious. Though this would come back to bite him by the end of his presidency, Van Buren managed to climb his party's ladder through crafty politicking.

He was elected as a New York state senator, a U.S. senator, and as the governor of New York in the decades leading up to his presidency. Following those roles, he was selected as secretary of state and vice president. He achieved this feat, in large part, because of his strong friendship with Jackson.

Seemingly different in so many facets of life, Van Buren and Jackson still managed to get along really well. Where Jackson was impulsive, Van Buren was very cautious in his decision making. Where Jackson was very comfortable in the spotlight, Van Buren preferred to work in the shadows. Their personalities meshed in a very yin and yang fashion, and when Jackson's second term came to an end, he endorsed Van Buren as the next president.

As president, Van Buren walked into a bit of misfortune from the get-go. Just weeks after being elected, the Panic of 1837 struck, largely due to policies enacted by Jackson. Banks across the country suspended their conversion of paper money into gold and silver, sparking panic among Americans and led to a six-year economic depression.

The economic woes were predicated on factors outside Van Buren's control but poor timing generally left him shouldering the blame. His biggest fault was in waiting too long to take action. He briefly created an independent treasury meant to restore public credit, but it took Congress until 1840 to pass it. They repealed the Independent Treasury Act a year later, and it wasn't reinstated until 1846.

Jackson also passed along the Second Seminole War to Van Buren. The Seminoles fought in an attempt to resist forced removal from Florida to the west, but Van Buren continued Jackson's Native American policy and the resistance was snuffed out in 1842.

While Van Buren struggled domestically, his foreign relations proved to be a strong suit. He successfully navigated the Caroline Affair, a dispute between Canadian rebels and their British rulers that took place in U.S. waters and killed one American. He also organized a truce to end the Aroostook War, a bloodless "war," after a disagreement between the specific borderlines that separated Maine from Canada. By avoiding bloodshed and improving the American navy, the rest of the world gained esteem for the United States.

Most likely sport: Basketball

Van Buren was the ultimate team player. A guy who was great at setting up his teammates to succeed and also benefited from said success. His strategic mindset and the ability to elevate those around him would have made him a solid basketball player.

Van Buren's ability to control a team and influence teammates would have made him a natural fit for a point guard role. He would have been strategic and disciplined, able to step into the spotlight at times but probably better off setting up teammates.

Best Comparison: Nick Van Exel

In a true sign of kismet, the Van (Buren/Exel) Boys flashed similar signs throughout their careers, intersecting at what could only be conceived as the Van-Nexus of the universe.

The two Vans share more in common than just name alone. There was a myth throughout much of Van Exel's career that he was brash and struggled to get along with coaches. That notion was laid to rest by one of Van Exel's former coaches, Del Harris. A couple of shouting matches were blown out of proportion—the result of a young, confident, and ambitious player.

This ambitious optimism that guided his career helped stoke an internal fire that allowed him to succeed in the face of long odds. A struggling education forced Van Exel to attend junior college for two years before he was able to transfer to the University of Cincinnati, a Division 1 school. After two years there, Van Exel was drafted in the second round by the Los Angeles Lakers.

Likewise, education was also a struggle in Van Buren's upbringing. Stopping his formal education before turning 14, he would go on to spend seven years as a law apprentice where his charming, optimistic demeanor and his ambitious desire helped guide him into the pros.

As an NBA player, Van Exel was regarded as a relatively flashy point guard. For sure, Nick the Quick had some pizzazz in his game. He could fake a behind-the-back pass like a soccer player selling an injury. But he has never really been credited for how well-rounded and fundamentally sound his game was.

As a ball-dominant player averaging nearly 33 minutes per game, Van Exel averaged just a hair over two turnovers per game. In fact, the lightning quick lefty never finished top-20 in turnovers during any season of his career.

Van Buren's game also had some sizzle on the surface. He donned garish outfits that garnered him a reputation for being fancy and seeking aristocracy. Though he dressed the part, Van Buren was much more down to Earth. Stories of lavish White House decorations and golden spoons became attached to his image. Of course, none of it was true. The furniture was old and largely remained unaltered from previous presidencies and the one set of golden spoons in the White House had come decades earlier from President Monroe.

For both men, it is fair to say they surpassed reasonable expectations given their paths to the pros. Van Exel worked his way through junior college and became a second-round draft pick before making a nice career for himself. Van Buren grew up relatively poor, lacked much formal education, and quietly ascended to the presidency.

Ultimately, Van Exel was an above average player who performed well on his own but would have been better off playing alongside a superstar throughout his career. Had Van Exel stuck with the Lakers for their early 2000s dynasty, his legacy would likely be remembered very differently than it is today.

Van Buren was also solid on his own, though he proved to be much more effective when he was considered a cog in the machine. His ability to work political back channels as a member of the larger Democratic party, was where he truly thrived. That, and his bromance with Jackson, made him a much better secondary option than primary option.

The Van Boys proved capable of holding their own, but it certainly isn't enough to get them into the Hall of Fame.

Trading Card Stats

Martin Van Buren	Name	Nick Van Exel
•The Little Magician •Little Van •Martin Van Ruin	**Nickname**	•Nick the Quick •Nick at Nite
•1837-1841	**Experience**	•1993-2006
•55	**Age Entering the League**	•22
•5'6"/164	**HT/WT**	•6'1"/170
•Democrat	**Team**	•Los Angeles Lakers •Denver Nuggets •Dallas Mavericks •Golden State Warriors •Portland Trailblazers •San Antonio Spurs
•Panic of 1837 •1837 Caroline affair •1839 Aroostook War •Second Seminole War	**Stats**	•14.4 points and 6.6 assists per game •1-time All-Star •NBA All-Rookie Second Team
•Theater •Gambling •Opera •Fishing	**Hobbies**	•Collects baseball cards, hats and books
•"As to the presidency, the two happiest days of my life were those of my entrance upon the office and my surrender of it."	**Quote**	•"1, 2, 3...Cancun!" -Said as the team broke huddle after practice during the 1998 playoffs as they were on the precipice of being swept by the Utah Jazz
•Tried curing his upset stomachs by putting a soot and charcoal mixture into water	**Interesting**	•Last Laker to ever score at the Boston Garden
•No	**Hall of Fame**	•No

9

William Henry Harrison (1841)

Well, that was brief. The presidency, that is. Not the speech.

Harrison's inaugural speech lasted a record one hour and 45 minutes on a cold, blustery day in which he insisted on forgoing hats, gloves, and overcoats. He became sick shortly after and wound up dying from pneumonia having served only 31 days as president.

That's probably not what Harrison was expecting when he made a campaign promise to be a one-term president. But thems the breaks.

Harrison grew up in a wealthy family with his initial sights set on becoming a doctor. At 14, he enrolled in college classes for premedical instruction. During his apprenticeship in 1790, Harrison found out his father had passed away. His father had requested that Harrison continue his studies but after running out of money in 1791, Harrison ditched medicine and joined the army.

As a professional soldier, he would fight in the Indian Wars and the War of 1812, eventually rising to major general. Some of his other professions included governor of the Indiana territory, U.S. representative, Ohio state senator, U.S. senator, and U.S. minister to Colombia.

In his run up to the presidential nomination, Harrison was cast as the log cabin and hard cider candidate compared to the image of palaces and champagne attached to Van Buren. Much of the public ate up this notion even though neither were true. Harrison's campaign was really the first to feature partisan songs, decorative objects, and much of the hoopla we consider to be part of the modern-day campaign trail.

Most likely sport: Baseball

Harrison was laid back and a strategic thinker. And if his speech was any indication, Harrison didn't mind playing a long game. Therefore, his best fit would have been on a baseball field.

With his unpretentious and affable personality, Harrison would have been willing to play any position asked of him, making him a suitable utility man who would be capable of either chasing balls down in the alleys as an outfielder or getting his uniform dirty as an infielder.

Best Comparison: Joe Cassidy

Just as Harrison's career had been cut short, so too was Cassidy's.

In 1902, an 18-year-old Cassidy began playing semi-pro baseball in Pennsylvania. The following season, Cassidy played in an independent league. By 1904, Cassidy had caught the eye of Washington Senators Manager Tom Loftus and signed a deal with them.

Cassidy earned his way into the spotlight with his slick glove work. He had a knack for quickly and smoothly fielding a ball at any position he played. Cassidy may have been small in stature, but he played big with his defense.

Like Harrison, Cassidy was unpretentious and just wanted to help his team be successful. He played shortstop, third base, and outfield during his two years in the big leagues.

Cassidy was spiked in the ankle during an August game in 1905. Though he would go on to finish out the rest of the season, Cassidy would have surgery in January to repair the ankle. In February, it was announced that he was suffering from typhoid, though his doctor would later diagnose it as malaria. By the end of March, Cassidy had died from the illness.

Both Harrison and Cassidy were credited with having good habits and morals, which contributed to their success.

Unfortunately for both men, their playing careers lasted about as long as this chapter. And, ultimately, their true potential went untapped. Neither man played long enough to receive Hall of Fame consideration.

Trading Card Stats

William Henry Harrison	Name	Joseph Cassidy
•Tippecanoe •Old Granny	Nickname	•Joe
•1841	Experience	•1904-1905
•68	Age Entering the League	•21
•5’8”/139	HT/WT	•5’9”/144
•Whig	Team	•Washington Senators
•Tried to end the spoils system used by Jackson and Van Buren	Stats	•2 home runs •23 triples •40 stolen bases •.228 batting average
•Morning walks •Horseback riding •Reading the Bible	Hobbies	•Bowling •Hunting •Fishing
•“Some folks are silly enough to have formed a plan to make a president of the U.S. out of this Clerk and Clod Hopper.”	Quote	•“I am ready when God calls me.” -Spoken just before his death
•The one platform he managed to carry out from his brief tenure was the promise to forgo a second term	Interesting	•Tricked a baserunner, Fielder Jones, into looking at the scoreboard during a game, which led to Jones getting picked off second base
•No	Hall of Fame	•No

10

John Tyler (1841-1845)

Some people are good at alienating others. John Tyler was good at alienating everyone.

His alienation game was so strong that by the time Tyler finished his presidential term, he was essentially a man without a political party.

"His Accidency," as Tyler was often referred, was initially thrust into the limelight after Harrison's fatal bout with pneumonia. But that limelight quickly turned into a searing spotlight that marred any chance he had at an effective presidency.

Tyler's journey to the presidential position was unlike any other up to that point. After studying law, Tyler served as a member of the Virginia House of Delegates, a U.S. representative, Virginia governor, and U.S. senator. When Harrison chose to run in 1840, Tyler was selected as his Whig running mate to help garner Southern support.

As vice president, Tyler had been relatively kept in the dark about Harrison's health. When news of Harrison's death finally reached Tyler, he was shocked. Tyler, by default, had become the new, acting president. Except Tyler wasn't acting.

Tyler was presidenting hard and letting others know it. He informed cabinet members that unlike Harrison, there would be no more majority votes on decisions. He would be Tyler the Decider. During the first few months of his tenure, Tyler would receive mail addressed to the "Acting President of the United States" to which Tyler would promptly return the mail as "addressee unknown." Tyler had no time for anyone who didn't show him the respect he thought was well deserved.

While in office, Tyler experienced limited success thanks to a hostile Congress and perhaps his own lack of readiness for the center stage. He signed the Webster-Ashburton Treaty, which set the present-day boundary between Maine and New Brunswick, Canada, resolving the dispute from the Aroostook War. Tyler also signed the Treaty of Wanghia, which provided the U.S. access to Chinese ports.

His most memorable action came three days prior to vacating the presidency when he signed a congressional resolution to annex Texas. Despite disagreement from Mexico over who actually laid claim to the area, Texas would officially become part of the United States. In doing this, the United States was able to add a big chunk of land to its ever-expanding ownership. Equally as important for Tyler was that it lay below the Mason-Dixon line and would be admitted as a slave slate.

Tyler had an aristocratic way about him that Americans often found off-putting, as he seemed to hold himself above all others; but particularly those who were not white. From an era of well-known racists, Tyler stood out for being more racist than most and wasn't shy about his beliefs. As someone who had no problem taking a firm stand in what he believed, Tyler's utter lack of compromise would leave him stuck in the mud.

Tyler was well aware of the contempt held for him and chose to forgo an attempt at re-election as a third-party candidate mostly out of fear that he would take votes away from James Polk who also supported the annexation of Texas. Tyler was concerned that by taking votes away from Polk, it would allow Henry Clay, a man he once stumped for to be president instead of Harrison, to find his way into the White House and jeopardize the Texas acquisition.

Most likely sport: Baseball

Tyler was stubborn and independent, making him a candidate for an individual sport; however, he also liked playing a feature role in decision making that impacted others, which ultimately keeps him in a team sport. As Tyler would require a sport that placed a little more emphasis on individual outcomes and letting them be themselves within the broad confines of a team dynamic, his best sport would have been baseball.

As a man who was independent and at times was off in his own world, he's a guy who would not be asked to play and produce for long stretches of the game. Having been called in from the bullpen to relieve Harrison of his duties, relief pitching would have been Tyler's calling.

Best Comparison: John Rocker

When it comes to athletes alienating others, it's hard to find many people more disagreeable than Rocker.

Tyler and Rocker share a common personality trait for being irritating and a penchant for welcoming the discord. Neither had a problem being the black sheep. Though as well-known racists, they might not be fond of the *black* portion of that label.

Rocker entered the league as a fireball-throwing lefty who could reach the upper 90s. He complimented the heat with a nasty slider to surprisingly step into a primary role at the backend of an Atlanta Braves bullpen during their heyday when the playoffs were as consistent as the sunrise.

For a couple of years, it looked as though Rocker was a rising star, destined to remain one of the league's premier closers. However, that career arc changed pretty dramatically after Rocker started opening his mouth.

Rocker had no problem telling it how he saw it. If that meant offending other people, all the better. In an interview at the tail end of 1999, Rocker went off on New Yorkers in a way that took out people of all creeds and colors. Some of the groups he disparaged included the LGBTQ community whom he attached AIDS to, ex-convicts, single mothers, and all foreigners. Oh, Rocker's derogatory comments made it clear he doesn't like kids with purple hair, either, in case anyone was wondering. Rocker made it abundantly evident what his stance was on other people and was unafraid of the backlash.

Tyler was also undeterred by potentially offending others. Tyler originally identified as part of the Democratic-Republican party but as the party broke into two distinct parties, Democrats and Republicans, Tyler sided with Jacksonian Democrats for their belief in states' rights—and his disdain for JQA as the leader of the Republican party. However, Tyler grew angry over President Jackson's support for federal rights, causing him to break with Democrats and turn to the Whigs.

Upon stepping into his presidential role, Tyler still found it difficult to toe the party line. When a Whig-led Congress wanted to re-establish the previously dismantled Bank of the United States, Tyler put the kibosh on that proposal. This sent the Whigs into a tizzy. Five of Tyler's six cabinet members resigned, ultimately resulting in his estrangement from the party. That's five people in some of the highest-ranking positions in the U.S. who decided quitting was a better alternative than continuing to work with Tyler.

Tyler elicited such hatred that at times he was burned in effigy and often dealt with bomb threats. The threats became so frequent that Congress passed "Tyler's Bill," providing the first federally-funded presidential security. The "doormen" as they were referred to unofficially became the first secret service members at the White House.

Despite these additional dangers, Tyler was steadfast in his ways. He arrogantly and stubbornly continued to fight with others and refused to compromise. Rocker also remained combative throughout the remainder of his career and into retirement. At various times he has disparaged sensitivity training, verbally taken people working inside MLB to task, campaigned for everyone to speak English, and stated the Holocaust never would have happened if Jewish people had been able to defend themselves by bearing arms.

Both men had a knack for asserting their presence and opinions. Even if they didn't actually think they were better than everyone else, it sure as hell came off that way to the public.

Tyler and Rocker both came on quickly and unexpectedly in relief. Sadly, for them, their personalities largely contributed to derailing their chances of success. These are two world-class alienators, but as far as their professional work goes, both men fall well short of the Hall of Fame.

Trading Card Stats

John Tyler	Name	John Rocker
•His Accidency	**Nickname**	•Captain Redneck
•1841-1845	**Experience**	•1998-2003
•51	**Age Entering the League**	•23
•6'0"/160	**HT/WT**	•6'4"/210
•None	**Team**	•Atlanta Braves •Cleveland Indians •Texas Rangers •Tampa Bay Devil Rays
•Webster-Ashburton Treaty (1842) •Treaty of Wanghia •Signed congressional resolution to annex Texas	**Stats**	•3.42 ERA •88 saves •11.7 strikeouts per 9 innings
•Violin •Playing with animals •Hunting	**Hobbies**	•Hunting •Fishing •Golf
•"Popularity, I have always thought, may aptly be compared to a coquette—the more you woo her; the more apt is she to elude your embrace."	**Quote**	•"The biggest thing I don't like about New York are the foreigners. I'm not a very big fan of foreigners. You can walk an entire block in Times Square and not hear anybody speaking English. How the hell did they get in this country?"
•One bomb threat against him resulted in two staff members hacking a package to pieces with a meat cleaver as Tyler peered out from behind a marble column	**Interesting**	•Rocker was a contestant on the show *Survivor: San Juan del Sur*
•No	**Hall of Fame**	•No

11

James Polk (1845-1849)

Have you ever felt you were so overworked that you might actually work yourself to death? Well, Polk actually did.

Ok, so officially his death was attributed to cholera—a bacterial disease contracted through food or liquid consumption—not long after leaving the Oval Office. But ask historians who have studied Polk's career and many will suggest that the cholera was simply the final straw that broke the overworked back of Polk.

Polk wasn't the most brilliant president, but what Polk lacked in intelligence, he made up for through hard work—not to mention a pretty sick mullet. He initially studied law before serving as a member of the Tennessee House of Representatives, a U.S. representative, and Tennessee's governor. He was also commissioned as a captain of a militia cavalry regiment and later rose to colonel.

Polk is widely considered the original dark horse candidate. During the 1844 Democratic Convention, it wasn't until the eighth ballot that Polk received his first votes for the party's presidential nomination. He wound up securing the nomination shortly after and rode a wave of annexing Texas and acquiring Oregon as his platform into the White House.

As the populace made it clear they supported Polk's desire to annex Texas, Congress did so, too, by passing a joint resolution three days before he took office. While in office, the U.S. also agreed to the Oregon Treaty of 1846 with Great Britain which set the present-day boundary of Oregon at the 49th parallel.

In an effort to increase free trade, Polk also worked to reduce tariff rates and implemented the Independent Treasury Act of 1846, essentially restoring the system originally created by Van Buren. This required all federal funds to be deposited in treasuries independent of private banks, which helped stabilize nearly a decade's worth of economic turmoil.

Under Polk's watch, the Mexican War was conducted. Seeing himself as a younger, albeit quieter, version of President Jackson, Polk aggressively pursued what he wanted and was unafraid of confrontation. Polk sought to acquire more land for the U.S. as a big believer in Manifest Destiny, or the cultural ideology that Americans were destined, by God, to expand their presence across North America.

Most critics believe Polk ordered troops to occupy disputed Mexican territory as an aggressive means to provoke an attack. This would create the appearance that Mexico was the aggressor, justify Polk's desire for war, and subsequently justify a fight over Texas. Once Mexico attacked, war began. Ultimately, a treaty was signed that ended two years of fighting and forced Mexico to relinquish more than 500,000 square miles of territory. While the vast acquisition of land helped improve U.S. size and strength, it hurt its reputation for being a fair and peaceful nation.

Despite that negative outside perception of the U.S., Polk was generally well liked by most, though he had few close friends due to his introverted nature. He forced himself to mingle with others out of political necessity, not out of enjoyment.

Most likely sport: Baseball

Polk proved to be capable of working with others and succeeding within a team structure, though he preferred operating alone. Baseball would have been Polk's sport of choice, allowing him to operate in a team setting but still creating some space for independence.

Thanks to Polk's generally poor health, he would not have survived as an everyday player. As a pitcher, Polk would not have had the stamina to start. So, like his predecessor, Polk would have excelled best as a relief pitcher.

Best Comparison: Joe Borowski

Joe Borowski was like the Six Flags theme park of pitching. You walk into the park and can already see it contains peaks and valleys. The next thing you know, you're in a tunnel getting water splashed in your face. For Borowski, like Polk, his career was an up-and-down adventure.

Borowski had a few cups of coffee in the majors during the late '90s. He was unable to stick with a team, though, and pitched in the Mexican League in 2000. In 2001, he appeared in one major league game for what would be his fourth different team. His career seemed to be going nowhere fast.

The following season, Borowski burst onto the major league scene notching back-to-back stellar campaigns. During those two years, he recorded a 2.69 ERA and 35 saves in 164 innings pitched.

While injuries and ineffectiveness would sabotage most of his 2004 and 2005 seasons, Borowski bounced back in 2006, saving 36 games. He then secured 45 saves in 2007 and won the AL Reliever of the Year award.

The 2008 season was a befitting end to his roller coaster career. Coming off his award-winning season, Borowski struggled mightily and was put on the disabled list with an injured triceps. By the middle of the season, and lacking any discernible improvement, Borowski was released, signaling the end of his career. He finished pitching for seven teams across 12 seasons in total.

Borowski had been drafted in the 32nd round. He was never considered a guy with "plus stuff"—pitch velocity, movement or control. Borowski simply outworked his competition. He studied his craft and worked himself into a position to experience success.

The same holds true for Polk. Nobody had really predicted greatness from Polk. He was relatively unknown when he snuck into the presidential conversation. His presidency saw plenty of ups and downs, largely defined by his actions in carrying out his plan for Manifest Destiny.

On the one hand, Polk carried out his presidential platform and secured a sizable portion of the land America has today. On the other hand, Polk did this in a sleazy fashion by seriously provoking the Mexican government if not outright being the reason the Mexican-American War started all together. Polk's tenure, especially in hindsight, offers a bit of a roller coaster ride experience.

Polk and Borowski were each rightfully considered underdogs who harnessed workaholic tendencies to achieve some success. Neither man was physically gifted, and both suffered numerous physical maladies, but through hard work and a single-mindedness, they were able to max out their talents.

Both Polk and Borowski carried a bulldog mentality to overcome some limitations in talent. Although Polk and Borowski weren't the most talented or successful men in their roles, there can be no mistaking, or dismissing, their work ethic. But a killer work ethic alone can't get you into the Hall of Fame.

Trading Card Stats

James Polk	Name	Joe Borowski
•Young Hickory •Napoleon of the Stump	**Nickname**	•Jumpin' Joe
•1845-1849	**Experience**	•1995-2008
•49	**Age Entering the League**	•24
•5'8"/174	**HT/WT**	•6'2"/225
•Democrat	**Team**	•Baltimore Orioles •Atlanta Braves •New York Yankees •Chicago Cubs •Tampa Bay Devil Rays •Florida Marlins •Cleveland Indians
•Walker Tariff of 1846 •Independent Treasury Act of 1846 •Oregon Treaty of 1846 •Mexican War	**Stats**	•454.1 innings pitched •4.18 ERA •131 saves
•Cooking •Tending to horses •Politics	**Hobbies**	•Football •Basketball
•"No president who performs his duties faithfully and conscientiously can have any leisure."	**Quote**	•"I despised baseball at that time." -Said after he was released in 2000
•Considered to be the original "dark horse" candidate	**Interesting**	•Signed a letter of intent to play at Rutgers University but never did
•No	**Hall of Fame**	•No

12

Zachary Taylor (1849-1850)

Zachary Taylor used to spit tobacco on the White House floor when a spittoon wasn't in reach. How's that for class?

Taylor was the epitome of the "everyman" who just happened to become the 12th president of the United States. In fact, he was a simple man who never even envisioned himself as a president. Prior to it, he knew very little about the world of politics. He was not well-versed in history. Funny enough, he had never even voted prior to being elected president.

Taylor didn't let the presidency change his personality or his style. Taylor's hat and clothes would be so torn and tattered that many Americans mistook the president for a farmer.

As for his journey to become president, it almost didn't happen.

Taylor lived for 40 years as a career military officer, rising from first lieutenant to major general. He served in the War of 1812, the Black Hawk War, the Second Seminole War, and the Mexican War. Taylor became well known and well respected for his work on the battlefield and was lauded tactically for how he treated everyone with respect, whether they were soldiers or generals.

When it came time for Whigs to nominate a candidate in the 1848 election, they pretty quickly settled on Taylor. Although Taylor had some reticence and even refused to campaign on his behalf, he found his way into the Oval Office.

Taylor's biggest successes during his brief stint as president came in the realm of foreign relations as he managed to avert war on a few different occasions. Most notably, he was able to diffuse rising tensions with Great Britain by agreeing to the Clayton-Bulwer Treaty of 1850 that said any canal built across Central America was to be neutral where neither side could occupy it or exert full control of the area.

Taylor also stopped the rising American desire to annex Canada. He enforced the Neutrality Act of 1818 on Germany, detaining a ship that posed a threat to make war on a friendly nation. He had also chosen not to retaliate after a white man had been killed by Native Americans, effectively avoiding another Seminole War.

On the domestic front, Taylor had a much calmer year. The economy was still stable, and the most prominent issue remained slavery. While Taylor was a big-time slaveholder, he opposed the extension of it and was committed to the Union. He denied the right for any state to secede.

Taylor's success was short-lived, however. Cholera had become rampant in the nation's capital during 1850. The public had been warned to avoid fresh fruit and unknown sources of water. But on a sweltering 4th of July, Taylor succumbed to temptation and downed a bowl of cherries, water, and ice milk that ultimately made him sick. In an ironic twist, Taylor had spent his entire life risking mortality, only to fall to his eventual demise five days later thanks to a bowl of fruit and his parched palate.

Most likely sport: Football

Taylor had always been tough, not to mention a bit unkempt. He was not charismatic, but he did fit in well with others and did what he thought was best for his team. He would have been best suited to play football.

You don't earn a nickname like "Old Rough and Ready" without being willing to stick your nose into a fight. Taylor would have enjoyed being physical and laying the wood on opponents. For this, he would have been a perfect fit leading his defense as a linebacker.

Best Comparison: David Griggs

When it comes to toughness, Taylor and Griggs are the epitome of the classic double-Spiderman meme.

Griggs made his way through the NFL with toughness rather than extraordinary talent. He grew up in New Jersey before attending college in Virginia. While there, Griggs had no issue scuffling with teammates to instill a more physical style of play. Fighting his college teammates became routine in an effort to set the right tempo.

When the NFL draft came around, he was selected in the seventh round by the New Orleans Saints for his gritty demeanor. Griggs, like Taylor, made it to the pros based largely on their "collegiate" reputation and winning background. However, the Saints eventually waived him, and Griggs latched on with the Miami Dolphins.

He spent five of his next six seasons there, building his status as a great fighter. Teammates, coaches, and fans all respected the way Griggs carried himself on the field and his fiery passion for the game.

Similarly, Taylor gained the respect of all Americans for how he handled himself on the battlefield. He encountered success in all four wars. The capper was his role at the Battle of Buena Vista in the Mexican War. Despite being heavily outnumbered, Taylor dealt a huge blow to the Mexican Army, inducing roughly three times as many casualties as his troops had suffered. Taylor became a national hero, a fan favorite.

Although Taylor and Griggs were far from nice on the field, they were known for being kind to those closest to them. They were both considered to be regular guys who connected with commoners. And, unfortunately, Griggs, like Taylor, died young.

Griggs died after losing control of his car one night and slamming into a pole. He had been driving 30 mph over the speed limit, and it was later discovered that his blood alcohol content level was twice the legal limit.

Griggs and Taylor were both guys who died just before entering the prime of their professions. Though their toughness and willingness to fight precedes them, neither man merits Hall of Fame consideration.

Trading Card Stats

Zachary Taylor	Name	David Griggs
•Old Rough and Ready	Nickname	•None know of
•1849-1850	Experience	•1989-1994
•64	Age Entering the League	•22
•5'8"/170	HT/WT	•6'3"/245
•Whig	Team	•Miami Dolphins •San Diego Chargers
•Clayton-Bulwer Treaty of 1850 •Enforced the Neutrality Act of 1818 on Germany	Stats	•14.5 sacks •1 interception •4 fumbles recovered
•Spending time with friends •Chewing tobacco	Hobbies	•Mentoring kids
•"Tell him to go to hell." -In reference to Mexican General Santa Anna's demand to surrender	Quote	•"I'm sure I made some enemies there, but that's life." -On his penchant for fighting teammates while at Virginia
•As a very cheap person, Taylor almost missed out on his presidential nomination as he had stopped accepting mail that wasn't prepaid and the nomination letter sat around for weeks before the Whigs found out what happened and sent him a prepaid letter	Interesting	•Got into a fight with local high school kids from another school, which ended in him running away from a group of roughly 30 kids, some of whom began firing gunshots at him
•No	Hall of Fame	•No

13

Millard Fillmore (1850-1853)

For a while, Fillmore's life read like that of a Hollywood movie. A boy comes from nothing. He is born in a log cabin, works the land, and receives little education throughout his childhood. He becomes a self-made man, teaching himself to read and write along the way, eventually rising to the position of president.

Fillmore was apprenticed to a clothmaker at age 14. With little by way of a formal education, he bought a dictionary when he was 17 to begin improving his vocabulary. At 19, he enrolled in an academy to begin studying law. Eventually, he was offered to work as a full-time clerk in a law office, once he had amassed enough money to buy himself out of indentured servitude.

Fillmore was elected as the New York State Assemblyman following years of law practice which he followed up with roles as a U.S. representative, the comptroller of New York, and vice president.

Interestingly, he was chosen by his party to be vice president despite having no working relationship with the presidential candidate, Taylor. The first time the two men ever spoke to each other was after their ticket won the election. The two never really grew close as Fillmore was often left out of Taylor's decision making.

After Taylor's death in 1850, Fillmore was handed the reins. As president, Fillmore adhered to what he genuinely thought were the best interests of all Americans, such as sending Commodore Matthew Perry (no, friends, not *that* Matthew Perry) to Japan with the intent to open up trade in the Far East. This eventually led to the Treaty of Kanagawa in 1854 during the Pierce administration, opening the doors for trade between the U.S. and Japan.

On the home front, the issue of slavery was beginning to dominate the national conversation. While Fillmore was anti-slavery, he was also anti-abolitionist and thought slaves should eventually be freed and sent back to Africa.

Fillmore's most controversial decision during his presidency was to fully support the Compromise of 1850, which admitted California as a free state. The territories of New Mexico and Utah were created. Their fates, as it related to being free or slave states, would be left to popular sovereignty, allowing the citizens of that state to decide.

The Fugitive Slave Act was also part of the compromise. It required all citizens and the federal government to play a more active role in returning any fugitive slaves to their Southern owners. Of course, the new law affected not only runaways but free blacks, too. Many free black people in the North were wrongly identified as runaway slaves and forced to go to the South. Black people had no recourse of action as they were denied the right to a trial.

The final part of the compromise stated that the slave trade would be abolished in the District of Columbia. Slavery itself, however, would still remain intact.

In supporting the Compromise of 1850, Fillmore was doing what he thought was best for all Americans—avoiding Civil War. Most Americans (well, white Americans) and historians at the time thought he handled the situation well. He had done enough to appease Northerners and Southerners to avoid secession or war, successfully kicking the can down the road.

In hindsight, Fillmore only delayed and, perhaps, exacerbated the hostilities when they rose again shortly after his term ended. Fillmore had viewed slavery as a political issue rather than a moral issue. While Fillmore's rise to prominence may have begun like a Hollywood movie, it ended with a straight-to-DVD finish.

Most likely sport: Baseball

Baseball would have been Fillmore's best sport, guided by his slowed down approach to life. Fillmore spoke slowly and deliberately. He was also measured, unhurried by life whirring around him. Additionally, his inclination to think logically and thoroughly about his plans would have made baseball's strategic nature all the more appealing.

Despite Fillmore's good looks and well-built body, he did not have an athletic background. And despite good intelligence, he lacked the acceleration, speed, or range of motion needed to adequately play most positions. First base would have been the best fit.

Best Comparison: Ed Konetchy

Like Fillmore, Konetchy grew up as an underdog.

He received little education growing up and by age 14 was working at a candy factory. There, baseball entered his life, and he began playing recreationally. Konetchy walked two miles to work to complete his 10-hour shift, walked another two miles to a ball field, and then played until it was dark.

At 16, Konetchy began playing for the factory's competitive baseball team. By 19, he had successfully earned a spot on LaCrosse's Class D Wisconsin State League team. Konetchy posted a couple of good seasons in LaCrosse and was then purchased to play professionally for the St. Louis Cardinals.

Konetchy played for five teams across a 13-year span, taking a one-year hiatus to play in the Federal League, which was known as the "third major league" next to the National and American leagues. During that time, Konetchy amassed 74 home runs, nearly 1,000 RBI, and a 46.4 career WAR. He even cracked the top-15 in MVP voting during his 1912 campaign.

Konetchy was regarded as a well-rounded player. He took naturally to first base, fielding with soft hands and displaying an innate ability to dig out low throws. At the plate, he had worked himself into being a good hitter, possessing extra-base power and the ability to steal bags, as well.

Throughout the late aughts and into the teens, Konetchy was considered one of the game's better players. He could play offense, defense, and was also considered to be a generally good guy. In 1911, the Cardinals were involved in a train wreck in which a dozen passengers were killed. Konetchy was credited with leading the rescue effort as he carried out a number of injured commuters, ultimately increasing his baseball notoriety, as well.

As time has gone on, however, it's easier to take a more objective look at his numbers and see that while Konetchy was a pretty good player, he was closer to being an average ballplayer than a great one. His career WAR falls more than 20 wins short of the average Hall of Fame first baseman. Baseball Reference has Konetchy's similarity score being most like Wally Pipp who was a good player but is most famous for getting hurt, being replaced by Lou Gehrig, and then subsequently losing his job.

Similarly, Fillmore was originally thought to be a great president, though retrospection proved otherwise. Although his presidency was generally a time of peace and prosperity, he never did much to address the crucially important social and moral dilemmas facing the nation. He simply pushed it to the back burner until he exited the Oval Office. Apparently, kicking the proverbial can down the road wasn't the best solution.

Both Fillmore and Konetchy were held in high regard during their heydays. But just because something seemed great at the time doesn't mean it was. Think popped collars, jorts, MTV, and of course everyone's favorite: Nickelback.

Anyway, this is not to bash Fillmore and Konetchy. The two had, at worst, average careers. Unfortunately, that's not good enough to put them in the Hall of Fame.

Trading Card Stats

Millard Fillmore	Name	Ed Konetchy
•His Accidency	Nickname	•Big Ed
•1850-1853	Experience	•1907-1921
•50	Age Entering the League	•21
•5'9"/164	HT/WT	•6'2"/195
•Whig	Team	•St. Louis Cardinals •Pittsburgh Pirates •Pittsburgh Rebels •Boston Braves •Brooklyn Robins •Philadelphia Phillies
•Compromise of 1850 •Fugitive Slave Act •Commodore Matthew Perry's mission to Japan •1854 Treaty of Kanagawa	Stats	•2,085 games played •74 home runs •255 stolen bases •.749 OPS
•Reading •Civil affairs •History	Hobbies	•Running a chicken farm
•"It is a national disgrace that our presidents, after having occupied the highest position in the country, should be cast adrift, and, perhaps, be compelled to keep a corner grocery for substance."	Quote	•"I know I tried to play baseball as soon as I was big enough to raise a bat from the ground."
•Turned down an honorary degree from Oxford University saying, "No man should...accept a degree he cannot read."	Interesting	•Has the most career triples (182) of any player not in the Hall of Fame
•No	Hall of Fame	•No

14

Franklin Pierce (1853-1857)

Well, that didn't go as planned.

Pierce entered the White House with high expectations and grand plans to lift the nation to new heights, just like most presidents when entering the White House. But unlike most presidents, Pierce reached a level of failure so extreme it makes Blockbuster look successful for declining to acquire Netflix in 2000.

Pierce's ascent to the White House started as a member of the New Hampshire legislature before serving as a speaker of the New Hampshire legislature. After that, he served as a U.S. representative, followed by a stint in the Senate.

Not long before the 1852 election, Pierce was about as dark a dark horse candidate as you could imagine. It took 35 votes before a member of the Democratic party listed Pierce's name on the ballot and it wasn't until the 49th ballot when a Democratic delegate made an impassioned speech on Pierce's behalf. This caused momentum to swell, and Pierce quickly won the party's presidential nomination.

Pierce entered his presidency as an ardent supporter of slavery, though he was firmly against the notion of secession. As a U.S. representative, Pierce had supported a gag rule that would prevent the mere consideration of anti-slavery petitions. He wholeheartedly supported the 1854 Kansas-Nebraska Act, which gave settlers in existing territories the ability to vote on whether their new states would be free or slave-owning.

Residents in Nebraska easily rebuffed the idea of slavery. But the battle for Kansas was venomous and vitriolic. Hard core Northern abolitionists and slavery-supporting Border Ruffians bitterly detested the other group. Eventually violence broke out, thanks to John Brown's infamous raid, in which he led a group to rebel against pro-slavery supporters. More than 200 casualties were suffered as a result of the rebellion known as "Bleeding Kansas."

Pierce was also very land-hungry as president. Through the Gadsden Purchase, the U.S. bought more than 45,000 square miles of land for $10 million to complete the modern outline of the 48 contiguous states. He also "negotiated" (at gunpoint) 52 different Indian treaties, taking 174 million acres of Indian land for $11 million where Pierce then involuntarily put the displaced Indians in two reservations.

Pierce wasn't done there, however. He even had plans to annex Cuba from Spain. Pierce was planning the Ostend Manifesto, which would buy Cuba from Spain and then go to war if Spain didn't agree to sell. What was meant to be an internal memo between the president and his secretary of war was leaked to the press, though, causing a public outcry. This forced Pierce to back out of his intended plan.

To top off Pierce's shiny humanitarian resume, he also opposed the government doing anything to help poor people and opposed the right of labor to organize.

By the end of Pierce's first term, he had proven his inability to control the unfolding drama that was leading the country down a path to Civil War. He couldn't find any support, and gave up on his hopes for a potential re-election bid when his own party coined the slogan, "Anybody but Pierce."

Most likely sport: Football

Often considered one of the most handsome presidents ever, Pierce sure looked to fit the desired mold entering his presidency. He was strong, active, and a bit devilish as a youngster when he was quick to fight if he thought the situation called for it. His tough demeanor and strong physical appearance would have lent himself best to football.

It would be hard to find a much better natural position for Pierce than quarterback based on his physique and pre-presidential success. He wasn't a huge person, but Pierce had a good build, was good looking, and showed a lot of potential from an early age. The combination of stereotypical quarterback looks and being the most talented person in his field prior to the presidency would have pegged him to that position dating back to his peewee football days.

Best Comparison: JaMarcus Russell

Well, that also didn't go as planned.

Pierce was not alone in his unexpectedly horrific, professional performance. Russell stayed stride for stride in his disappointing career.

A few years before Russell blew up in weight, going from about 265 pounds to more than 300, he blew up the minds of professional scouts. He showed steady improvement throughout his time at LSU. During his junior campaign, Russell threw for more than 3,000 yards and 28 touchdowns, while completing nearly 69% of his passes.

Although his college numbers were solid, it was his pre-draft workout that set the stage for his NFL future and the high expectations that were soon to follow. The workout was the stuff of legends. A God masquerading in the body of a mortal.

A quarterback with his size is always sought after. A quarterback with his footwork, ability to roll out of the pocket, and make throws on the run is rare. A quarterback with his arm strength doesn't exist.

Russell had the ability to throw the ball more than 80 yards and blew scouts away with his size and skillset. By the end of his pre-draft workout, Russell had become the consensus top prospect. That's exactly what he was when tabbed as the number one overall pick by the Oakland Raiders in that year's draft.

As a Raider, however, Russell never recaptured the form he displayed during his magical pre-draft workout. He suffered through a miserable three seasons before being released and never stepped foot on NFL soil again.

Russell and Pierce both shared an atrocious work experience. They failed in both strategy and execution on most fronts. A lot of their issues, though, stemmed from their personal habits.

Both men were widely considered poor decision makers who didn't quite understand the ramifications of their choices. Russell never harnessed the great power his arm possessed and it often got him into trouble. He tried to force too many balls into spots where his receivers weren't open, leading to a career 52% completion rate and more interceptions than touchdowns.

Off the field, Russell experienced a series of moments ranging from brain-fart to what's-the-matter-with-you status. In one embarrassing episode, Raiders coaches suspected Russell hadn't been studying tape to help his development, so they gave him blank tapes as a test. When Russell returned to the facility the next day, he told the coaches about having studied blitz packages. I repeat. They gave him blank tapes.

He was also once arrested for illegally possessing codeine syrup, and he admitted to having previously tested positive for it as a rookie in the NFL, though he was never indicted. He's certainly not the only athlete who was using codeine, back during a time when lean (or purple drank) was pretty popular. But it does signal either a dependency or a strong lack of judgement for someone who had just been released by the Raiders and was actively seeking another job opportunity.

For Pierce, his inability to see and understand the bubbling hostilities over the issue of slavery prove his troubled decision-making. The Bleeding Kansas episode brought the crisis of sectionalism to a dangerous new height. But Pierce saw the issue as an abolitionist problem and lacked the ability to inspire or persuade the nation to band together in any direction. He simply stood by as events unfolded and the nation unraveled.

Part of the reason for that was Pierce struggled on and off with alcoholism throughout his adult life. Though, if there was ever something to bring a person to drinking, losing three children before age 11 might do it—the third of which happened two months before Pierce's inauguration as the result of a train accident. While cause-and-effect can't be proven, it certainly stands to reason that the substance abuse didn't do his decision making any favors.

In the end, Russell and Pierce both seemed overwhelmed by the job, unable to perform up to their own standards and those of the public. The public lost trust in both of these men, and as a result, their teams and their professions also lost trust and lost interest. Both men are considered to be two of the biggest busts in history, effectively denying any Hall of Fame consideration.

Trading Card Stats

Franklin Pierce	Name	JaMarcus Russell
•Young Hickory of the Granite Hills	**Nickname**	•OffDaMarcus
•1853-1857	**Experience**	•2007-2009
•48	**Age Entering the League**	•22
•5'10"/144	**HT/WT**	•6'6"/265
•Democrat	**Team**	•Oakland Raiders
•1854 Kansas-Nebraska Act •Bleeding Kansas •1853 Gadsden Purchase	**Stats**	•4,083 passing yards •18 touchdowns •23 interceptions
•Fishing	**Hobbies**	•Bowling •Video games
•"There is nothing left...but to get drunk." -Referring to his plans after not being nominated by his party for a second presidential term	**Quote**	•"I am a better man because of my struggles, and I simply desire an opportunity (to) redeem myself. I do not want my legacy to be a trail of unfulfilled dreams and missed opportunities."
•Friends with Nathaniel Hawthorne, and he was a classmate of Henry Wadsworth Longfellow	**Interesting**	•Reportedly threw the ball 70 yards from his knees while in high school
•No	**Hall of Fame**	•No

15

James Buchanan (1857-1861)

Timing is everything.

And for Buchanan, that sentiment certainly rang true.

It was great timing that brought Buchanan into the White House. Buchanan's path began with his law studies while in school. His working background included being a member of the Pennsylvania House of

Representatives, a U.S. representative, the U.S. minister to Russia, a U.S. senator, the secretary of state, and the minister to Great Britain.

It was this last role that propelled him to the top of Washington politics. Because Buchanan had been out of the country as the Kansas-Nebraska Act consumed the nation, he never had the opportunity to anger any region or demographic by publicly commenting on the situation.

His absence ultimately played a large part in securing the presidency. But what lucky timing giveth, lucky timing taketh away. Buchanan had no grasp of just how big and volatile slavery had become in the U.S., and this was the biggest factor in his presidential ineptitude.

Before ripping into Buchanan, he does deserve some credit. When it came to foreign affairs, Buchanan actually performed well. During his term, the U.S. opened the door to diplomatic relations with nations in Asia. In all, Buchanan opened trade with three different continents via treaty. He helped decrease escalating tensions on the San Juan Islands after war was threatened over an English pig that was shot by an American.

Buchanan even showed political and military might by invoking the Monroe Doctrine in the Caribbean and Central America to protect U.S. interests. His quick, decisive action led lurking European interveners to back down. Looking comprehensively at Buchanan's foreign track record, one could make an argument that he was nearing "great" status as president. Sadly, for Buchanan, his domestic policies completely overshadowed all of his successes.

And, now, it is time to rip into Buchanan. From the start, Buchanan was hit with the Panic of 1857. While Buchanan wasn't to blame for the economic recession, he was responsible for much of the ensuing suffering. He stood on the sideline and offered his sympathy to poor people who were devastated by the depression but the only support he offered was by ensuring Americans that they would prevail on their own.

Then there was that whole slavery thing. Buchanan quickly lost his hold on Northerners when he supported the Lecompton Constitution, which would have made Kansas a slave-owning state. The idea was concocted by pro-slavery settlers who essentially offered Kansas two options: be a state with unabashed slavery or be a state where slavery was permitted but future slaves could not be imported from outside the state. Anti-slavery activists refused to vote, and Congress ultimately refused to implement the Lecompton Constitution.

From that point forward, hostility grew toward Buchanan and Democrats lost control of both houses in the following midterms. Speaking of hostility, the outlook only grew bleaker as the race debate waged on.

By the end of Buchanan's term, seven states had seceded from the Union. The president's solution? He watched from afar.

Buchanan didn't believe the Constitution could legally prevent states from seceding. His plan was to patiently wait so as not to anger the remaining Southern states, while also hoping that states which had already seceded would be unable to work together and find that a return to the Union was their only option.

Buchanan even refused to act after a South Carolina ship opened fire on a Northern vessel. The lame-duck president was prepared to watch his country dissolve.

Most likely sport: Baseball

Buchanan did work hard and was devoted to his craft. As someone who moved at a leisurely pace in his everyday life and had an ease about him, Buchanan would have been best suited for a slower, grind-it-out sport like baseball.

Buchanan possessed good stamina as a president but had trouble seeing consequences clearly. He also spent many days standing off to the side watching as the nation unraveled, almost as if he were off from work those days. Buchanan, as a result, may have had poor pitch command because of his vision, but he fits the bill of a starting pitcher.

Best Comparison: Gus Weyhing

Buchanan wasn't the only one who had a hard time with his vision at work. Meet Gus Weyhing.

The native of Louisville, KY, spent the better part of his 14 years in professional baseball bouncing around from team to team. He spent time on 11 teams in total with seven of those teams being just a one-year stop along his journey.

Weyhing, like Buchanan, had moments where it looked like he possessed greatness. He had three separate seasons posting an ERA under 3.00 and won 30+ games four straight seasons from 1889-1892.

Weyhing pitched 448 complete games, good for 12th most all time. He had proven stamina, recording 4,337 innings pitched in his career, putting him at 33rd all time. He even has a no-hitter to his name.

But like Buchanan, Rubber-Winged Gus is better known by baseball historians for what he didn't do well. Weyhing had seemingly little control of his pitches. Whether the cause was related to eyesight, command, or just an unidentified case of the yips, it was a problem that plagued Weyhing throughout his time in the big leagues.

Weyhing finished his career 10th on the all-time list of walks allowed by pitchers with 1570. He issued more walks than a doggy daycare. Only one player on the list, Amos Rusie, climbed above him on the list in fewer seasons pitched than Weyhing. And Weyhing holds the dubious honor of hitting the most batters all time, having done so on 277 professional occasions. The next closest person still falls 58 hit batters shy of Weyhing's impressive feat.

Buchanan also could not see as he lacked foresight into how his actions (or inactions) would affect the country. While he struggled to see situations politically, he also literally could not see well physically. He had an eye disorder where one eye was nearsighted and the other farsighted. His left eye was also higher in its socket than the right eye. So, who would really blame Buchanan for having poor control of his pitches?

Weyhing had the makings of a great pitcher. Had he been able to harness that control, it's very likely he would have ended up being remembered for different reasons. The same holds true for Buchanan. In his dealings with foreign nations, Buchanan proved himself talented enough to have been a great president. But his inability to handle domestic issues is why he's better remembered for watching his country spiral into chaos and bloodshed.

While both men serve as great case studies on the duality of talent and success, that doesn't make them great candidates for the Hall of Fame.

Trading Card Stats

James Buchanan	Name	Gus Weyhing
•Ten-Cent Jimmy •Bachelor President •Old Buck	Nickname	•Cannonball •Rubber Arm Gun •Rubber-Winged Gus
•1857-1861	Experience	•1887-1901
•65	Age Entering the League	•20
•6'0"/198	HT/WT	•5'10"/145
•Democrat	Team	•Philadelphia Athletics •Philadelphia Phillies •Pittsburgh Pirates •Louisville Colonels •Washington Senators •St. Louis Cardinals •Brooklyn Superbas •Cleveland Blues •Cincinnati Reds
•Panic of 1857 •Pig War of 1859 •Allowed secession to begin and did nothing to stop it	Stats	•264-232 record •3.88 ERA •1,570 BB •277 hit batters
•Reading •Entertaining friends •Playing cards	Hobbies	•None known of
•"My dear sir, if you are as happy on entering the White House as I on leaving it, you are a very happy man indeed." -Said to Lincoln in 1861	Quote	•"Weyhing has a weakness for fine pigeons; in fact, is quite a pigeon fancier, and this fact makes the charge appear plausible." -A Louisville newspaper article in 1862 reporting on a local pigeon theft
•Morally opposed slavery and bought slaves to free them	Interesting	•All-time leader in hit batters
•No	Hall of Fame	•No

16

Abraham Lincoln (1861-1865)

Let's go ahead and punch Lincoln's Hall of Fame ticket now and move on to Andrew Johnson.

Wait, what? You still want to discuss his career? All right, have it your way.

While Lincoln's track record isn't flawless, it's pretty damn good.

Lincoln was a skilled rail-splitter growing up and became very handy with an axe. Having received only one year of formal education, Lincoln learned to read and write by practicing it on his own and with the help of various individuals. He eventually became a postmaster, leading the post office of New Salem, Illinois, before studying law and becoming a member of the Illinois legislature for eight years before serving as a U.S. representative.

As president, Lincoln would go on to have unprecedented success in almost every facet. One of the most underappreciated areas of success during his tenure was with foreign policy where, on multiple occasions, Lincoln de-escalated rising tensions to avoid war with other countries. He navigated the Tent Affair in which Confederate diplomats had been seized and removed from a neutral ship, averting potential war with England and France.

He traversed another quagmire with England after the U.S. seized one of their ships for supposedly carrying contraband to Mexico. Lincoln also offered diplomatic recognition to Haiti and Liberia, which were both governed by black people.

Lincoln even knew when to let some threats slide from other countries. He recognized Mexico's Maximilian regime even though Lincoln knew he was a puppet for Napoleon III, thus violating the Monroe Doctrine. Lincoln deemed this didn't elicit enough cause for concern at the time when he had bigger fish to fry.

Like a Civil War.

Lincoln oversaw the first and only Civil War in United States history after decades of rising tension spilled into bloodshed. The tall, lanky president displayed a deft handle of the situation as he desperately fought to keep the union together. As time wore on, Lincoln transitioned from opposing the future spread of slavery to adamantly advocating for the abolishment of slavery. Though the war would last nearly the entirety of Lincoln's presidency, the North did prevail. The Union remained intact. And Lincoln laid the foundation for granting all people of color their freedom.

Other significant, though less notable, highlights during Lincoln's time in office included the Homestead Act and the Morrill Act. The Homestead Act granted up to 160 acres of land to anyone settling on public land who stayed there for five years. This law significantly contributed to the settling of the Great Plains after the Civil War. Meanwhile, the Morrill Act granted public lands to each state, relative to its congressional representation, to be sold in an effort to finance colleges focused on financial, agricultural, and mechanical endeavors.

The Civil War had hardly been over for one week when Confederate sympathizer John Wilkes Booth shot Lincoln dead at Ford's Theatre in the nation's capital. Lincoln was just beginning his second term and had his sights set on piecing a broken nation back together.

Following his death, Lincoln became a martyr as much of the nation grieved. Whether a person was anti-slavery, a Northerner, a person of color, a pro-Union supporter, or just a person who believed in humanity, what Lincoln had tried to do for his country deserved admiration. His legacy began to crystalize more over time, but make no mistake, hate him or love him, Lincoln earned the vast majority of the nation's respect.

Most likely sport: Basketball

Lincoln was a great leader who worked well with teammates but always knew how to operate on his own when necessary. He had good size and disproportionately long arms and legs, resulting in an elite wing span. (Drink up, Jay Bilas fans!)

Lincoln was also one of the most talented presidents ever who could control a game or situation all by himself. He probably would have been talented enough to pursue a number of sports if he had dedicated himself to it, but basketball would be his true calling.

Lincoln had good size and an all-around skillset. If you put the ball in his hands, he would know how to handle it and run a team. He had superior vision. He was strong enough mentally to be the focal point of a team and outwardly brushed off criticism.

He was strong enough physically to take a pounding at the rim and keep coming back for more. He once famously got into a wrestling match with Jack Armstrong, the leader of an Illinois gang. It was reportedly a fierce competition and though details of who won remain sketchy, Lincoln had certainly won the gang's respect as they would attend all of Lincoln's debates as a show of support.

And, of course, Lincoln was unafraid to shoot the rock and put the outcome of a game on his shoulders. As a result of his well-rounded game, he would have been primarily a wing who could successfully operate at any position required of him to win.

Best Comparison: Michael Jordan

From one great to another, there isn't much room for debate here. Jordan is widely, and with good reason, considered the GOAT.

Jordan combined elite skill with a relentless drive for excellence on his way to six championships. He was able to claim a myriad of records and awards in the process. To many, his name is synonymous with winning and greatness.

However, the start of Jordan's career wasn't perfect. Jordan's game went through an evolution process before he reached success. He entered the league as a talented player but had to endure some growing pains. It was a mix of inexperience, injuries, and rival teams that put roadblocks in front of Jordan.

The Chicago Bulls immediately used Jordan as the focal point of their team during his rookie season but were unable to escape the first round of the playoffs. A broken foot cost Jordan most of his second season. The third season ended just like the first two—with a first-round exit in the playoffs.

Then came his battles with the Detroit Pistons who defeated the Bulls three straight seasons, putting Jordan through the ringer physically and mentally. It wasn't until his seventh season that he finally broke through en route to six straight titles. Experiencing the losing early on better taught Jordan how to win later on. His game also evolved over time from more of an athletic, acrobatic aerial attack to a smooth-shooting, high-IQ all-around game that devastated opponents

Similarly, Lincoln also had to evolve before finding his own success. Like Jordan, Lincoln came into office talented but lacking in experience. His first, and most important, task was to keep the Union intact by preventing Southern states from seceding.

By the time Lincoln was sworn in, he morally opposed slavery but felt bound by the Constitution to uphold it. He tried to delicately massage the topic in hopes of bringing Southern states back into the fold. Lincoln made it clear he was willing to do whatever necessary to keep Southern states from seceding, including letting the institution of slavery continue, because his top priority was to keep the country from disbanding.

When this tactic did not work, and the South still seceded, Lincoln became more stern. The war began, and Lincoln began taking away the Constitutional protections from Southern states. This included refusing to return any runaway slaves who had escaped from seceded states to eventually announcing the emancipation of all slaves residing in rebelling states.

Lincoln had grown intent on seeing the war through, while first implicitly, then later explicitly, setting the stage to end the system of slavery all together. As the war trudged on, Lincoln masterfully learned how to tie slavery's abolishment to his main objective of keeping the union together. His ability to maneuver between those two, both publicly and politically, drew plenty of ire and criticism.

But it was also what allowed him to have the best chance of winning the war, making the union whole again, and abolishing slavery.

Lincoln and Jordan were also able to find success in their ability to connect with the average person. Lincoln made a habit of holding office hours in which he personally interacted with dignitaries and commoners, alike. Jordan on the other hand knew how to reach the masses through his NIKE shoe endorsements and commercials. Both men proved how important it was to be able to make a connection with the broader population, something that buoyed their post-playing legacies.

Despite the connection these two greats made, there were still plenty of doubters back when their careers were starting. Jordan and Lincoln learned how to take in all the criticism they heard on the outside and harness that negativity into motivation. Lincoln heard the cries of him being too supportive of slaves, not supportive enough, too inept to run a country, too aloof to win a war. Jordan heard that he wasn't a winner, was just an athlete and nothing else, and that he wasn't a good enough teammate. Both men used the criticisms to fuel their drive.

That drive took them to the upper-most echelons of their professions. They could have flown even higher, however, if their careers had not been shortened. For Jordan, it was a choice. Or two choices. Or one choice and one silent suspension, depending on what conspiracy theories you want to chase.

Either way, Jordan retired from the game on three separate occasions. The first retirement was because Jordan wanted to play baseball (or maybe because he was kicked out of the league for gambling…like I said, it has been denied, but there's still some mystery around it). This took place smack dab in between his two three-peats. Had he not missed that time, it's very conceivable he would have won eight straight titles. The second retirement came after his second three-peat when he was still putting up superstar numbers and would have continued to compete at a high level. It wasn't until his third, and final, retirement with the Washington Wizards that it was clearly time to hang it up and take a bow.

For Lincoln, the shortening of his career was a bit more permanent when he was assassinated just weeks into his second term in office.

Despite the abbreviated careers, these two not only punched their Hall of Fame tickets. They also managed to achieve GOAT status along the way.

Trading Card Stats

Abraham Lincoln	Name	Michael Jordan
•Honest Abe •The Railsplitter •The Great Emancipator	**Nickname**	•MJ •Air Jordan •His Airness
•1861-1865	**Experience**	•1984-1993 •1995-1998 •2001-2003
•52	**Age Entering the League**	•21
•6'4"/180	**HT/WT**	•6'6"/195
•Republican	**Team**	•Chicago Bulls •Washington Wizards
•Civil War •Homestead Act •Morrill Act	**Stats**	•30.1 points, 6.2 rebounds and 5.3 assists per game •6-time NBA champion •6-time NBA Finals MVP •5-time MVP •14-time All-Star •2-time Olympic gold medalist
•Reading •Theater •Chess •Telling jokes	**Hobbies**	•Golf •Baseball •Gambling
•"If I had another face, do you think I would wear this one?" -Said in response to being called a two-face	**Quote**	•"I can accept failure, but I can't accept not trying."
•Wrestled a gang leader in New Salem, IL; the winner is unclear but Lincoln handled himself so well that the entire gang would go support Lincoln at debates	**Interesting**	•Jordan started the trend of wearing baggier shorts when he wanted to wear his North Carolina shorts underneath his Chicago Bulls shorts
•Yes	**Hall of Fame**	•Yes

17

Andrew Johnson (1865-1869)

There are plenty of things you can say about Andrew Johnson. He was not a great leader, he lacked charisma, and he did not have a warm personality. But one thing you can't say about the man was that he lacked cojones.

Johnson was the only Southern congressman who opposed secession on the eve of the Civil War. His support for the Union never wavered. Not even after his support of the Union nearly had him hanged during a trip to his home state of Tennessee in spring 1861.

While riding the train through Virginia, Johnson had to use his pistol to keep civilians away from his car. Another angry mob, however, managed to pull him off the train. The secessionist group beat Johnson and only refrained from hanging him because they thought his home state should have been afforded the honor.

That's generally how rough life was for Johnson as a Union-supporting Southerner during the war. Johnson, though, was unfazed by rough times.

He had grown up in abject poverty and, at age 14, Johnson became an indentured servant at a tailor shop. After two years, Johnson ran away and eventually opened his own tailor shop where his professional career slowly started evolving. He became alderman, which is similar to a city councilman, of Greeneville, TN, and then later became the city's mayor.

Johnson then spent time in the Tennessee House of Representatives and Senate, became the governor of Tennessee, a U.S. senator, and spent a month as Lincoln's vice president.

Johnson became the third person to take the reins from a predecessor after Lincoln was shot and killed. Johnson, in some ways, was lucky to have taken over for Lincoln because Johnson would have been dead too as part of the larger plot to kill several Union leaders had it not been for a bout of cold feet from the would-be killer, George Atzerodt.

In terms of policy, while Johnson wasn't quite at Lincoln's level, he was strategically able to hold his own. He was left to pick up the pieces in Lincoln's wake and oversaw the Reconstruction effort as a result. Johnson wanted to carry out a lenient Southern Reconstruction after the war, but Southerners and radical Republicans made life difficult.

Unfortunately for Johnson, his leadership qualities were nowhere near those of Lincoln. He had trouble inspiring others to follow his lead and was surrounded by hostile, corrupt, and undermining cabinet members.

Personally, though, Johnson was an ethical man and always tried to act in the best interest of the people while he was in office. Interestingly, at one point Johnson owned slaves but wound up championing for their rights after the war. His administration passed the 13th and 14th amendments to outlaw slavery, while also granting citizenship and equal protection to black people. Johnson also showed reverence for Native Americans, demanding that a railroad be re-routed out of respect for Sioux lands.

In other political matters, the U.S. purchased Alaska for $7.2 million. Johnson then restored the Monroe Doctrine by expelling the French from Mexico and executing Maximilian. Johnson's showing in office proved to other nations he would go to great lengths to protect American interests but had no desire to interfere with those nations.

Johnson's term was marred by his impeachment in 1868. He is one of only three presidents who have been impeached in the United States' history. He was brought to trial for ignoring the Tenure of Office Act, forbidding the president from removing certain public officials without the Senate's consent. This law had been recently implemented to show support for Secretary of War Edward Stanton, a radical Republican, who was at odds with Johnson's approach to Reconstruction. Senate Republicans were worried that Johnson would attempt to oust Stanton over their differences and preemptively passed legislation to prevent it.

Johnson ignored the law, deeming it unconstitutional, and tried to get rid of Stanton anyway. The president was brought to trial where the Senate fell one vote shy of kicking Johnson to the curb. After nearly being removed from office, Johnson was unsurprisingly passed over when it came time for the 1868 Democratic presidential nomination.

Most likely sport: Baseball

Though Johnson could be feisty at times, his largely reserved demeanor would have suited him well for the ebbs and flows of a long baseball season.

As someone who covered a lot of ground going from Southerner to Northern-supporter and slave-holder to slavery-ender, Johnson would have had a knack for broadly roaming the outfield of major league parks.

Best Comparison: Harry Leibold

Ah, good old Harry Leibold—otherwise known as Nemo thanks to his pint-sized nature.

Everyone is familiar with Leibold. And, of course, by everyone, I do mean no one.

Leibold grew up as a poor kid in Detroit's inner-city. As a teenager, Leibold quit school and started working at a factory to help support his family. He played semi-pro ball in 1910 before signing with the Milwaukee Brewers to play minor league ball for a couple of years.

Leibold would crack the majors with the Cleveland Naps in 1913. In total, he spent 13 seasons in the big leagues, winning two titles. He wasn't much of a hitter; but what Leibold lacked in offensive prowess, he made up for with speed and defense.

Leibold's scrappiness epitomized the Deadball era in baseball when scoring runs came at a premium and homerun power was almost nonexistent. After his playing career ended, Leibold stuck around the game as he managed in the minor leagues for 21 seasons.

Perhaps the most notable item on his resume was for something he didn't do—cheat. In 1919, eight players from the Chicago White Sox were found to have purposefully thrown the World Series in exchange for money. The incident became known as the Black Sox scandal for its corrupt nature.

Leibold was eventually absolved of any culpability despite having roomed with Buck Weaver, one of the eight found guilty. Leibold had found himself surrounded by teammates acting corruptly. He lost out on a potential third championship and, for a time, had his name besmirched as he dealt with an investigation into his knowledge of the scandal.

Similarly, Johnson also had to deal with teammates who made life more difficult than he would have liked. Secretary of War Stanton was, at best, disrespectful. Emotionally unstable and extremely disobedient, he overstepped his bounds on numerous occasions. Stanton was spying on the White House administration and utilizing information before Johnson could deal with it.

Stanton revoked Johnson's order to end martial law after the war. He even intercepted a message from the Louisiana governor and hid it from Johnson prior to riots that took place in New Orleans, which killed 200 people. When death penalties for the Lincoln assassination were being carried out, Stanton tore out a page from the court documentation recommending leniency for one of the involved parties before Johnson got to review it. The man was hasty, if not altogether crazy.

His replacement, General Grant, would ultimately break his promise to Johnson and turn his power back over to Stanton after the Senate ordered Stanton's reinstatement. In the war's aftermath there was a general lack of unity and morality from inside and outside the administration that led to an untenable situation for Johnson.

The one personality trait that likely kept Johnson from folding was his courage. Johnson always stood firm on what he believed in. It took a certain grit and scrappiness to never waver. He even deviated at times from his normally mild-mannered approach to support his beliefs. During a particular bout of heckling, a miffed Johnson compared himself to Jesus Christ and claimed that God had struck down Lincoln in order for him to become president.

Leibold was also known to carry an indignant disposition on occasion That manifested in a regrettable incident in 1946 when Leibold punched Forrest Peters, an umpire, after the two began arguing. Leibold was suspended indefinitely but returned after just six games.

Neither Leibold nor Johnson had the early trajectory of someone who would make it to the pinnacle of their profession, but both guys actually turned out to be serviceable, though unspectacular. However, "serviceable" still leaves them far short of the Hall of Fame.

Trading Card Stats

Andrew Johnson	Name	Harry Leibold
•King Andy •Sir Veto	**Nickname**	•Nemo •Half-pint
•1865-1869	**Experience**	•1913-1925
•56	**Age Entering the League**	•21
•5'10"/174	**HT/WT**	•5'6"/175
•Democrat	**Team**	•Cleveland Naps/Indians •Chicago White Sox •Boston Red Sox •Washington Senators
•Reconstruction •Purchased Alaska	**Stats**	•.266 batting average •3 home runs •136 stolen bases
•Checkers •Vegetable gardening •Watching the circus and minstrel shows	**Hobbies**	•Coaching
•"Of all the dangers which our nation has yet encountered, none are equal to those which must result from success of the current effort to Africanize the southern half of the country." -On the subject of black suffrage	**Quote**	•"We could not believe that eight of our teammates let us down."
•Never had one formal day of education	**Interesting**	•As a manager, he used volleyball to improve his team's reflexes and agility
•No	**Hall of Fame**	•No

18

Ulysses Grant (1869-1877)

How many other presidents are actively remembered for what they've done outside of their presidency rather than in it? Not many is the answer. When that's the case, chances are they probably weren't too great at the whole Oval Office thing.

Even the bad ones are better remembered for their poor or corrupt performances at the helm. For Grant, though, that's not the case. In his meager defense, Grant is rightly remembered for his Civil War successes on the battlefield, even though some may consider him a butcher for losing so many of his men. Grant's presidency, however, was a different story due to his gross incompetence.

As a young man, Grant became a professional soldier at the behest of his father. He served in the army from 1843-1854, fighting in the Mexican War. Eventually, he began boozing to the point that he was forced to resign and spent the next half-dozen years failing at every occupation he tried. Farming, real estate, clerking, and selling firewood account for some of his failed ventures.

Luckily for Grant, the Civil War saved his fledgling professional career as he was once again given the opportunity to command troops. It was one of the few things he excelled at during his life, a prophecy predicted by his father who used to call his son "Useless" when Grant was a child.

Riding high from the Union's victory in the Civil War, Grant's war hero status easily catapulted him into the White House, where he continued the Reconstruction efforts and mandated a federal occupation of the South. He suspended habeas corpus, the ability for a court to rule that a person had been unlawfully detained, in an attempt to halt KKK activity in South Carolina. He introduced the Civil Rights Act of 1875 that initially granted black people equal use of accommodations and facilities until it was declared unconstitutional in 1883. In a sense, Grant can be considered the first civil rights president for his genuine attempt at bringing equality to African Americans.

Economically, he endured the Panic of 1873, which was the worst recession seen up to that point. Grant's solution to the devastating economic recession was to stop public works and internal improvement projects across the country. His policies proved themselves to be largely counterproductive, ultimately transforming the economic recession into a five-year depression.

On a brighter note, Grant did institute the 15th amendment, giving blacks the right to vote. He also, in theory, supported Native Americans. Congress appropriated $2 million to help Native Americans, though they left no instructions on how the funds were to be utilized. While Grant created a board of philanthropists to fashion an Indian policy, he did not excel at reining in the Army when they began displacing Natives and quarreling with them. In essence, Grant allocated money to help Native Americans but did not have an organized plan to disperse the funds and did not intervene when troops began treating Natives poorly.

From a foreign policy perspective, Grant's approach was a bit of a mixed bag. On one hand, he favored big business over the common man, and his insistence on supporting big businesses led to him utilizing a high protective tariff, ultimately hurting world trade. On the other hand, the U.S. did receive a $15.5 million settlement from Great Britain for damage done to American ships in British ports during the Civil War. He also opened Samoan ports to American shipping.

A lack of vision, specificity, and assertion was Grant's biggest pitfall as president. Because he lacked a concrete vision for what he would like to accomplish while in office, Grant ceded the power to his subordinates and trusted them to figure it out. This led to widespread corruption and incompetent decision making from inept personnel around him. Personally, he was soft-spoken, naïve, and didn't do a good enough job holding cabinet members responsible for their departments.

Grant had a mix of toughness and fragility that isn't often seen. For example, the sight of blood made Grant squeamish. Even a rare steak nauseated the man. Yet, he was the leader of the Union army during the bloodiest war in the nation's history. It's about as stark a dichotomy as you'll find.

Most likely sport: Football

Grant's willingness to be in a gruesome environment while he internally grappled with the sight of physical calamity would have placed him, uncomfortably, in the sport of football.

Grant wasn't naturally talented and often struggled as a leader, but when placed in the biggest of moments, he led his team to victory. His ability to be at the helm and guide his team to victory would have put him at the quarterback position.

Best Comparison: Tim Couch

Draft-day busts don't get much more synonymous than Tim Couch.

It happens a lot. A player comes into a situation where they have performed at a certain level that creates high expectations. They enter an organization that has been yearning for something to grasp hold of—something to give their heartache and exasperation a break, something to let a little sliver of hope cascade through the fanbase until it swells and bursts open the floodgates.

It's like when the football team in *Remember the Titans* wins its first few games. The community starts to swell with pride. Citizens of different colors and backgrounds start to become friends. The whole town starts to feel a united optimism that pulls them out of the uncomfortable racial tension they've resided in for decades because they found common ground.

Except for Couch, this wasn't *Remember the Titans*. Or *Remember the Browns*. Or anything he likely would want to remember at all. But Couch's presence did, however briefly, give an entire city a reason for hope.

Couch's journey to the pros began at the University of Kentucky. While there, Couch put up eye-popping numbers for a school that had rarely been good. In his junior season, Couch won SEC Player of the Year, set an SEC-record of 4,275 passing yards that stood for more than two decades, and led his team to a seven-win season. That was the most wins for Kentucky in 14 years.

Couch entered the NFL draft at the same time as the Browns were making their way back into Cleveland. After spending 50 years in Cleveland, the original Browns were moved to Baltimore in 1995 to become the Ravens. When football was brought back to Cleveland in 1999 in the form of an expansion team, the city was stoked. And they thought they had their franchise quarterback to guide them.

Couch struggled in the NFL due to poor performance and injuries. At Kentucky, Couch could do no wrong, bringing an underwhelming football program to national prominence. Accomplishing what Couch had done, one could argue, was made more impressive by the fact that it was a small school relative to your usual Division I powerhouses.

He went from being a big fish in a small pond to a small (inadequate?) fish in a big pond. So, too, did Grant. Before politics, Grant became a war hero and the general of the Union army largely because there were so few good candidates from which Lincoln could choose. Lincoln was desperate for any of his army leaders to be more assertive in their fighting. That, coupled with a modicum of success, gave Grant the spotlight. But it didn't last when he became president and had to contend with other political figures who could rival Grant's clout.

Neither man was well-suited for their time under the lights, but they also didn't receive any favors from their teams in the process. As mentioned, Couch was part of an expansion team. It was a young team with new ownership, new management, new coaching, and new players. Rarely does that pan out well.

The Browns were the rule, not the exception. They lacked talent and when a quarterback controversy broke out at the end of Couch's fourth season, despite the team making the playoffs, the writing was on the wall. Couch had lost the confidence and support of his coaching staff, ultimately lasting one more season in the NFL. He finished his career with a 22-37 record, and more interceptions (67) than touchdowns (64).

Grant, meanwhile, was taken advantage of by cabinet members and appointees whom he trusted way too easily. There were monetary kickbacks, patronage, and even scandals involving his personal secretary for illegally pocketing liquor taxes as part of a widespread and illegal conspiracy. Grant, however, never did anything wrong—outside of being a terrible judge of character. But the amount of immoral behavior within his administration was enough to infringe upon any potential success.

Both Grant and Couch faced a bit of unfortunate luck on their way to being two of the biggest busts in their professions. But many of the struggles were self-inflicted as a result of talent limitations and decision making. Neither man comes anywhere near the Hall of Fame.

Trading Card Stats

Ulysses Grant	Name	Tim Couch
•Useless •Unconditional Surrender •Hero of Appomattox •Sam	**Nickname**	•Tim Ouch
•1869-1877	**Experience**	•1999-2003
•46	**Age Entering the League**	•22
•5'8"/156	**HT/WT**	•6'4"/220
•Republican	**Team**	•Cleveland Browns
•Reconstruction •Panic of 1873 •Treaty of Washington	**Stats**	•64 touchdowns •67 interceptions •166 sacks
•Smoking •Drawing •Painting •Riding fast horses	**Hobbies**	•Coaching •Investing in businesses •Broadcasting
•"Labor disgraces no man; unfortunately, you occasionally find men disgrace labor."	**Quote**	•"All the losses pile up. It's very easy to lose your confidence. I know I did at times."
•Graduated 21st of 39 members from West Point, often receiving demerits for being tardy, dressing sloppily and missing church	**Interesting**	•He initially planned to play basketball at Kentucky in addition to football but decided not to after injuring his ankle as a high school senior because he wanted to avoid jeopardizing his football scholarship
•No	**Hall of Fame**	•No

19

Rutherford Hayes (1877-1881)

How the hell did that happen?

One minute, Hayes is going to bed on election night a loser. The next night, he's the country's new president. It was an insane turn of events. Imagine the confusion of the 2000 election (Bush/Gore) coupled with the shock of the 2016 election (Trump/Clinton). That was the 1876 election.

When the 1876 election rolled around, Hayes narrowly defeated James G. Blaine for the Republican nomination, leading him to face off against Democrat Samuel Tilden. The election turned into one of the biggest political controversies the country had seen to that point.

Tilden led in electoral votes 184-166, just one vote shy of securing victory. However, disputes in Florida, Louisiana, and South Carolina—as well as one revoked vote for an illegal elector in Oregon—allowed chaos to reign.

A 15-man electoral commission was created to choose the president where Hayes won 8-7 as everyone voted along party lines. Hayes had become president despite losing the popular vote and having nearly lost the electoral vote.

Democrats and Southerners were livid. A mutiny was ready to unfold, and the fear of plunging into another Civil War briefly became a real possibility. Tilden, though, did not pour gasoline on the fire. He talked the vengeful mob down in an effort to quell the anger.

Hayes also did his part by promising to leave the White House after one term. It's believed that Hayes promised Democrats he would end Reconstruction of the South by removing the military if they would peacefully stand down during the election upheaval. Though Hayes denied making any promise, he did end Southern Reconstruction, which helped smooth over differences with some Southern demographics, but also restored white supremacy and left black people more vulnerable over the coming decades.

Prior to his presidency, Hayes practiced law for more than a decade before becoming Cincinnati's city solicitor. He then volunteered to fight in the Civil War as part of the 23rd Ohio Infantry Regiment, where he fought in roughly 50 separate engagements while rising to major general. After the war, he served as a U.S. representative before becoming Ohio's governor.

While president, Hayes put a halt to a number of fights and potential fights across the country. Out west, when skirmishes broke out in New Mexico as settlers fought for control of the land, Hayes implemented a territorial governor to shut it down. He helped end a number of Indian Wars, as well. Although Hayes wasn't exactly best friends with Native Americans, he was much kinder than his predecessors had been in terms of treating them fairly and with respect.

Hayes also appropriately managed a dicey situation when France wanted to build a canal in Panama, which was viewed as a violation of the Monroe Doctrine. He effectively utilized his military to show force without aggressively agitating France, ultimately avoiding war as a result.

Hayes was not prejudiced against anyone. He refused to ban Chinese immigration, though Congress still passed a treaty that restricted immigration. He also supported the 15th amendment, giving African Americans the right to vote. Although his lax policies eventually allowed Southerners to return to their racist roots, Hayes refused to withdraw federal marshals from Southern polling locations during his tenure.

Hayes had a very respectable career, despite the fact that the average person wouldn't be familiar with him. Also, relative to many of his bigoted and racist contemporaries, Hayes was actually considered very progressive for his time. He had his warts, such as struggling to compromise or being able to personally inspire the public, but Hayes was pretty underrated when put in the proper context.

Most likely sport: Basketball

Overall, Hayes was a good team player who cared about, and got along with, others. He had a laid-back personality but was unafraid to step up and lead when needed. Hayes' temperament and skillset would have made him a basketball player because he knew how to set up his teammates with an assist but was also willing to take the last shot.

Hayes was very astute and prided himself on being a keen observer of human nature. He understood his teammates, put them in a position to succeed, and trusted them to do their jobs. He was also poised, which allowed him to remain calm under pressure, leading him to be a natural point guard on the court.

Best Comparison: Baron Davis

B-Diddy was the talk of the NBA for a time. In basketball circles, he was a bit of a cultural phenomenon as his star burned brightly at times but didn't last exceedingly long.

He wasn't Mick Jagger, still rocking out with one foot in the grave, but he also wasn't a Vanilla Ice one-hit wonder. Davis had a mix of handles, quickness, and rim-rocking power that helped him find success before injuries robbed him of the back-half of his career.

Davis' career began at UCLA where he was named PAC-10 Freshman of the Year in 1998. He was drafted by the Charlotte Hornets after his sophomore season and would spend parts of the next 13 seasons with five different franchises. For his career, Davis averaged 16.1 points, 7.2 assists, and 3.8 rebounds per game, while notching two All-Star appearances.

He also led the "We Believe" Warriors to one of the biggest upsets in NBA history as Davis' eight-seeded Golden State Warriors beat the number one seed Dallas Mavericks in the first round of the 2007 playoffs. It was a dramatic upset that shocked the world. At the time, it was just the third instance in which an eight seed defeated a one seed.

Like Hayes, Davis remains underrated when looking at his bonafides. He averaged nearly 20 points, 8 assists, 4 rebounds, and 2 steals per game over the span of seven seasons. And while he seemed relaxed and easy-going on the court, he had the ability to spark an arena with his play.

Davis was never as talented as Isaiah Thomas, John Stockton, or Jason Kidd. And he didn't quite measure up to more modern-day athletes like Steph Curry, Russell Westbrook, or Damian Lillard. In the pantheon of great guard play, Davis would be deemed as more of an average player. But don't let the gravitas of a flashy name fool you. Davis could hold his own.

Hayes was also never as talented as the great presidents before or after him. While policy-making was not his forte, he is underrated in terms of what he did for the office of president and the vision he had. As president, Hayes eradicated governmental corruption. He openly communicated with Congress and the public. Also, unlike Johnson and Grant before him, Hayes restored the power and prestige of being president. In preventing Congress from dominating his term as they did the previous terms, Hayes restored balance in the three branches of American government.

Both men could also be a bit stubborn during their careers. Davis had a number of run-ins with coaching when he was a younger player. He and Hornets Head Coach Byron Scott didn't always see eye-to-eye. Davis was willing to accept critiques but didn't always appreciate how hard his coach was on him, which led Davis to resist acquiescing to his coach's requests and compromising his personal approach to the game earlier in his career.

Hayes also welcomed constructive criticism but was resistant to compromise. Generally, when Hayes set his sights on doing something, he didn't like to budge, which occasionally gave him tunnel vision and affected the policies he enacted. For example, his economic policies favored business interests over farmers and laborers. That, in and of itself, wouldn't be so bad if he had been more willing to compromise to benefit the working class, as well. As a result, monopolies began to form, and Hayes failed to utilize the government's resources in a way that could adequately help the poor.

In the end, both men bowed out of their profession a little quicker than most. Hayes kept his promise to stick to one term, while injuries ravished what was left of Davis' career. Had they stuck around for longer, their chances at enshrinement could have merited some discussion. As it is, neither man is worthy of the Hall of Fame.

Trading Card Stats

Rutherford Hayes	Name	Baron Davis
•Rutherfraud Hayes •His Fraudulency •Granny Hayes	**Nickname**	•B-Diddy
•1877-1881	**Experience**	•1999-2012
•54	**Age Entering the League**	•20
•5'8"/170	**HT/WT**	•6'3"/209
•Republican	**Team**	•Charlotte Hornets •New Orleans Hornets •Golden State Warriors •Los Angeles Clippers •Cleveland Cavaliers •New York Knicks
•Compromise of 1877 •Bland-Allison Act •Panama Canal	**Stats**	•16.1 points, 7.2 assists and 3.8 rebounds per game •2-time All-Star
•Hunting •Fishing •Exercising •Reading •Chess •Landscaping	**Hobbies**	•Acting •Producing •Broadcasting
•"I am heartily tired of this life of bondage, responsibility and toil."	**Quote**	•"I was actually abducted by aliens two weeks ago."
•Spent every single night singing gospel hymns	**Interesting**	•Created the Black Santa Company that generates content to reflect a more diverse America
•No	**Hall of Fame**	•No

20

James Garfield (1881)

What could have been if not for a gun-toting job seeker and a few unhygienic doctors.

Garfield had long been considered a rising star; a gregarious and gifted orator oozing with potential who, unfortunately, never really got to start his presidency. Shortly after Garfield's inauguration in 1881, he was shot by Charles

Guiteau, a fellow Republican, who had voted for Garfield as president a mere eight months before shooting him. What was Guiteau's motive, you ask? Well, after being turned away from a role in office working for Garfield, Guiteau ultimately decided if Garfield would not hand him a position, then Garfield did not deserve one himself.

Garfield was shot twice, with one of the bullets being lodged in his back, but he died largely from unsanitary doctor treatment. His doctors struggled to find the bullet but continued to poke and prod inside with fingers and medical instruments that had not been sanitized. Garfield's health vacillated for nearly three months before he was done in by blood poisoning related to his doctor's efforts.

Garfield did not enact any policies due to his limited time (six months) as president. Prior to his presidency, Garfield worked his way through school as a carpenter, janitor, and teacher before studying law and spending two years as an Ohio state senator. When the Civil War began in 1861, Garfield served for the Union, rising from a lieutenant colonel to major general. After his two-year service, he spent the next 18 years as a U.S. representative.

Garfield had initially become known as a radical republican, advocating for the immediate and permanent eradication of slavery, without compromise. He even viewed John Brown as a hero, though he didn't condone Brown's bloody raid on Harpers Ferry. While his views became slightly more moderate following his Civil War involvement, they still erred on the side of radicalism.

Most likely sport: Football

The 20th president was about as tough as they come. As a kid, Garfield was aggressive and a bit belligerent, getting into a number of fights when other children made fun of him for being poor and fatherless. Though he became more amiable as he matured, that inherent toughness never dissipated.

It was further exemplified on the battlefield where, during the battle of Chickamauga, Garfield bravely rode his horse through enemy fire to convey vital information from one flank to the other. Garfield was unintimidated by the dangers of what he did, which would have led him to play football. His strength, fearlessness, and sense of purpose makes him an ideal candidate to play safety.

Best Comparison: Sean Taylor

"Meast" (Half-man, Half-beast) as they called him, was a hard-hitting, ball-hawking playmaker who was killed on his way to football-playing greatness.

Taylor was only 24 years old, and in the middle of his fourth season, when he was shot by burglars who had broken into his home. Taylor was struck in the leg, which severed his femoral artery and led to his death.

Taylor was in the midst of an All-Pro season prior to being shot. During his three-and-a-half-year career, Taylor earned All-Pro honors once, made the Pro Bowl twice, and had earned a reputation for being one of the game's best defensive players.

His raw talent was second to none. Nearly all professional athletes can be declared as having won the genetic lottery as they are the one-percenters of the sports world. However, Taylor had a combination of size, speed, strength, athleticism, and instinct that made him one percent of the one-percenters.

He was a terror on the field. Just three preseason games into his professional career, Taylor had already forced four turnovers on a number of bone-crushing hits. That bruising, playmaker mentality would come to define his time in the NFL. Taylor consistently toed the line between an appropriate level of skull bashing and a more questionable code of on-field conduct that alienated some.

Take the time that Taylor was ejected from a playoff game for spitting on an opposing player, for example. He even decleated a punter in the Pro Bowl—a game in which tackling is generally more optional than mandated—but that was how Taylor got the most out of his talent. By going full bore on every play and combining that with his Freakazoid-like skills, Taylor had an effect on the game that was unlike most players.

Garfield had a similar level of untapped potential stripped away by his early demise and was even considered to be a political prodigy by many. He had been elected to Congress when he was 32 years old. He was an academic and had served valiantly in the Civil War. Garfield became a bit of a Swiss army knife for the Republicans and was someone who often bordered on radical Republicanism, which alienated some Democrats. Yet, he was also viewed as someone who could turn on the charm and compromise with the other side of the aisle.

Learning to work with others was something that took time for Garfield. His pugnacious attitude in youth that resulted from being made fun of as a kid eventually dissipated. Garfield, like most people, grew in maturity as he aged. He better understood how to control his frustrations and turn someone from a foe to a friend.

Taylor was also experiencing his own maturing process when he was killed. He had been arrested on separate occasions for driving while intoxicated and for assault. Taylor was ultimately acquitted of the former and placed on 18 months of probation for the latter.

But Taylor's teammates have often pointed out how he seemed to be learning from his mistakes—particularly after the birth of his daughter before the 2006 season. Even Taylor himself pointed out the momentous impact of his daughter's birth and how it had changed his outlook on life.

Both Taylor and Garfield were lessons in what it means to mature as you age. That, along with some of the best talents in their professions, gave them Hall of Fame potential. Unfortunately, both men were robbed of the chance to fulfill that potential. As a result, neither guy makes it to the Hall of Fame.

Trading Card Stats

James Garfield	Name	Sean Taylor
•The Preacher •The Teacher President •Martyr President	**Nickname**	•Meast
•1881	**Experience**	•2004-2007
•49	**Age Entering the League**	•21
•6'0"/184	**HT/WT**	•6'3"/220
•Republican	**Team**	•Washington Redskins
•No major policies enacted	**Stats**	•299 tackles •12 interceptions
•Hunting •Fishing •Chess •Euchre •Billiards •Reading	**Hobbies**	•Track •Basketball
•"My God! What is there in this place that a man should ever want to get into it?"	**Quote**	•"You can't be scared of death. When that time comes, it comes."
•First left-handed president and last to be born in a log cabin	**Interesting**	•Taylor did not trust the media and rarely spoke to reporters
•No	**Hall of Fame**	•No

21

Chester Arthur (1881-1885)

The circle of life dictates that when one door closes, another one opens. When Garfield was shot by Guiteau and eventually died, Arthur ascended to the presidency. Sometimes what's behind the new door is an improvement and a much-ballyhooed evolution. Think horse and buggy to the car or box televisions to flat-screens.

Transitioning from Garfield to Arthur? Not so much.

Arthur's rise to prominence began as a teacher. He also clerked in a law firm while studying law in school before serving as the Collector of the Port of New York, responsible for collecting import duties on foreign goods brought into the country. After that, he was selected as Garfield's running mate to become vice president.

Arthur belonged to a faction of the Republican party called the Stalwarts, which Garfield had been hoping to team with in order to placate the more conservative Republican base. However, Arthur only spent about six months in his VP role before taking over for Garfield.

As president, Arthur didn't have the best go of it. His most notable contribution was signing the Pendleton Act, which created the modern-day civil service system. This helped reform the existing spoils system, requiring a more thorough application process to be held. Arthur's support for this transformation was ironic seeing as he had come to be New York's Collector of the Port through the spoils system and repaid the favor by using his money and influence in the New York customs house to bring in additional Republicans to the ledger.

Arthur's other enacted policy of note was the Chinese Exclusion Act, which suspended Chinese immigration for 10 years. This was the result of decades of bubbling resentment toward the Chinese who created competition for white men during the gold rush and subsequently provided very cheap labor out west. The act also forbade the courts from granting citizenship to any Chinese person already living in the country. This would be renewed on two separate occasions before finally being repealed in 1943.

A few other noteworthy moments from the Arthur era include his desire to make only tobacco and liquor taxable items (no dice). He also focused more on businesses instead of helping common citizens or making internal improvements. Meanwhile, Arthur did secure the construction of a building to house the Library of Congress.

Arthur's administration also oversaw a slow descent into recession. He took little action throughout his tenure and was passive when it came to taking control of his own policy. In one instance, Arthur demanded a significant decrease in tariffs, Congress countered with less than a 1.5% reduction, and Arthur silently signed the Mongrel Tariff. But the new tariff rate ultimately had little impact and only created divisiveness that would grow along party lines.

Delegating tasks became all too common under Arthur, although it may have been with good reason. The man suffered from Bright's disease, which was a then-fatal kidney ailment. It is a painful disease that saps a person of their energy.

Arthur was never a fan of interacting with the press and it was no different when it came to his illness. He fought to keep the press and public from finding out, and it wasn't until the backend of his term that rumors began to spread due to his changing physical appearance.

Most likely sport: Football

Based on what Arthur endured with his illness, there's no questioning his resiliency. He finished out his term as president, though he would ultimately succumb to a combination of the Bright's disease and a bout of malaria. His quiet strength and willingness to play through pain would have made him an ideal fit for football.

Arthur was defensive by nature—both in terms of combativeness with the press and in his passivity with policy making. He was also extremely emotional, oftentimes wearing his emotions on his sleeves. Despite Arthur's good size and physicality, his team would not have looked to him to be a leader, just as his party did not look to him as a leader. His best fit defensively would have been as an outside linebacker.

Best Comparison: Darren Hambrick

Hambrick isn't exactly a household name, but some football fans of the late 1990s and early 2000s will likely remember him. Perhaps for his on-field performance but more likely for his spotted past.

Hambrick grew up excelling athletically in Florida. He committed to the University of Florida to play football and was the only true freshman to start on defense during the 1993 season. He played two seasons there, while also competing on the track team.

Just prior to the 1995 Sugar Bowl, though, Hambrick got into an altercation with a teammate, Anthony Riggins, in which he hit Riggins in the face with a glass. The blow required 40 stitches to close, and Hambrick was dismissed from the team. After sitting out a season, he would finish his college career at the University of South Carolina.

Hambrick was selected by the Dallas Cowboys in the fifth round of the 1998 draft but wound up playing on three teams across five solid seasons. Many of Hambrick's most notable professional moments in the spotlight, though, have been obscured by his legal background.

In addition to fighting Riggins at Florida, Hambrick also has a rash of other troubles on his resume. He has served probation on multiple occasions for misdemeanor battery and for reporting a check he had cashed as being stolen.

Hambrick is also famous for one prickly encounter he had with the media when asked about why he skipped voluntary, summer workouts with the Cowboys. He shot back with a, "What do 'voluntary' mean?" line that has been hailed as an unofficial mantra for football players frustrated by the implicit understanding that "voluntary" workouts have long been considered mandatory by coaches and executives who like lording over their players as if they were dictators (Hello, Tom Coughlin!).

Hambrick nailed the line, but it's hard to deny that it has played a role in overshadowing his playing career. While Hambrick, the player, was always known as a tough person on the field, Hambrick, the person, was viewed as rough around the edges. Although, in recent years, he has been working to mentor kids playing youth football.

Arthur was also rough around the edges, or at least that's what he portrayed in the public eye. Arthur was known for his corrupt political past as New York's Collector. It likely did him no favors that his relationship with the press was strained, at best.

He saw no need to communicate with the media. Arthur went so far as to ask reporters not to quote him on anything. He believed it was undignified to share his opinions unless it was done through a formal message. His combination of shady background and unfriendly disposition with the public largely overshadowed his presidency.

Right or wrong, both Arthur and Hambrick are better remembered for their temperament and off-the-field incidents. However, when you cut through their ancillary sideshows, neither man had a great career, leaving both unworthy of the Hall of Fame.

Trading Card Stats

Chester Arthur	Name	Darren Hambrick
•Elegant Arthur •Our Chet •Prince Arthur	**Nickname**	•D-Ham
•1881-1885	**Experience**	•1998-2002
•51	**Age Entering the League**	•23
•6'2"/224	**HT/WT**	•6'1"/227
•Republican	**Team**	•Dallas Cowboys •Carolina Panthers •Cleveland Browns
•1882 Rivers and Harbors Act •1882 Chinese Exclusion Act •1883 Pendleton Act	**Stats**	•262 tackles •3.5 sacks •3 interceptions
•Late night conversations •Fishing •Hunting	**Hobbies**	•Teaching kids who play youth football
•"I may be president of the United States, but my private life is nobody's damned business."	**Quote**	•"I missed a voluntary camp. What do 'voluntary' mean?"
•Held an auction on the White House lawn featuring 24-wagon loads of items from past administrations	**Interesting**	•In high school, he became the first Florida athlete to qualify in five different events at the state track meet
•No	**Hall of Fame**	•No

22 & 24

Grover Cleveland (1885-1889, 1893-1897)

If at first you don't succeed, try again.

It is a cliched mantra that implores perseverance and hard work. It's also befitting of Cleveland's time in office. Though for him, it was more like, "If twice you don't succeed, try thrice."

Cleveland is the only president to have served two, non-consecutive terms. He won the election in 1884, lost in 1888, only to win again in 1892. Now, this isn't exactly a fairytale, Tiger Woods-style comeback story, but it was a good bounce back for one of the most real and transparent presidents of all time.

Growing up in New York, Cleveland was a responsible boy who had dropped out of school in order to help support his struggling family. He initially worked in a general store as a clerk before teaching at the Institution for the Blind in New York City. Following that, he began studying law, like most presidents before him.

Cleveland was drafted for the Civil War but chose to purchase a substitute soldier, which the Conscription Act of 1863 legalized. He ended up paying $150 to George Brinske, a 32-year-old Polish immigrant, who served in his place. After practicing law for several years, Cleveland served three years as the sheriff of Erie County in New York. He would also briefly go on to serve as mayor of Buffalo and then as the governor of New York.

Cleveland's lack of time in politics did not prepare him well for his presidency. It was an exceptionally conservative tenure that was largely won due to Cleveland's earned reputation as an honest man and politician, which appealed to a country that had grown weary of dirty politics since the Civil War.

In Cleveland's first go as president, he vetoed hundreds of pension and private relief bills that he viewed as an unwarranted drain on the Treasury. Anything remotely resembling a handout was denied. He also tried to prevent railroad companies from consistently favoring large corporations by creating the Interstate Commerce Commission to help regulate railroad company practices, though he lacked any real enforcement power. Cleveland also strenuously argued for a tariff reduction in hopes of not only lowering tariff rates, but also as part of his larger plan to set up an 1888 re-election campaign bid.

Except that didn't work out so well for Cleveland. His opponent, Benjamin Harrison, ran on a platform that supported a protective tariff designed to make imported goods cost more than domestic-made goods.

The country voted for a new leader, and Cleveland rode the pine for the next four years. Eventually, though, Cleveland returned to the big show, winning the 1892 election. Unfortunately for Cleveland, his second stint was much busier than his first, and not in a good way, as most of his time was spent dealing with an economic crisis.

The Panic of 1893 began just before Cleveland entered office for the second time. The reasons for the downturn were widespread, ranging from railroad failures and industrial overexpansion to depleted gold reserves and crop harvests across much of the country. Cleveland was unable to rein in the depression during his tenure despite his various policies and efforts to stabilize the economy.

Although Cleveland got along well with others, he lost the leadership role in his party after internal tensions arose during the Panic of 1893 and Democrats became divided over whether to use gold or silver currency.

Most likely sport: Baseball

In his private life, Cleveland quite enjoyed being outdoors, despite rarely exercising. He would have much rather eaten, drank, and smoked. Because of this, Cleveland's life as an athlete would have been an acceptable fit within baseball.

Cleveland was, at times, care free and liked to exuberantly banter with everyone; other times, he was tough and stubborn. During these times, he was solely focused on his work and responsibilities. His inability to grind day-in-and-day-out would make it hard for him to play every day, so he would have been best suited as a starting pitcher.

Best Comparison: Lynn Nelson

When your professional occupation is a pitcher and your nickname is "Line Drive," it probably doesn't portend great success.

Such was the case for Nelson who acquired that moniker thanks to all of the line drives that hitters sent whizzing back in his direction.

Nelson grew up in North Dakota, briefly playing semi-pro ball before taking up boxing. Nelson befriended a man named Billy Petrolle, a professional fighter, whose trainer, Jack Hurley, convinced Nelson to become a boxer. However, Nelson had already agreed to play baseball for an independent team whose manager didn't want him fighting. Eventually, a compromise was made that allowed Nelson to box as long as he donned a mask.

Nelson became known as the Masked Marvel and dominated his 21 professional bouts, securing early knockouts in all of them. Despite his success in the ring, Nelson had pitched well in independent ball during the 1925 season and subsequently agreed to a deal with the American Association's Kansas City Blues. He spent the next four years there before being traded to the Chicago Cubs.

However, Nelson's baseball career lacked any real stability. He spent one year with the Cubs followed by two years in the minor leagues; then two more years with the Cubs followed by another two-year stint in the minors. Nelson managed to make his way back to the big leagues once more for a four-year period with two different teams.

Nelson was described by peers as a simple and easy-going person who continued to play minor league baseball after his big-league days were done. He finally hung it up in favor of working his job at an airplane factory during World War II. Nelson went on to earn an honest living after the war, as well. One report surfaced that he was running a saloon, while another stated he worked as an electrician.

That integrity and commitment to honest work was just as easily seen in Cleveland. He wholeheartedly believed in his own slogan that "public office is a public trust." Cleveland was a plain, candid, and even ordinary person who was able to connect with the public in that way.

It helped that he was a good teammate to all Americans. Though not a persuasive party leader, Cleveland worked for the interests of the public. He didn't sacrifice his principles or morals for political gain. Nelson also showed off his willingness to put the team first. He became accustomed to adjusting his role for the benefit of the team. Nelson was frequently moved back and forth between starting and the bullpen, while also being used as the primary pinch-hitter, showing an ability to adequately handle the bat.

Perhaps what Cleveland and Nelson had most in common was their perseverance. Cleveland didn't give up after being voted out of office after one term. He returned to practicing law after his ouster but remained politically engaged. By staying involved, Cleveland found himself ready to go for another chance at re-election, which he successfully secured in 1892. Nelson also had that stick-to-itiveness quality. Despite a number of stints in the minor leagues, Nelson continued to pursue his passion.

Unfortunately, the reality is that neither guy was particularly good at his job. Cleveland didn't have the most spectacular first term and his second term was marred by an inability to pull the nation out of an economic depression. Nelson walked more hitters than he struck out and possessed an ERA over five-and-a-half. Neither man is entering the Hall of Fame without a paid ticket.

Trading Card Stats

Grover Cleveland	Name	Lynn Nelson
•Uncle Jumbo •Buffalo Hangman •His Obstinacy	Nickname	•Line Drive
•1885-1889 •1893-1897	Experience	•1930-1940
•47	Age Entering the League	•25
•5'11"/260	HT/WT	•5'10"/170
•Democrat	Team	•Chicago Cubs •Philadelphia Athletics •Detroit Tigers
•1886 Presidential Succession Act •1887 Interstate Commerce Act •1887 Dawes Severalty Act •1887 Hatch Act •Panic of 1893 •1894 Pullman Strike	Stats	•33-42 record •676.2 innings pitched •5.25 ERA
•Fishing •Hunting •Euchre •Walking •Cribbage •Pinochle •Poker •Smoking cigars	Hobbies	•Boxing •Bowling
•"Sensible and responsible women do not want to vote."	Quote	•"The opposing batters had a habit, most annoying to me, of hitting liners past my ears and one of the writers decided I should have a nickname along those lines."
•Enjoyed occasional pranks like ringing the school bell at night or unhinging a neighbor's front gate	Interesting	•Recorded 21 early knockouts in 21 professional boxing matches as a middleweight
•No	Hall of Fame	•No

23

Benjamin Harrison (1889-1893)

Ah, the portly filling to our Grover Cleveland sandwich. And, yes, we're talking one of those insanely massive *Man vs. Food* type of sandwiches. Just as these presidents would have liked it.

Harrison, the grandson of William Henry Harrison, fared longer than his grandfather who died of pneumonia just 31 days into his tenure. The younger

Harrison was voted in between Cleveland's two stints. The election seemed to swing on the tariff debate, and although Cleveland secured a plurality of the popular vote, Harrison won the electoral vote.

Prior to his presidency, Harrison had studied law. He also spent time as the secretary of the Republican State Central Committee and as a supreme court reporter for Indiana before serving with the 70th Indiana Infantry Regiment. Harrison was reputed for excelling at fighting, though he did not relish it. After the war, Harrison returned to reporting and studying law with his last role before the presidency being a U.S. senator.

The success of Harrison's presidency was a mixed bag. The Sherman Anti-Trust Act was passed in 1890, which intended to curb abuses of monopolies like the Standard Oil Company run by John Rockefeller. The Act, though, was too vague and essentially rendered ineffective. He tried to pass the Force Bill, which would have insured black people the ability to vote freely. However, it was killed by the Senate. He worked hard to support African-Americans and veterans, but he did little to try and help Native Americans.

Internationally, Harrison's success was also varied. The McKinley Tariff Act set the average tariff rate at 48%, which was the highest rate up to that point during a time of peace. Consumer prices rose, the cost of living went up, and people of limited means began to struggle.

An aggressive foreign policy was employed during Harrison's term as he tried to claim American dominion over the Bering Sea, ultimately causing a dispute with Britain. When an American warship had removed the Hawaii monarchy, Harrison rushed (but failed) to annex the island nation before Cleveland's return to office. He demanded more respect be shown to the U.S. by strongly protecting their interests and building out their Navy. He also narrowly avoided separate wars with Chile and Italy after a couple of deadly citizen spats had tensions rising. Harrison alienated a handful of nations during his tenure, but he also managed to attain broader, global respect by flexing America's muscle via their national defense.

Ultimately, Harrison's lasting imprint from his term, unfortunately, was the economy. The Sherman Silver Purchase Act was passed in 1890, requiring the Treasury to purchase 4.5 million ounces of silver per month. The payments were to be made in treasury notes meant to increase paper circulation. While the Silver Purchase Act helped briefly until Americans began redeeming their notes in gold, this sparked fear of depleted gold reserves and touched off what would ultimately be the Panic of 1893.

Most likely sport: Basketball

While Harrison wasn't exactly a physical specimen, he was physical. He didn't fear a challenge or back down from opponents. And though he wasn't a great athlete, he also wasn't in terrible shape as he tended to enjoy three-to-four mile walks each day as president. This would have led Harrison to a career in basketball as a professional athlete.

His operational style was predicated on being detail-oriented and Harrison preferred having control in all endeavors. Thanks to a high level of intelligence, he would be able to command a team despite a lack of leadership and an inability to make his teammates better. Point guard would have been his best fit.

Best Comparison: Raymond Felton

Many fans thought Felton was destined for greatness after a decorated college career at a decorated school. Instead, Felton turned into a nomadic wanderer of sorts, gracing nearly a quarter of the league's teams with his presence.

While Felton's professional career wasn't nearly as decorated as his previous resume, it wasn't terrible, either. Like Harrison, it was a mixed bag of success for Felton.

The point guard grew up in South Carolina where he led his high school team to two state championships. His success continued in college where Felton made an All-ACC team in each of his three seasons at the University of North Carolina. He also took home the Bob Cousy award, which honors the best collegiate point guard in the country and secured a national championship in 2005.

As an NBA player, though, Felton's career saw some adversity. Through his 14 seasons, Felton averaged nearly 11 points and five assists across seven different teams. He has been viewed in a variety of different lights: from promising starter to disappointment, from rejuvenated to disgruntled, and from out-of-shape player to veteran leader. Felton's career was a tale of two sides.

Right or wrong, Felton gained a reputation for being a bit prickly. This was earned, in part, thanks to his upbringing and personality. He grew up at an early age with his dad instilling toughness, insisting that fear and weakness were not options. Felton then brought that stern demeanor with him to the basketball court.

It peaked for him during his seventh NBA season when he became a lightning rod for criticism on a Portland Trailblazers team that drastically underperformed. Felton was panned for coming into the season out of shape, which became an even bigger deal when he put up what were career lows for him at the time. He drew the ire of fans who had expected more, which led to Felton's contentious relationship with the city of Portland and its media. It's a reputation that was built quickly but took a long time to shed.

His public reputation has also been made worse by an off-court incident that was settled in 2014. Felton pled guilty to possessing a pair of guns without a license. This arose after he was accused by his ex-wife of brandishing the weapons in front of her during arguments as an intimidation tactic. Felton was sentenced to a fine and community service.

While Harrison never had any run-ins of that nature, he was fully familiar with weaponry having fought in the Civil War. Harrison's irritable nature was specific to how he dealt with other people. He disliked small talk and was known for being extremely cold to others. The guy even cut his own kids out of his will after they disapproved of him marrying his late wife's niece.

As a result of lacking charisma and interpersonal skills, Harrison never leveraged his cabinet very well. Oftentimes, he tried doing too much on his own and refused to seek second opinions. His stiff personality made it difficult to be a true leader of men, let alone an entire nation.

Although Harrison wasn't the best leader for his team, he usually earned the respect of his contemporaries for his intelligence. He was also as honest as they come. While his inability to work with his teammates and make them better is what really held him back, it was Harrison's intellect that allowed him to reach the pinnacle of his profession in the first place. Harrison had always been considered the brightest of his seven siblings growing up and earned the respect of his colleagues at every professional stop he made.

Felton also started racking up similar compliments for his cerebral approach. As his time in the NBA increased, Felton's various coaching staffs pointed out his mental acuity and credited him for teaching younger players.

But greatness on the court isn't achieved through mental prowess alone. Neither man's performance would stand out in the crowd or get them a spot in the Hall of Fame.

Trading Card Stats

Benjamin Harrison	Name	Raymond Felton
•Little Ben •White House Iceberg	**Nickname**	•Felts •Duck
•1889-1893	**Experience**	•2005-2019
•55	**Age Entering the League**	•21
•5'6"/160	**HT/WT**	•6'1"/205
•Republican	**Team**	•Charlotte Bobcats •New York Knicks •Denver Nuggets •Portland Trailblazers •Dallas Mavericks •Los Angeles Clippers •Oklahoma City Thunder
•1890 Dependent and Disability Pensions Act •1890 Sherman Anti-Trust Act •1890 Sherman Silver Purchase Act •1890 McKinley Tariff Act	**Stats**	•11.2 points, 5.2 assists and 3.0 rebounds per game •NBA All-Rookie Second Team
•Walking •Carriage rides •Duck hunting •Billiards •Smoking cigars	**Hobbies**	•Community service with Big Brothers Big Sisters organization •Bowling
•"We Americans have no commission from God to police the world."	**Quote**	•"Words don't break me. I stay right off Pearl District, in the Indigo, if you want to come see me."
•Last president to don a beard	**Interesting**	•Didn't start lifting weights until 2012 (halfway through his career)
•No	**Hall of Fame**	•No

25

William McKinley (1897-1901)

For a reportedly friendly and even-tempered man, McKinley sure didn't mind being ruthless every now and then. Aggression, hostility, and war ruled McKinley's time as president the same way the Kardashians have basically ruled the 21st century.

Wobbly Willie, as he was known, began his professional career as a teacher after being forced to drop out of college due to physical exhaustion from studying and a lack of finances. He then moved onto clerking for a postal office before participating in the Civil War. He fought for more than four years without ever succumbing to injury or illness and was also the last president to have served in the Civil War.

Like most presidents before him, McKinley began studying law after the war. Eventually, he would serve two separate stints as a U.S. representative followed by four years as Ohio's governor.

While his presidential opponent, William Jennings Bryan, stumped across the country aiming to secure votes, McKinley did so from his front porch only. While it may seem to be a counterintuitive way to earn the nation's support, it worked well for McKinley as he won the election with relative ease.

As president, McKinley is perhaps best known for authorizing the Spanish-American War. The hostility was first caused by Spanish aggression toward Cuba as a revolution was taking place. McKinley had initially advocated neutrality until the *Maine*, a U.S. battleship, exploded in a Cuban harbor. Though it was ultimately discovered that the *Maine*'s explosion was a self-inflicted accident, McKinley caved to outside pressure demanding retaliation. Yellow journalism, a newspaper practice meant to exaggerate and distort information, fanned the flames of an American public that had a burning desire to fight during this era. Ultimately, Spain relinquished its right to Cuba and ceded Puerto Rico, Guam and the Philippine Islands to the U.S. for $20 million.

The Filipinos, however, resisted U.S. rule in favor of their own independent government in which McKinley used military force to squash the dissent. Although he did not want these countries' citizens to become American citizens, he did try to provide internal improvements to help those who were sick and impoverished. McKinley also annexed Hawaii by a joint resolution after the Senate refused to do so.

Inside the contiguous borders of his country, McKinley oversaw the ending of the economic depression. McKinley, who had once been a bimetallism supporter, switched to a gold standard proponent. He then implemented the Gold Standard Act, formally placing all U.S. money on the gold standard, backed by gold at a fixed price. Both the Sherman Silver Act and the protectionist McKinley Tariff were considered partly responsible for the economic downturn in the first place.

And who helped frame those acts initially? That's right—U.S. Senator John Sherman!

Oh, yeah…and McKinley, too.

So, McKinley had supported and helped lead the charge for policies that led to an economic depression. Then he capitalized on how it played out during Cleveland's second term, and in the end, it contributed to his own presidential nomination.

Heady play, sir.

While McKinley was elected to a second term, it was short-lived. On September 6, 1901, McKinley was shot by anarchist Leon Czolgosz who walked up to the president with a revolver wrapped around his bandaged hand to conceal the weapon. Two shots were fired, one of which struck McKinley in the stomach. While the shot itself didn't kill him, gangrene ultimately did a week later.

Most likely sport: Baseball

McKinley was generally an easy-going guy. He was well liked and got along with nearly everyone. However, he did not deem exercise to be of any importance and subsequently was not very fit. Baseball would have been the best fit for McKinley.

While McKinley's lack of physical prowess would not have enabled him to be a very active player, he did prove durable (if not lucky) given his clean bill of health during the Civil War. And while he was usually laid back, he did show a propensity in office for intensely attacking his opponents. As a result, McKinley would have been best served as a starting pitcher where he could lock into the task at hand once every few days.

Best Comparison: Hal Carlson

One day you're preparing to start a major league baseball game. The next day you're dead.

That was the shocking reality for Carlson who, like McKinley, suffered an unexpected death.

Carlson grew up during the turn of the 20th century. He played semi-pro and minor league baseball for six years before receiving an opportunity in the majors. The Rockford, IL, native spent the next 14 years pitching for three different clubs.

Carlson was an average pitcher during his career, starting 236 of his 377 career games while sporting a 3.97 ERA. His career likely would have been better had the pitch he was best known for not been banned. The spitball was Carlson's forte. For the non-baseball nerds among us, the spitball is thrown with a baseball that has been altered by a foreign substance—typically spit—causing the ball to move atypically in the wind.

He developed the pitch as a minor leaguer when it was legal, spending years working to perfect it. He utilized it to his advantage during his first three seasons to a tune of a 2.81 ERA. Unfortunately for Carlson, the spitball was banned starting in 1920, during his fourth major league season. Carlson was forced to abandon his best pitch and adjust, doing so with moderate success.

Just as McKinley had taken a break from his professional career to participate in a war, so did Carlson. McKinley had participated in the Civil War, while Carlson fought in World War I. The pitcher turned machine gunner served valiantly during 1918 and 1919. This in spite of the fact that he, along with many others, was hit with poisonous gas that would cause him permanent health complications, plaguing him off-and-on for the rest of his life.

Often, Carlson would come down with illnesses and unexplained aches and pains. One day Carlson sought out a team trainer looking for a massage on his sore elbow. The trainer, Andy Lotshaw, asked Carlson to lie down. Without telling Carlson what he was doing, Lotshaw began rubbing Coca-Cola into the extremity. Carlson's start that day went so well that he began receiving this treatment consistently. It's a wonder Coke hasn't replaced Tommy John surgery as the therapy of choice among modern-day pitchers.

In 1930, Carlson retired early to his apartment one night while feeling ill. He was scheduled to pitch the following day but woke up in the middle of the night with stomach pains. Carlson died that night from stomach hemorrhaging.

Carlson was regarded as a hard-working and self-reliant man. He had also gained a reputation as a practical joker among his family and teammates. Similarly, McKinley also enjoyed a good (clean) joke and was self-sufficient in his day-to-day presidential duties.

Both men were highly regarded by their teammates and nearly all of their contemporaries. They both lived full and vibrant lives and served their country with honor and valor. They lived life to the fullest and, unfortunately, died awful, literally gut-wrenching deaths. One final similarity between the two: neither man makes it to the Hall of Fame.

Trading Card Stats

William McKinley	Name	Harold Carlson
•Wobbly Willie •Idol of Ohio •Napoleon of Protection	**Nickname**	•Hal •The Silent Swede
•1897-1901	**Experience**	•1917-1930
•54	**Age Entering the League**	•25
•5'7"/199	**HT/WT**	•6'0"/180
•Republican	**Team**	•Pittsburgh Pirates •Philadelphia Phillies •Chicago Cubs
•Spanish-American War •Annexation of Hawaii •Open Door Policy and the Boxer Rebellion •1897 Dingley Tariff Act	**Stats**	•114-120 record •2,002 innings pitched •3.97 ERA
•Opera •Theater •Euchre •Cribbage •Smoking cigars	**Hobbies**	•Practical jokes
•"We need Hawaii just as much and a good deal more than we did California; it is Manifest Destiny."	**Quote**	•"I feel pretty bad. You better call a doctor."
•First president to have their inauguration captured on film; last president to have served in the Civil War	**Interesting**	•Served as a machine gunner in the U.S. Army at the Battle of Argonne Forest (WWI) where he was exposed to poison gas
•No	**Hall of Fame**	•No

26

Theodore Roosevelt (1901-1909)

While most presidents end up abhorring their time in the Oval Office, Roosevelt is a clear exception to the rule. The dude had energy out the wazoo. He had a zest for life, and his presidency was palpable.

Roosevelt was a spindly, asthmatic child who struggled with his health. Through rigorous exercise and sheer will, he turned himself into a brawny go-getter. That path ultimately led him to the military where he spent time in the New York National Guard, rising from second lieutenant to captain. He also fought in the Spanish-American War as the leader of the Rough Riders, which was the First U.S. Volunteer Cavalry Regiment. Roosevelt really forged his public persona as an exceptionally tactical militarist.

Outside the military, Roosevelt spent a brief time attending law school before dropping out to enter politics. He would go on to become a New York State Assemblyman, member of the U.S. Civil Service Commission, and New York City police board president. Following that, he spent time as the assistant secretary of the Navy, governor of New York, and vice president.

Roosevelt stepped into the president's role after McKinley was assassinated and immediately took on the role as his own. During his presidency, Roosevelt tried legislating antitrust policies, attempting to balance free enterprise and corporate responsibility as he went after railroad, beef, oil, and tobacco companies, among others. He also instituted the Meat Inspection Act, as well as the Pure Food and Drug Act, which helped improve and sanitize goods for commerce.

Roosevelt also tackled workers' rights head on by laying down the hammer on the Anthracite coal strikes of 1902 when 150,000 Pennsylvania coal miners went on strike for better overall working conditions. When mine owners refused to negotiate with the workers, Roosevelt threatened to seize their mines all together if an agreement was not reached with their workforce.

Few presidents have done as much for the environment as Roosevelt did, and certainly nobody before him had done more to protect the planet. Some of his accomplishments in this realm included reserving 125 million acres in forests, 68 million acres in coal lands, 2500 water-power sites, the first national wildlife refuge, and the first national monument.

The one brief blip on Roosevelt's domestic radar was the Panic of 1907. It was sparked by the fall of roughly a dozen banks and railroads collapsing financially. There was disagreement about whether it was the result of Roosevelt's antitrust policies or the fault of big businesses. Either way, the panic was short-lived as recovery began in spring 1908.

Roosevelt also oversaw the terms of the Hay-Pauncefote Treaty in which the U.S. was given the right to construct and operate a canal across Central America. Eventually it was agreed to set up the canal through Panama.

As much as Roosevelt enjoyed being the aggressor and getting into a tussle of some sort, he also had the ability to play peacemaker. That's exactly what he did in mediating the Russo-Japanese War by helping Russia and Japan resolve their conflict, earning him the 1906 Nobel Peace Prize. His award was the first one given to an American.

Most likely sport: Boxing

Roosevelt balanced his listening skills with a speaking ability that appealed directly to the interests of Americans. He was patient but also ambitious. And Roosevelt was always ready for a fight—whether it was physical combat or political, he never ran from a confrontation. Roosevelt's best sport would have been as a boxer thanks to his mentality and background.

Best Comparison: Jack Johnson

Bold? Check.

Brash? Check.

Arrogant? Check.

A legend? Check that, as well.

Johnson combined brute strength and the ability to move like a jellyfish with a big personality that extended well beyond the boxing ring.

The small-town boy from Galveston, TX, became a big-time celebrity with his dominance in the ring. Johnson's career record was 79-8. He recorded 12 draws, 14 no-decisions, and won 46 fights by knockout. In 1903, Johnson secured his title as "Colored Heavyweight Champion of the World." It would be another five years before he was given the chance to fight a white man for the world heavyweight title. Johnson dismantled the reigning titleholder, Tommy Burns, in the 14th round to become the first African-American to be named the heavyweight champ.

Johnson would go on to solidify his greatness after dispatching Jim Jeffries in 1910. Jeffries was dubbed "The Great White Hope" by the white media who sought a competitor to dethrone Johnson from atop boxing's perch. It was billed as the fight of the century, but Jeffries proved no match for Johnson.

Roosevelt also had a passion, and even a skill, for fighting. He participated in the intramural boxing and wrestling programs while at Harvard. He continued to fight and spar for much of his life—even while in the White House. Roosevelt eventually stopped boxing all together after his friend and heavyweight champion, John Sullivan, hit Roosevelt so hard during a match that his retina detached. The president went blind in his left eye because of the blow, which was kept a secret for nearly a decade. Oh, and if that's not tough enough for you, Roosevelt also killed a Spaniard with his bare hands while charging up San Juan Hill during the Spanish-American War.

Roosevelt combined his toughness with a public bravado that displayed confidence and inspired many. While campaigning in Milwaukee in 1912, Roosevelt prepared to give a speech when he was approached by a man with a gun. John Schrank said former President McKinley had appeared in a dream and told Schrank to avenge the assassinated president's death by killing Roosevelt. Schrank fired his gun, striking Roosevelt in the right pectoral.

Luckily for Teddy, the bullet had to travel through his folded-up speech and an eyeglasses case before piercing through his skin and lodging in his chest. Largely unharmed and wholly undeterred, Roosevelt proceeded to give his speech with a fractured rib and a bullet that would remain inside his chest muscle for the rest of his life. Boasting his resiliency, Roosevelt informed the crowd, "I don't know whether you fully understand that I have been shot, but it takes more than that to kill a Bull Moose." For this, and many other reasons, he was viewed as an inspiration to Americans.

Johnson also knew how to inspire and show off for a crowd. As if his greatness in the ring at a time of intense racial discord didn't speak enough volumes, his actions outside the ring certainly did. Johnson had a penchant for driving flashy, yellow sports cars. He owned a nightclub and had his own jazz band. He had gold teeth and a gold-handled walking stick. The guy even owned a pet leopard that he would take on walks for crying out loud.

It became a habit for Johnson to date and marry some of the most popular white women from his era. It was a move that did not endear him to a large portion of the white population, but he refused to adhere to society's racial norms.

Johnson, like Roosevelt, was fearless. They were ambitious and excelled in the biggest moments. Each man was a trailblazer in his own way and used his immense skills to make the future better for those who followed. Without a doubt, both men have punched their ticket to the Hall of Fame.

Trading Card Stats

Theodore Roosevelt	Name	Jack Johnson
•Hero of San Juan Hill •The Bull Moose •The Great Conservationist	**Nickname**	•Galveston Giant
•1901-1909	**Experience**	•1897-1931
•42	**Age Entering the League**	•20
•5’8”/210	**HT/WT**	•6’0”/185-242
•Republican	**Team**	•Independent
•Antitrust policy •1906 Pure Food and Drug Act •Conservation •Hay-Pauncefote Treaty •Russo-Japanese War	**Stats**	•First black, world heavyweight champion •79-8 career record •46 knockouts, 12 draws and 14 no-decisions •7-0-2 defending his title
•Zoology •Wrestling •Boxing •Jujitsu •Horseback riding •Tennis •Hiking •Skinny-dipping •Hunting •Polo •Rowing	**Hobbies**	•Driving sports cars •Playing in a jazz band •Owning a nightclub •Acting
•“Speak softly and carry a big stick.”	**Quote**	•“The search for the ‘white hope’ not having been successful, prejudices were being piled up against me, and…decided if they could not get me one way, they would another.”
•Tried to have American English spelling changed to become more phonetic	**Interesting**	•Owned a pet leopard that he would take on walks while sipping champagne
•Yes	**Hall of Fame**	•Yes

27

William Taft (1909-1913)

Imagine sitting in a bathtub and getting stuck because of your paunchy build. Now imagine that this happens to you as the president of the United States and your advisors have to help free you from said bathtub.

If that sounds a little embarrassing, welcome to Taft's world.

Taft found himself stuck in bathtubs and requiring help on several occasions while in the White House. Talk about some hide your kids, hide your wife moments. It reached the point that Taft had his bathtub replaced with a seven-foot tub that was deemed to have the width of four, average-sized men.

Big Bill had always been on the bigger side while growing up, but it held little relevance on the path to his presidency. He studied law and acted as a part-time newspaper court reporter. He held various jobs in Ohio cities, counties, and the state, such as assistant prosecutor, collector of internal revenue, assistant solicitor, judge, and U.S. solicitor general. He also served as a professor of law and the dean of the University of Cincinnati before leaving Ohio to serve as the Commissioner and Governor-General of the Philippines at the start of the 20th century. He eventually spent four years as the secretary of war.

In 1908, Roosevelt decided not to run for a third term. Instead, he handpicked Taft to be his successor on the Republican ticket. Taft secured the nomination rather easily thanks to how widely popular Roosevelt had been during his tenure.

Though Taft and Roosevelt would eventually grow apart due to different policy views, Taft did follow in Roosevelt's footsteps in many regards. He enforced Roosevelt's antitrust policies in as stringent a manner as his predecessor and even scored victories by curbing the American Tobacco Company and the Standard Oil Company practices.

He executed the Mann-Elkins Act, which authorized the Interstate Commerce Commission to fix excessive rates charged by railroads and prevented these companies from charging more for short hauls than longer ones. It also gave the ICC supervision of the telegraph and telephone industries.

Globally, Taft oversaw a time of peace as America stayed out of war. He pushed a policy known as Dollar Diplomacy. The intent was to encourage American financial and political investment in Central American countries. It acted as an extension of the Monroe Doctrine, protecting their interests in this region. It also promoted American business while displaying U.S. military might to any would-be interlopers.

Taft also signed the Payne-Aldrich Tariff Act into existence which effectively lowered the tariff rate from 46% to 41%. While the act generally led to a rate reduction, it ultimately became extremely controversial as specific items such as coal, iron ore, and animal hides saw a rate spike. It even led to a large splintering of the Republican party, pushing Roosevelt away from his protégé and leading to the creation of the Bull-Moose party as a future challenger to Republicans and Democrats.

Most likely sport: Football

While Taft was overweight and out of shape, he was deceptively athletic because of his size. He played baseball in his early days and was the first president to venture into golf after his presidency. However, Taft's sheer size, without question, would make him best suited for football.

Not surprisingly, Taft's potential positions would be pretty limited playing football. His lack of speed, endurance, and mobility would have kept him at the line of scrimmage. He was generally laid back, lacking in offensive aggression. However, he did a good job of disrupting the Republican party, making him a good fit as a defensive tackle.

Best Comparison: William Perry

There's big. Then there's bigger than life.

Perry falls into the latter category.

Perry was always bigger than his peers, weighing in at more than 200 pounds as a sixth grader. By the time he was 14, nearly everyone in his home state of South Carolina knew about him. Perry wasn't just expected to be big. He was expected to be a big success.

Perry would attend Clemson University and become a three-time All-American, helping lead his team to a national title in 1981. He set the Clemson record for most career sacks at 25—a record that would be broken just a few years later by his younger brother, Michael.

While at Clemson, Perry earned one of the most iconic nicknames in sports and pop culture. As a freshman, he entered an elevator with one of his teammates, Ray Brown. Perry noticeably took up the majority of the elevator, causing Brown to remark that he was the size of a refrigerator. The moniker has stuck with Perry ever since.

The Fridge was drafted by the Chicago Bears in 1985 and immediately contributed as a rookie to a Super Bowl winning team that is widely considered one of the best in NFL history. Perry would go on to have a successful 10-year career, playing eight-and-a-half seasons with the Bears before finishing with the Philadelphia Eagles. In total, Perry recorded 29.5 sacks, more than 500 tackles, and 3 offensive touchdowns. He even scored one as a running back during his lone Super Bowl appearance.

Despite the talent, much of Perry's fame came because of his size. Now, 300-plus behemoths are the norm in football. Back in the 1980s, however, he was more along the lines of a freak show because of how he stacked up relative to his contemporaries. He struggled with weight for much of his career, often tipping the scale closer to 400 pounds than 300.

Perry's level of skill is often overshadowed by his on-going weight issues. But Perry had a freakish level of athleticism and mobility that you don't see in most people—regardless of their weight. He could dunk a basketball, throw a football 70 yards, and bench-press 485 pounds. Perry even ran a 5.05 second 40-yard dash. And, no, they didn't place a ham sandwich at the finish line. Perry had a big smile and a jovial personality that combined with his natural talent to make him a lovable, though somewhat underrated, player.

The same can be said of Taft who is also overshadowed in the history books. Taft's weight also played a (*ahem*) large role in how he is remembered. Most Americans think of Taft—if they think of him at all—as being the fat president. After all, the man did have a custom bathtub built for himself. He also had banisters installed to help him climb the White House stairs.

His weight likely even contributed to some type of sleeping disorder. Taft was reported to have often fallen asleep in some strange places—like campaign rallies, cabinet meetings, and funerals. While the sleeping disorder suggestion is reckless speculation, it feels less reckless to say those aren't typically places where a person plans their sleep.

Another reason for Taft's commonly overlooked place in history is due to whom he followed. He was trying to fill Roosevelt's shoes after being hand-picked for the job. And let's face it, being president is hard enough, but following in the place of a Hall of Famer while being saddled with those same expectations isn't easy.

But Taft was very good in his own right and typically doesn't get the credit he deserves. Like Perry, Taft fit the stereotype of a jolly, fat guy. He was cheerful, friendly, and had an infectious chuckle. Everyone liked him, and he possessed real skill, too. His trust-busting, conservation efforts, and elite judiciary skills should have been more appreciated.

Both Big Bill and The Fridge had very respectable careers when properly analyzed. Unfortunately, their greatness didn't quite match their size. Neither man makes it to the Hall of Fame.

Trading Card Stats

William Taft	Name	William Perry
•Big Bill •Big Lub	**Nickname**	•The Refrigerator •Fridge
•1909-1913	**Experience**	•1985-1994
•51	**Age Entering the League**	•23
•6'2"/316	**HT/WT**	•6'2"/335
•Republican	**Team**	•Chicago Bears •Philadelphia Eagles
•1910 Mann-Elkins Act •Antitrust policy continued •1909 Payne-Aldrich Tariff Act •Dollar diplomacy	**Stats**	•524 tackles •29.5 sacks •2 rushing touchdowns •1 receiving touchdown
•Dancing •Oration •Math •Composition •Following baseball •Theater •Golf •Swimming •Ice skating	**Hobbies**	•Fishing •Music •Swimming •Basketball
•"What's the use of being president if you can't have a train with a diner on it?"	**Quote**	•"Even when I was little, I was big."
•Fractured his skull in a carriage accident when he was nine	**Interesting**	•Boxed for charity against Manute Bol in 2002
•No	**Hall of Fame**	•No

28

Woodrow Wilson (1913-1921)

Wilson may have typically been the smartest man in the room, but at his presidency's most critical juncture, his voice fell on deaf ears.

As the only president to earn a Ph.D., Wilson was certainly one of the smartest to reach the Oval Office as his rise to political prominence came via the educational system.

He began his foray into the professional world by studying law at the University of Virginia before teaching political economy and public law at Bryn Mawr College. He then became a professor of history at Wesleyan University, a professor of jurisprudence and political economy at Princeton, and capped it off with an eight-year run as Princeton's president. Next, he spent two years as New Jersey's governor until he was elected U.S. president.

While Wilson won the 1912 election largely because the Republican vote was split between Taft and Roosevelt, he entered his new gig with a progressive and reformist attitude designed to shake up the status quo.

Domestically, Wilson supported the Federal Reserve Act, creating the modern reserve system by establishing 12 regional banks governed by a board. This helped make the country's financial system safer, more elastic, and more stable. The Federal Trade Commission was created to investigate business practices conducted by most interstate corporations. Though the powers of this group were ultimately limited by the Supreme Court, the intent was to help small businesses and put an end to monopolies.

He implemented two different acts meant to curb child labor laws, though they were both struck down by the Supreme Court. Wilson also helped pass the Adamson Act, which averted a railroad strike. As part of the act, trainmen were limited to working eight hours a day, which eventually led to the widespread acceptance of eight-hour work days.

In foreign affairs, Wilson replaced the Payne-Aldrich Tariff with the Underwood Tariff, which reduced the average rate from 41% to 27% and also provided a federal income tax in accordance with the 16th amendment. In order to secure these changes, Wilson became the first president to personally address Congress since John Adams.

Tensions consistently ran high with Mexico during Wilson's tenure that coincided with the 1913 Mexican Revolution. Though the ire on both sides was drawn and troops were sent to the region, no war erupted. However, the feelings of mistrust culminated in 1917 when Mexico joined an alliance with Germany, stipulating they would provide each other with mutual support should the U.S. become involved in World War I. While this provocation by Mexico pissed off the U.S., it mainly galvanized the country against Germany.

Until then, the U.S. had resisted the temptation to join the war that began three years earlier. Wilson had stressed the need to remain neutral and support a peaceful negotiation to end the fighting. Eventually Germany's relentless submarine warfare took its toll on Wilson who felt compelled to ask for a declaration of war in the interest of humanity.

While the U.S. engagement on the battlefield helped bring on-field fighting to a close, Wilson began creating a 14-point set of principles that would guide the world in upcoming peace talks. The Treaty of Versailles brought WWI to an end and also provided for the creation of the League of Nations. The idea was to have a large contingent of nations enter into a pact to aid in promoting global peace.

However, Wilson suffered a stroke while stumping across America to sell the nation on this idea. When a group of Republicans fought to add reservations to the treaty, Wilson stubbornly refused to budge from his position while cooped up in bed. Wilson, though, was publicly unable to voice his argument for the existing framework of the proposed deal due to the stroke. As a result, the Senate failed in ratifying the treaty, and the U.S. never joined the League of Nations.

Ironically, though, Wilson was awarded the 1919 Nobel Peace Prize for his creation. But without U.S. involvement and Wilson's guidance, the League of Nations was less effective than it likely could have been. Although the League of Nations eventually folded, it did lay the groundwork for what is now the United Nations.

Most likely sport: Football

Wilson was very confident and possessed a true talent for leading others—at least those he was interested in leading. Not unlike most of his predecessors, Wilson didn't have the greatest track record with race relations or civil rights; but he was actually best when leading larger groups rather than smaller ones. With this in mind, football would have been his best sport.

Wilson was incredibly intelligent. He worked hard, was a great communicator, was able to explain his decision making to the press, motivated others, and had a true passion for what he did. Oh, he also sought attention and craved affection. Wilson had "quarterback" written all over him.

Best Comparison: Joe Theismann

When a grown man who makes a living out of trying to destroy quarterbacks is fervently calling for assistance after doing his job, you know something bad has happened.

That turned out to be just the case on November 18, 1985 when Joe Theismann was dropped in the backfield. And it wasn't just an ordinary opponent waving to Theismann's bench for assistance before putting his hands on his head as if to ask "What have I just done?" This was Lawrence Taylor. One of the baddest men ever to make a living in this gruesome sport.

Taylor jumped on Theismann's back, pulling him toward the grass. The weight of Taylor's body pinned Theismann's right leg to the ground. Milliseconds later, Taylor's teammate, Gary Reasons, finished the play by driving Theismann's upper body into the turf. His leg pinned and pointing one direction, the rest of his body going in another. Theismann's tibia and fibula were both broken, which was painfully evident given the bone poking through his sock.

It is a play that has lived on in sport and pop culture anytime a significant injury occurs and broadcasters look for a similarly gruesome injury with which it can compare. It was on Monday Night Football, the world's centerstage, at a time when live, cable TV was the main source for connecting with the rest of the world.

To that point, Theismann's career had been going really well. He was playing in his 12th NFL season, all of which came with the Washington Racial Slurs. He had thrown for more than 25,000 yards and 160 touchdowns. He was a Super Bowl champion and an MVP. Before that, Theismann had played three successful seasons in the Canadian Football League after being a four-year player and first-team All-American at the prestigious University of Notre Dame.

Theismann's career had certainly been a success, but the injury completely derailed its ending. He never again played in an NFL game.

The injury cut Theismann's career short, stripping him of the control all athletes fear losing—the ability to finish on their own terms. For Theismann, his lasting memory could have been as one of the best quarterbacks of all time with a few more years of solid production. Instead, he is largely remembered for his shattered leg.

In a similar fashion, Wilson's stroke prevented him from finishing with a bang. Wilson remained incapacitated from the time of his stroke in 1919 until he left office in 1921. During that time, he was unable to convince the U.S. to support his own idea that had been presented to the rest of the world. This was an embarrassing failure that has stuck with Wilson, largely damaging his legacy.

In spite of the less-than-ideal endings, both men were also inspirational in their speaking ability. Wilson was a top-notch orator. He knew how to communicate with the masses and did so via his press interactions. Wilson was very persuasive when he spoke. He motivated millions of people around the world with his progressive ideas that generated a devout following of his Wilsonian ideology as a political approach to foreign policy. Meanwhile, Theismann was also a good communicator who turned to broadcasting and motivational speeches after his career. His ability to overcome the leg injury and come out of it still seeing the positives in life inspired many.

Had Wilson and Theismann been able to avoid the injury/illness bug that derailed the end of their careers, their legacies would have been different. Both men may have gone down as two of the very best at their respective jobs. As it is, both men fall excruciatingly short of reaching the Hall of Fame.

Trading Card Stats

Woodrow Wilson	Name	Joe Theismann
•The Schoolmaster •Big One of the Peace Conference	**Nickname**	•Captain Bubbly •Hollywood
•1913-1921	**Experience**	•1974-1985
•56	**Age Entering the League**	•25
•5'11"/170	**HT/WT**	•6'0"/192
•Democrat	**Team**	•Washington Redskins
•1913 Federal Reserve Act •1914 Clayton Antitrust Act •Child labor laws •1916 Adamson Act •WWI •League of Nations	**Stats**	•25,206 passing yards •160 passing touchdowns •138 interceptions
•Golf •Horseback riding •Theater •Mimicry •Telling dialect jokes •Singing •Billiards •Poetry •Reading •Enjoyed baseball and football	**Hobbies**	•Acting •Broadcasting •Collecting memorabilia
•"The use of a university is to make young gentlemen as unlike their fathers as possible."	**Quote**	•"Nobody in the game of football should be called a genius. A genius is somebody like Norman Einstein."
•Only president to earn a Ph.D., which he acquired in political science from Johns Hopkins University	**Interesting**	•Theismann went 20 years without watching a replay of his leg breaking
•No	**Hall of Fame**	•No

29

Warren Harding (1921-1923)

Harding really had no business being president.

What Harding had going for him was good looks, a friendly demeanor, and a driven, if not bossy, wife.

His rise to prominence came largely via the help of his domineering wife, Florence, who pushed her husband to reach for more. One could argue he didn't even know what the hell he was doing to which even Florence would likely agree. In fact, Florence is even on record as taking credit for putting Harding in the White House.

Before the presidency, Harding had bounced around the workforce as an adult. He spent one term as a teacher after graduating from college. He studied law briefly at his father's insistence but quit to become an insurance salesman. After being kicked to the curb in insurance, he became a reporter. Eventually he helped purchase, and then became the owner, of the *Marion Star* newspaper.

Harding then entered politics by becoming an Ohio state senator which was followed by a stint as lieutenant governor of Ohio and then as a U.S. senator. Harding had enjoyed his foray into politics, finding that it required less work from him than his previous endeavors. That lack of effort was reflected in his timecard, too, as he had one of the poorest attendance records in the upper chamber.

In 1920, Harding was not expected to be nominated for his own party, let alone the president of the United States. But with ardent support from his wife who helped rally women voters to the polls to vote for the first time in U.S. history, perhaps the darkest of dark horse candidates arrived in Washington.

Harding had promised Americans to return the country to normalcy as he oversaw the official end to WWI. With that in mind and a crew of white-collar criminals secretly in tow, Warren G set out to regulate.

Harding's two years in office passed uneventfully. (*Spoiler alert: he died in the middle of his only term.*) He had a solid, if not uninspiring, track record in policy making. However, Harding was generally well-regarded during his time in office.

At home, he established the Budget Bureau, which created formal budgetary restraints on federal expenditures. Harding released a number of wartime protesters including, most notably, Eugene Debs, who was the leader of the Socialist party. Harding also was the first president since the Civil War to go to the South and stump for improved civil rights for black people.

Abroad, Harding oversaw the formal end of WWI. His vehement opposition to the League of Nations ensured America's absence from the group. In keeping with the theme of international peace, the U.S. agreed to a naval arms limitation at a time when a number of nations were jockeying for global supremacy. The pact included the U.S., Great Britain, Japan, France, and Italy. Each country agreed to an aggregate tonnage limit of battleship cruisers and carriers to prevent any rising tensions.

Though Harding wasn't spectacular as president, he was mostly lauded at the time of his passing. It wasn't until after his death that the more scandalous side of his cabinet came to light, ultimately hurting his reputation.

Most likely sport: Basketball

While Harding was not much of a strategic or long-term thinker, he was humble and able to stay calm under pressure. He had good size for a president and would have been best suited to play basketball.

Although Harding did not excel at anything in particular, he was pretty well-rounded in his skillset. This, coupled with his size, would have put him on the wing as a forward.

Best Comparison: Lamar Odom

Even with some relative recency bias, it seems fair to say this about the end of Odom's career, and his life in general.

Damn. *That* was crazy.

Odom morphed from a solid basketball player to a Hollywood celebrity to a scandalous, nationwide, medical marvel over the course of several years. He slowly flew across the sports and pop-culture scenes like a rising meteor before it all ended in a blinding explosion of addiction.

For Odom, though, it all started back in the late 1990s as a teenager. He had been let go from the University of Nevada at Las Vegas program after some minor indiscretions and found himself at the University of Rhode Island where he played extremely well as a freshman, receiving several conference awards in the process. After his freshman year, Odom was testing the NBA waters when he ultimately decided he wasn't yet ready for the NBA and wanted to return to Rhode Island to play out his sophomore year.

Alas, Odom had already signed with an agent, forcing him to forgo the remainder of his college career. As a pro, Odom played on four teams over 14 seasons, averaging nearly 13 points and 8 rebounds per game for his career. He is best remembered for his time with the Los Angeles Lakers where he won a Sixth Man of the Year Award and contributed to two, title-winning teams.

Odom was a solid, all-around-player. He had good size, pretty good skill, and was well liked as a person and teammate. But he had some sizable skeletons in his closet that did not come to light until the twilight of his career. In December 2011, he was traded to the Dallas Mavericks because Odom and the Lakers were unable to mend fences after an earlier proposed trade involving Odom had been shockingly vetoed by the NBA. His rocky tenure with the Mavericks led to him taking a mid-season sabbatical before they split all-together prior to the season's end.

During a two-week period in 2013, Odom went missing for 72 hours, surfacing when he was arrested for a DUI and was in a car crash. A couple years later, Odom hit rock bottom while partying in Las Vegas where he was found unconscious at a brothel. While he was in a coma at the hospital, the 35-year-old Odom suffered 12 strokes and six heart attacks. At the same time, the outside world was just beginning to fully comprehend Odom's addiction to drugs, alcohol, and his infidelity to his estranged wife, Khloe Kardashian. Remarkably, Odom managed to recover from that incident despite being given only four hours to live at one point.

Odom wasn't the only one with skeletons, though. Harding had some of his own that only began to publicly manifest at the end of his career (life). He had voted in favor of prohibition as a senator in 1920 only to consistently drink bootleg liquor at the White House. It was also unearthed that he had a pair of extramarital affairs and a secret child from one of the women. Yet, it was the decision making of those surrounding Harding that proved most problematic for his legacy. While Harding had a few good men in his cabinet, there were far too many miscreants for him to go unscathed. Several different Harding subordinates had committed and been convicted of varying acts of fraud, conspiracy, and bribery.

The most infamous incident was the Teapot Dome scandal where Secretary of the Interior Albert Fall allowed the Mammoth Oil Company to siphon the Teapot Dome federal oil reserves in Wyoming. Fall received $308,000 and a herd of cattle for this act of bribery. He also accepted money from another company after letting them tap a California reserve. Although no evidence has ever been found to indict Harding of any wrongdoing, he did seem to understand that his friends ran amuck, betraying him and putting him in peril just before his death.

Poor decision making combined with hypocritical and self-destructive habits led to each man's downfall. While neither man was bad at his job, their playing careers will ultimately be less known for policies and slam dunks than the tumultuous scandals that are now forever linked to their names. Neither of them has a case for the Hall of Fame.

Trading Card Stats

Warren Harding	Name	Lamar Odom
•Wobbly Warren	**Nickname**	•L.O. •Candy Man
•1921-1923	**Experience**	•1999-2013
•55	**Age Entering the League**	•20
•6'0"/173	**HT/WT**	•6'10"/220
•Republican	**Team**	•Los Angeles Clippers •Miami Heat •Los Angeles Lakers •Dallas Mavericks
•1921 Budget Bureau •Civil Rights reform •League of Nations •Formal WWI conclusion	**Stats**	•13.3 points, 8.4 rebounds and 3.7 assists per game •Sixth Man of the Year •NBA All-Rookie First Team
•Golf •Playing poker •Attending baseball games •Following boxing •Burlesque shows •Playing cards •Auto trips •Fishing •Yachting	**Hobbies**	•Music •Shopping •Designing clothes
•"I am a man of limited talents from a small town; I don't seem to grasp that I am president."	**Quote**	•"Death always seems to be around me."
•Kept the White House stocked with bootleg liquor despite reluctantly voting for prohibition as a senator	**Interesting**	•Famously had a candy addiction
•No	**Hall of Fame**	•No

30

Calvin Coolidge (1923-1929)

Knowing when to be quiet and listen is a great presidential characteristic to possess. Being an utter recluse whose disdain for human interaction largely dictates their entire presidency, however, is not exactly ideal.

Therein exists the conundrum for someone like Coolidge who was best known for being abnormally shy and closed off. That's not necessarily a bad trait in and of itself as nobody is asking for him to be the Ryan Seacrest of politics, but it does seem a bit problematic for someone who is the president of one of the most powerful nations in the world. His hermit-like nature eventually earned him the nickname, Silent Cal, which he put to good use over the years.

Coolidge's extreme introversion was not a new quality that emerged in the Oval Office. As a child, he would border on panic attacks anytime somebody visited their home and he was forced to greet them. Although he eventually worked his way out of that phase, Coolidge didn't stray much further from his introverted roots.

After graduating from college, Coolidge studied law. He was elected to the Northampton City Council (MA) at the turn of the 20th century before quickly moving on to city solicitor. He joined the Hampshire County clerk of courts, became a member of the Massachusetts General Court, and then was elected mayor of Northampton. Coolidge continued to climb the political ranks and became a state senator. He then moved on to become Massachusetts' lieutenant governor, followed by governor, and finally served two years as vice president before Harding's death propelled him into the hot seat.

As president, Coolidge's tenure was largely restrained, cautious, and a bit sluggish—just like he was. Coolidge wasn't lazy per se, he just didn't think the government was supposed to do much. His administration did pass separate revenue acts in 1924 and 1926 that greatly favored the wealthy, which created a ripple effect that ultimately abolished several taxes. This eventually led to the Great Depression by creating private investment funds that led to speculation, or investing in assets with the mere hope that they would become more valuable.

A separate policy that passed, despite his veto, was a veteran's bonus that awarded WWI vets pay based on their time of service and location during the war. Meanwhile, commercial aviation also made headway into American society during Coolidge's tenure. The Air Commerce Act was passed, and the first two commercial air routes were approved.

Regarding international relations, Coolidge implemented an incredibly restrictive Immigration Act that only allowed for up to 150,000 immigrants per year and put caps on some countries. The law barred Japanese immigration altogether. The Kellogg-Briand Pact was another Coolidge foreign policy aimed at renouncing war as a way to solve international disputes. The U.S. and France initiative began with 15 countries and eventually saw 47 more nations join.

Overall, Coolidge had a decidedly anti-agricultural approach to governing. And while he wasn't repressive to minority groups, he showed little interest in supporting them. In that sense, it acted as a microcosm for his approach to life.

Coolidge rarely reached out to others and was laid back to the brink of lethargy as president.

Most likely sport: Tennis

Due to Coolidge's personality and his severe preference to work alone as much as possible, he would have been best suited for an individual sport. Unfortunately for Coolidge, as a president he couldn't play solely by himself, ruling out golf. He had to compete with and against the interests of others on a daily basis. Tennis would have been his best sport.

Best Comparison: Kyle Edmund

Edmund isn't exactly a household name to Americans, but then again, neither is Coolidge.

However, travel to Great Britain and most Brits are well aware of their tennis hero. Edmund attributed his early foray into tennis to his mom who wanted him to find something to do because he was "probably annoying her." He began focusing on tennis full-time when he left school at 14 and joined the Win Tennis academy. His training quickly led him to the junior circuit where Edmund flashed his potential. He won the Junior Davis Cup in singles and snagged U.S. Open and French Open juniors titles in doubles. Edmund went professional at age 17, joining the Association of Tennis Professionals (ATP).

As a pro, his success has been more limited. Having competed in more than 200 singles tournaments, he sports a nearly .500 record. His first tournament victory was the 2018 European Open, and he has since added a second title at the 2020 New York Open. Edmund's game is known for his big forehand hits and a typically subdued approach to his craft.

That calm demeanor was likely borne from his naturally quiet disposition. Edmund keeps a close circle and is very introverted off the court. In that regard, Edmund and Coolidge are like two, uncomfortable peas in an introverted pod. Coolidge was a man of very few words—and friends. Unsurprisingly, he did not like consulting with others and was not a great communicator.

One of the most poignant examples to convey his level of shyness took place at a social engagement. Already notorious for being quiet, Coolidge was approached by a woman who insisted he had to talk to her because she had made a bet with a friend that Coolidge would say at least three words to her. Without even looking at her, Coolidge replied, "You lose," and the conversation ended. Willy Wonka didn't even deliver that line as masterfully as Coolidge.

That shy personality and closed off approach may not have always been the most beneficial to Coolidge, but it did prevent him from being surrounded by "yes-men" who might have given him a big ego. This isolation helped him stay humble and even level-headed in emergencies. When tensions with Mexico began to rise during his administration, Coolidge helped defuse the strained relationship and an agreement was struck that ensured peace. Likewise, Edmund has been known for his down-to-Earth nature. Edmund doesn't let the pressure of the moment rattle him. He continues to play with the same pace and attitude regardless of how the match is unfolding.

Despite their calm, easy-going presences, both Coolidge and Edmund have not had extremely successful careers. Neither man is worthy of the Hall of Fame.

Trading Card Stats

Calvin Coolidge	Name	Kyle Edmund
•Silent Cal	**Nickname**	•Kedders
•1923-1929	**Experience**	•2012-present
•51	**Age Entering the League**	•17
•5'10"/148	**HT/WT**	•6'0"/176
•Republican	**Team**	•Independent
•Tax reduction •Veterans bonus •Commercial aviation •1924 Immigration Act	**Stats**	•117-115 record in singles •2018 European Open champion •12-22 record in doubles •2020 New York Open champion
•Horseback riding •Walking •Window shopping •Fishing •Skeet shooting •Practical jokes •Being with animals •Attending the circus •Yachting •Smoking cigars	**Hobbies**	•Motorsports •Soccer •Music •Golf •Sports cars
•"When a great many people are unable to find work, unemployment results."	**Quote**	•"Mum just wanted me to do something because I was probably annoying her." -On why he started playing tennis
•Gifted a raccoon intended to be a Thanksgiving Day meal; Coolidge turned the raccoon, Rebecca, into a pet that lived at the White House for nearly two years	**Interesting**	•If not a tennis player, Edmund said he would likely be a cricket player or Formula 1 driver
•No	**Hall of Fame**	•No

31

Herbert Hoover (1929-1933)

Imagine a terrifying world in which you are responsible for seeing the country through the Great Depression. You know, only the single worst economic occurrence in U.S. history.

First of all, you're doing time travel, so that's cool—regardless of your very perplexing choice in era. Secondly, though, don't make the same mistake

Hoover did by lavishly eating seven-course meals every day and night at the White House as a way to garner the citizens' trust and respect.

Hoover strangely thought it would help maintain public confidence if the average citizen saw him eating well, as if that would assure the public that they could also eat well. Though in hindsight, and likely in real-time, it doesn't seem like the most well-thought-out idea ever.

Hoover, however, had grown accustomed to his well-off lifestyle after working his way into success. He had a very rags-to-riches story. At the age of two, Hoover nearly died as a result of croup, an infection of the airway that restricts breathing. Hoover's parents placed pennies over his eyes and drew a sheet over his face right before his uncle, a doctor, arrived and managed to revive him. Unfortunately, his parents both died young, causing Hoover to be orphaned at the age of nine.

After working his way through school, Hoover spent nearly two decades as a mining engineer. When WWI hit, he wound up playing an instrumental role in the American relief efforts. Hoover served in a variety of capacities and received global recognition for efficiently distributing food and supplies throughout Europe, ultimately distributing 34 million tons of American food, clothing, and other supplies. He even convinced Americans to observe wheatless and meatless days to help in the conservation effort.

Following WWI, Hoover served as the secretary of commerce. When Silent Cal chose not to run again, Hoover was the first, and only, choice for Republicans. He won the general election in a landslide, which was the first position he had been appointed to since he was elected class treasurer in college.

The economy was, by far, the largest obstacle of Hoover's presidency. There were signs leading up to the 1929 market crash, but nobody predicted what was to come when the markets took their first major hit on the 23rd of October that year. The country's economy was eviscerated.

A few of the main factors in causing the depression were an extreme surplus in agricultural products, a lack of restraint on the amount of financial credit given to the public, and high tariffs. National unemployment rose to 25% by 1933, roughly a quarter of all U.S. banks failed from 1929-1932, and crop prices dropped 30% in 1930 and 1931.

While it would be a mistake to blame Hoover for causing the Great Depression, he didn't exactly do much to help diminish the financial bludgeoning. Hoover and his team failed to recognize the severity of the depression right away, insisting on multiple occasions that the worst of it had already passed. While he did work diligently to drum up support and encourage volunteerism by corporations and the wealthy to help the general populace, the strategy never quite measured up to the intent.

Hoover also established the Reconstruction Finance Corporation, which lent out nearly $2 billion to a whole host of institutions and state government agencies by the time Hoover left office. He tried creating a Federal Farm Board to spur agriculture. Additionally, in 1932, he paid war veterans bonuses that had been initially promised to them by Coolidge in 1924 but were not meant to be doled out until 1945. Ultimately, none of it made much difference as American finances continued to hit new lows during Hoover's tenure.

Coming into office, one of Hoover's greatest strengths was his understanding of foreign affairs, entering the presidency as one of the more qualified individuals in that regard. Unfortunately, the economy never fully allowed him to dedicate his eye to a global lens.

Most likely sport: Baseball

Hoover wound up being president at one of the worst times imaginable. He was a tireless worker with a sterling reputation for getting after it every day while in office. Though he entered his presidential role with a good mix of policy-building background and personal characteristics, it wasn't nearly enough to overcome the dumpster fire that emerged under his watch.

Hoover was also a thinker, though he often went a bit too far, making plans based on humans behaving rationally. For example, he gave large contributions to private relief efforts during the Great Depression and believed in the humanitarianism of other well-off citizens to do the same, lifting their destitute neighbors out of poverty.

He viewed all problems as having rational, impersonal solutions because that's how he saw them. However, that led to problems as everyone but Hoover knows the general populace is far from rational. But his hard-working, thought-conjuring nature makes him best suited for baseball. It doesn't hurt that he also played baseball as a freshman at Stanford.

Hoover came into the White House with almost no experience in public office, but a seemingly well-rounded approach to the job. In baseball parlance, he was good enough to play a number of positions but not good enough to stand out at any one position over the course of his career. Therefore, he would have served as a utility man.

Best Comparison: J.R. Phillips

Sometimes you exceed expectations. Sometimes expectations exceed you.

Such was the case for Phillips, a highly touted prospect who never quite lived up to the expectations held by fans. Phillips was an exceptional athlete as a child, participating in football, track, and wrestling. Baseball, though, was where he really excelled.

In high school, Phillips was a dominant hitter and pitcher. He impressed scouts so much that the California Angels drafted him in the fourth round of the 1988 draft.

It took Phillips a handful of years, and a trade to a new organization, to get comfortable. During his sixth minor league season, Phillips appeared to finally break out. Phillips led his AAA league with 27 home runs in back-to-back seasons. In 1994, Phillips was ranked as the second-best prospect in the San Francisco Giants' organization by Baseball America. The following year, he climbed the ladder to claim the top ranking. He became a well-regarded prospect, expected to fill the first base void of then five-time All-Star, Will Clark.

Phillips, however, was unable to carry over his success to the majors. He played with four teams across seven, unspectacular seasons. He became the classically-thought of AAAA player; somebody who consistently does really well at the highest minor league level but is unable to sustain that success at the professional level.

One could argue he choked on the big stage or that he simply wasn't talented enough to be successful. The argument could also be made that he found himself in the wrong situation at the wrong time. Despite playing seven seasons, Phillips only played in more than 50 games once in his career. In fact, he amassed just 545 plate appearances, equivalent to about one season's worth of at-bats as he was never given the opportunity to play through his early struggles. Had Phillips been given a longer leash and not expected to immediately replace Clark's production, perhaps, he could have succeeded.

Of course, Phillips wasn't the only failed prospect. Hoover struggled mightily during his term, as well. Hoover had gained worldwide fame and quickly ascended the political pecking order, even being dubbed the "wundah boy" by Coolidge. But none of it mattered as Hoover was unable to successfully navigate America through the Great Depression. An optimist might say had Hoover been president at a different time, it's possible his talents would have shone in a more appreciable light.

On the other hand, a cynic could point out that all presidents have to play the hand they're dealt. Hoover's timing wasn't the problem, but his strategy was. He thought the wealthy would help support the poverty-stricken, pulling the country out of recession. He naively thought showing Americans that he still lived lavishly would help the public stay strong, knowing that their leader wasn't succumbing to economic hardship.

Similarly, it can be pointed out that Phillips wasn't a victim of "wrong place, wrong time." Rather, he was a victim of a terrible eye. In his 545 career plate appearances, Phillips struck out an unconscionable 180 times. That's good for a strikeout rate of 33%, putting him inside the top-25 all-time worst strikeout rates for hitters with at least 500 plate appearances.

Whether it was bad timing or just being plain bad, neither Hoover nor Phillips had the success they would have liked. Neither man is worthy of the Hall of Fame.

Trading Card Stats

Herbert Hoover	Name	Charles Phillips
•The Great Engineer	**Nickname**	•J.R.
•1929-1933	**Experience**	•1993-1999
•54	**Age Entering the League**	•23
•5'11"/187	**HT/WT**	•6'2"/205
•Republican	**Team**	•San Francisco Giants •Philadelphia Phillies •Houston Astros •Colorado Rockies
•Prohibition •Stock market crash and the Great Depression •1930 Hawley-Smoot Tariff	**Stats**	•.188 batting average •.247 on-base percentage •23 home runs
•Exercising •Fishing •Reading mysteries •Baseball •Football	**Hobbies**	•Football •Track
•"I outlived the bastards." -Referring to the many people who blamed him for the Great Depression	**Quote**	•"I love to have pressure on me. It doesn't bother me."
•At age 17, he became Stanford's youngest student in its inaugural class (1891)	**Interesting**	•Despite playing his last major league game in 1999, Phillips played in Korea, Mexico and the minor leagues until 2005
•No	**Hall of Fame**	•No

32

Franklin Roosevelt (1933-1945)

Elected as president four times, Roosevelt was truly the People's Champ.

He is the only president to ever be elected more than twice as no law forced a two-term limit until 1951. His highlights include helping pull America out of The Great Depression, which he then took a step further by bringing them into global prominence.

As a sufferer of polio, his paraplegic state was purposefully hidden from the world thanks to a "hush-hush" agreement with the press. His paralysis was covered up for many years in order to prevent any doubts about his competency from creeping into the American psyche. In actuality, Roosevelt was more competent, and more active, than the vast majority of presidents before him.

FDR rose to prominence with a law background, having studied it, though he never graduated law school after passing the bar exam. He would then serve as a New York senator, as the assistant secretary of the Navy, and then as New York's governor. Roosevelt earned the nod as the Democratic candidate in the 1932 election, and with the nation in a tailspin and President Hoover running as the incumbent, Roosevelt won easily.

Despite coming from a privileged background, Roosevelt truly sought what was best for the average American. Unlike Hoover's approach, Roosevelt wanted to act quickly and relentlessly to alleviate the downtrodden economic state and was willing to try almost anything to turn the economy around. If something didn't work, he simply moved on to his next plan.

Roosevelt's most well-known efforts were all encompassed as part of the New Deal, a comprehensive package of acts aimed at strengthening the economy. It included a series of new administrations and reforms that gave the federal government significantly more power and influence on the dire economic situation. Commissions and acts such as the Civilian Conservation Corps, Agricultural Adjustment Acts, Tennessee Valley Authority, Federal Emergency Relief Administration, National Industrial Recovery Act, Securities and Exchange Commission, National Housing Act, Works Progress Administration, Rural Electrification Administration, Wagner Act, and the Social Security Act were just some of the measures implemented and intended to provide economic relief.

Some of Roosevelt's other work included instituting the Hatch Act in 1939, barring federal employees from engaging in partisan political activity. Roosevelt also repealed prohibition shortly after being elected which allowed Americans to drink alcohol freely; and, man, was it needed during that era.

Of course, the biggest boon to the economy came from WWII. When the war began, the U.S. economy didn't just recover—it took off. He managed to generate strong support and boost morale once America was involved in the fighting. His ability to work closely with the Allied powers and demonstrate firmness, but fairness, while advocating for peace left an indelible mark on a global scale. He also sought to carry out the Good Neighbor Policy, which strengthened the bond of the Western Hemisphere. Roosevelt signed trade agreements, non-aggression treaties, made deals, as well as good-faith gestures to a number of Latin countries that were beneficial to international cooperation, ultimately garnering global respect for the U.S. and its power both during times of war and peace.

Most likely sport: Baseball

Despite a crippling illness, FDR came to play every day. He had great durability and longevity to match his natural talent. And while Roosevelt wasn't always consistent with making others responsible for their own actions, he always held himself accountable. He was also extremely superstitious. All of this adds up to the resume of a baseball player.

While Roosevelt would have been successful anywhere on the field thanks to his immense talent, his limited mobility would have been best suited as a designated hitter or hidden in the outfield when forced to play defense.

Best Comparison: Babe Ruth

As if Ruth's womanizing, whiskey-swilling, cigar-toting, human-garbage-disposal ways weren't enough to attract popular attention, his on-field play surely got the job done.

It's one thing to chase women, drink himself silly, smoke like a chimney, and put away any edible morsel that came within reach. Lots of people participate in those activities to excess. But almost nobody could indulge to the high degree Ruth did, while still performing with the same level of dominance at their job.

The man was a baseball savant.

Ruth learned to play baseball for the first time while he had been sent away to St. Mary's Industrial School outside of Baltimore when he was seven years old. Ruth's father worked long hours, while his mother was often sick. By the age of six, Ruth had been spending most of his time in his dad's bar where he learned to drink and use tobacco. He became so difficult to handle that his parents sent him to a reform school, which is where Ruth spent the vast majority of his adolescence.

Ruth quickly developed a knack, and a passion, for baseball at school. It didn't matter where Ruth played—pitcher, catcher, infield, outfield—he dominated all of his classmates. It led to him signing a minor league contract in 1914 to play with a Baltimore Orioles affiliate when he was just 19 years old. The Orioles, who were low on cash, sold Ruth to the Boston Red Sox during his first summer of professional baseball where Ruth continued to hit and pitch regardless of the uniform he wore.

Ruth was called up that same year and received his first taste of big-league ball. The first four seasons of Ruth's career were spent largely as a pitcher. It wasn't until 1918 that he began to shift his attention to hitting full-time. And while Ruth's pitching had been great, his hitting had become other-worldly.

In total, Ruth's career spanned 22 seasons, breaking all sorts of records in the process. Ruth compiled a 94-46 record to go along with a 2.28 ERA in just over 1200 innings pitched. While those numbers are great, his hitting was even better. Ruth ended his career as the all-time record holder in home runs with 714. He also had a .342 batting average, a .474 on-base percentage, and a .690 slugging percentage. His OPS (on-base + slugging percentage) still sits at an all-time MLB high of 1.164. The dude could mash.

Despite his success, the Red Sox couldn't get past some of Ruth's warts while he donned their uniform. His constant refusal to adhere to a team-mandated curfew was one issue. He continued to ask for more money, threatened to ditch baseball in favor of boxing, and acted in a way the Red Sox found to be selfish and inconsiderate. The Red Sox wound up selling Ruth to the New York Yankees where he played 16 of his final 17 seasons. While there, Ruth was fined or suspended on multiple occasions for barnstorming, which is when players participated in unsanctioned games to earn extra cash. Ruth also lobbed obscenity-laced tirades and jumped into the stands to fight heckling fans.

Similarly, Roosevelt had to navigate his own set of difficult circumstances and self-induced blemishes. An argument can be made that Roosevelt was a bit of a compiler, or someone who racked up accomplishments because they were around for so long. The New Deal contained a number of different programs with varying levels of impact. Combined with the fact that the depression still lasted roughly a decade, some of Roosevelt's success can be attributed more to timing and longevity than sheer policy. Roosevelt also had to manage tricky situations with the press and public as he didn't want the masses to discover his paralyzed state or the affairs he had been having. Hiding this required some serious cooperation from his staff and the White House press who had a gentleman's agreement not to divulge too many details. It was so well hidden that few Americans knew of either situation.

Part of what allowed Roosevelt to mask some of the warts was his endearing, good-humored nature, and his ability to perform in the clutch. Roosevelt was revered for being charming and a man of the people, even if he wasn't actually like them. FDR attacked the depression head on and tactfully navigated America through WWII in style. He never shied away from tough decisions, and he made love to pressure, Stephen Jackson-style.

Likewise, Ruth was viewed as a common man for whom it was easy to make a connection. He slummed it at local bars and enjoyed joking around with kids. Ruth also thrived under pressure. In World Series games, his OPS went up from 1.164 to 1.214 and his at-bats per home run went from 11.8 in the regular season to 8.6 in the postseason. Ruth is also widely famous for allegedly calling his own homerun in a 1932 World Series game against the Chicago Cubs. In a widely-circulated, and grainy, video from that game, Ruth is seen pointing. Most writers and fans have long interpreted the point as being out to center field where Ruth would subsequently launch the next pitch. Though the story has never been confirmed, Ruth's legendary prowess in the playoffs only added to his lore.

While neither Ruth nor Roosevelt were perfect, they were pretty close to it during their heydays. Without question, both men easily punch their tickets into the Hall of Fame.

Trading Card Stats

Franklin Roosevelt	Name	Babe Ruth
•FDR •The New Dealer •The Man in the White House	**Nickname**	•The Bambino •The Sultan of Swat •The Colossus of Clout
•1933-1945	**Experience**	•1914-1935
•51	**Age Entering the League**	•19
•6'1"/188	**HT/WT**	•6'2"/215
•Democrat	**Team**	•Boston Red Sox •New York Yankees •Boston Braves
•New Deal •1939 Hatch Act •Repeal of Prohibition •WWII	**Stats**	•714 home runs •1.164 OPS •94-46 record •2.28 ERA •2-time All-Star •1-time MVP
•Dancing •Swimming •Bird watching •Stamp collecting •Sailing •Fishing •Movies •Playing cards •Smoking •Football •Boxing •Baseball	**Hobbies**	•Golf •Fishing •Bowling •Partying
•"The only thing we have to fear is fear itself."	**Quote**	•"It's in the papers, isn't it?" -Said when asked about allegedly calling his own home run during a 1932 World Series game
•Came out of the womb blue and breathless, needing to be resuscitated	**Interesting**	•With his parents around very little, Ruth took to stealing, drinking and using tobacco by age six
•Yes	**Hall of Fame**	•Yes

33

Harry Truman (1945-1953)

When Roosevelt died at the beginning of his fourth term in office, nobody was looking forward to Truman taking the reins—Truman in particular.

He was unprepared for the reality of being the commander in chief. Nevertheless, Truman was foisted into a lead role that had him dropping a pair of atomic bombs on Japan when just four months prior, he hadn't even known of their existence.

Truman's rise to presidency was unlike any other during the 20th century. He never received a college degree as he instead prioritized assisting his family financially by working as a timekeeper for a railroad contractor after high school. From there, he became a mailroom clerk at the *Kansas City Star*, a clerk at the National Bank of Commerce in Kansas City, and a bookkeeper at the Union National Bank in Kansas City. He also occasionally helped his family on their farm.

He volunteered in WWI, serving in the Missouri National Guard where he rose from lieutenant to major. Following WWI, Truman established a haberdashery, or men's clothing store, that nearly bankrupted him. Then, after studying law, Truman became a judge of Jackson County, Missouri. Next, he spent a decade as a U.S. senator before serving as the vice president until Roosevelt's death.

As if his initiation into office wasn't enough of a shock to the country, his actual election in the 1948 presidential race surely did the trick. It had been widely speculated by political pundits that Truman's challenger, Thomas Dewey, was bound to win. The *Chicago Tribune*, eager to break the news by their early evening deadline, printed the now-famous headline "DEWEY DEFEATS TRUMAN." Apparently, early voting returns and hearsay can't always accurately predict an election. Who knew?

Truman ultimately thrived as president despite initially being ill-prepared to take over the Oval Office. His most notable achievement was ringing in the official conclusion of WWII. While Germany surrendered in May 1945, Japan refused to give in until Truman dropped atomic bombs on Hiroshima and Nagasaki. The Nuremberg Trials took place shortly after the war. A number of Axis leaders were put to trial internationally for waging aggressive war, violating established rules of war, and crimes against humanity. Nineteen of 22 Nazi leaders were found guilty in these trials and punished by varying sentence lengths.

Truman was a leading force in the creation of the United Nations in 1945. He oversaw the start of the Cold War with Russia and implemented the Truman Doctrine as a response to the increasing spread of Communism which stated that the U.S. was not looking to eradicate Communism where it already existed but was intent on stopping its spread. Truman aimed to do so through the creation of the North Atlantic Treaty Organization (NATO), which was a military alliance among more than a dozen countries who all wished to curb Communism's reach.

Several other notable items from Truman's foreign policy include: The Marshall Plan, which gave Europe $13 billion to help them rebuild after WWII. The U.S. recognized the creation of Israel. Truman implemented a four-point plan aimed at providing technical assistance to Third World nations. Americans also became tangled in the Korean War, trying to help expel North Koreans from the South. Their involvement, however, provoked China into retaliation. At the fear of setting off WWIII, Truman backed down, and a peace agreement was eventually reached during the next presidential administration.

Truman also had to deal with the Red Scare in his own backyard. The flames of fear were stoked wildly in the U.S. by Joe McCarthy. The Wisconsin senator claimed to have a list of more than 200 known Communists within the State Department alone. Despite not having any evidence to back his claims, McCarthy rose to fame over the issue and sent many Americans into a frenzy that would last beyond Truman's regime.

Truman's domestic policy also included the Fair Deal. Among the items that passed were increased minimum wage, extension of social security, and desegregation of America's armed forces.

Most likely sport: Basketball

Truman's personality was said to be a bit rough around the edges. What Truman lacked in charisma, however, he made up with good leadership, principles, and a desire to help others. He was regarded as a team player who wasn't afraid to take charge or take ownership of his actions. While Truman wasn't physically imposing, he had an underlying toughness that helped him thrive on the rough and tumble of politics. Basketball would have been Truman's best sport.

Truman had no problem making decisions, doing so thoughtfully and in a timely manner. He kept calm in emergencies and, most importantly, Truman refused to let personal agendas take precedence over the good of the team, making Truman a natural point guard.

Best Comparison: Rajon Rondo

If there was ever a man whose reputation preceded him so early in his career it would be Rondo.

Before ever stepping foot into the NBA, Rondo's reputation had been fairly established. He was an old-school point guard, immensely talented, and stubborn as hell. Mules were viewed as being more compliant than him. Rondo had strong opinions on what should be done during games and had no problem doing it, even if it went against the game plan. Ask Rondo, and he would say it was better to ask for forgiveness than permission.

Even as a college player at the University of Kentucky, Rondo had his own ideas of how to run a team. Unlike most college point guards who would acquiesce to their coach's demands, Rondo challenged them. In challenging his coach, he challenged conventional wisdom.

Rondo spent two, well-played but largely unspectacular seasons at Kentucky. Rondo had a desire to play up-tempo that ultimately earned him a seat on the bench. The most notable event from his time in college was being benched six games for refusing to play the slowed-down style of basketball that was requested of him.

Sports, at their highest levels, are about power and control as much as they are about talent and winning. Coaches willingly cede control to nobody—particularly an inexperienced sophomore in college. The truth was Rondo had a vision of how his skills were best utilized and it didn't mesh with the stymied offense of his college program.

A *meh* college career and reported tension with his coach led to lackluster expectations when he was drafted into the NBA. He has never been able to shake his reputation for being stubborn and butting heads with coaches. From Doc Rivers in Boston to Fred Hoiberg in Chicago, Rondo had a number of run-ins with different coaching staffs. In fact, the clashing got so tumultuous in Dallas with Head Coach Rick Carlisle that Rondo was sent home in the middle of a playoff series under the guise of a back injury.

Any personality or coachability issues aside, Rondo's career has managed to vastly exceed expectations. Concluding the 2020-2021 NBA season, Rondo has played 15 years with eight different teams. His 10.0 points, 8.1 assists, 4.6 rebounds, and 1.6 steals don't do his career justice in terms of the effect he's had on the game. As a four-time All-Star and a two-time NBA champion, Rondo's career has been defined more by his on-court leadership than his stats.

Rondo's tension with coaches often comes from wanting to play the game in a particular style. But part of his style has always included a high-level of unselfishness. He is known for putting guys in the best positions to succeed and ensuring that everybody receives an adequate number of touches in a game. His ability, and desire, to count the number of times his teammates touch the ball during a game is a prominent example as to what has made him such a good leader.

Similarly, one of Truman's best characteristics was his leadership. He set high standards for himself and put his principles above the rest. Truman refused to compromise for political success when he felt his principles were at stake which helped him advance a number of forward-thinking labor and civil rights legislation despite popular blowback. In that sense, Truman was known to act with a great nobility.

On the other hand, he also had the ability to be overly petty such as when he engaged in name-calling with a columnist or he threatened to hurt a music critic for the review of his daughter's singing performance. Rondo has also flashed a tendency to behave the same way. Despite his rocky ending with the Mavericks, Rondo remained effusive in his praise of Carlisle for the success he had achieved in the past. But Rondo's pettiness has also been evident at times. It is, perhaps, most evident in his beef with Ray Allen after Allen, a teammate of five years, left the Celtics to join their Eastern Conference rival Miami Heat. Since then, it has been nothing but cold shoulders between the two. Rondo has even gone so far as to say Allen's published, biographical book was just an attention-seeking, money grab, suggesting that Allen should have just called Rondo for a loan if he was desperate for money.

Incidents like those are what has formed the jagged edges around Rondo's and Truman's personalities. They may not be regarded as the kindest or cuddliest in their professions, but both have had major success doing it their ways rather than following a more conformist path. Although they both exuded flashes of brilliance, neither man enters the Hall of Fame.

Trading Card Stats

Harry Truman	Name	Rajon Rondo
•The Haberdasher •Give 'Em Hell Harry	**Nickname**	•Swag
•1945-1953	**Experience**	•2006-present
•60	**Age Entering the League**	•20
•5'9"/167	**HT/WT**	•6'1"/186
•Democrat	**Team**	•Boston Celtics •Dallas Mavericks •Sacramento Kings •Chicago Bulls •New Orleans Pelicans •Los Angeles Lakers •Atlanta Hawks •Los Angeles Clippers
•Conclusion of WWII •Rise of McCarthyism •United Nations creation •NATO creation •Fair Deal	**Stats**	•10.0 points, 8.1 assists and 4.6 rebounds per game •4-time All-Star
•Playing piano •Walking •Poker •Art	**Hobbies**	•Roller skating •Reading •Video games
•"I fired MacArthur because he wouldn't respect the authority of the president. I didn't fire him because he was a dumb son of a bitch, although he was, but that's not against the law."	**Quote**	•"I haven't played defense in a couple of years."
•Truman had the pilot of his airplane buzz the White House roof as a joke, activating the secret service and Air Force	**Interesting**	•He tried quitting high school basketball on multiple occasions only to be talked back into it by his mom
•No	**Hall of Fame**	•No

34

Dwight Eisenhower (1953-1961)

You like Ike. I like Ike. Everybody likes Ike—for president!

Okay, so maybe you don't like Ike. I, for one, am pretty indifferent to Ike. But the man did have a pretty catchy presidential slogan.

Though it wasn't like he needed any help getting to the White House. The country was practically begging for him to run for office after his success as a five-star general who led the U.S. during WWII.

Eisenhower tried to resist the presidential beckoning at first as he was a career military man with no political experience. He grew up with five brothers in a pacifist household, which certainly would have made holiday dinners a bit awkward when he decided to enroll at West Point and join the military.

Eisenhower thrived in the military, however, quickly becoming a professional soldier. Eisenhower never saw any action in WWI, though, much to his chagrin. Despite his lack of involvement, Eisenhower's organizational skills and ability to lead others helped earn the admiration of his bosses. By the time WWII rolled around, he was designated the assistant chief of staff in charge of war plans and would hold many positions and titles throughout the war, ultimately rising to General of the U.S. Army.

After the war, Ike briefly took on a couple of roles that fell outside the military realm. He was president of Columbia University for a short time where he mostly just served as a figurehead. Eisenhower followed that by serving as the Supreme Commander of the North Atlantic Treaty Organization.

Despite his other ventures, Eisenhower's name continued to resonate for his military success. He had killed it—literally and figuratively—during his service time. By 1952, the public urges for him to run for president were growing louder after he had completely rebuffed any public prodding for his political candidacy in 1948. Four years later, though, Eisenhower had a change of heart once convinced there was a public mandate for his leadership, and he was selected as president in a landslide.

The army-vet-turned-politician envisioned himself as a foreign policy president first and foremost. His biggest concern was the rise of Communism and America's ability to stand firm with Europe against Russia's red wave. In doing so, the U.S. vowed to aid any country that was threatened by Communist aggression. At home, the threat of Communism domestically was still just as important to Americans. However, the fall of Senator Joe McCarthy helped restore a certain level of sanity that had been lost. During the Army-McCarthy hearings in 1954, the senator was exposed for his lack of evidence and lying about American citizens he deemed Communists. He fell into disgrace and was ultimately censured by the Senate.

Eisenhower did as promised with his foreign policy emphasis by bringing the Korean War to a quick conclusion. The Cold War continued under his watch but never escalated to violence. He seemingly made attempts to defuse international tensions on the surface. However, those attempts were largely undercut by his brinkmanship policy. This strategy encouraged CIA-led revolts and counter-revolutionary operations in Third World countries without Eisenhower's direct knowledge in order for him to maintain deniability. You can think of Third World countries as merely pawns in the U.S.'s power struggle for global power.

Inside America's borders, Eisenhower's priorities revolved around civil rights. In 1954, the Supreme Court ruled that racial segregation in public school was unconstitutional. Eisenhower threw his support behind the ruling in 1957 when black students attempting to enter Little Rock Central High School were attacked. He nationalized the Arkansas State Guard to ensure the black students' safety.

Eisenhower also enacted legislation to protect African American voters. The Civil Rights Act of 1960 allowed for federal sanctions to be implemented against local officials who obstructed voter registration and rights of black people.

In infrastructural-related improvements, a widespread interstate highway system was authorized, which created a 42,000-mile interstate system. The result of this vastly improved America's interconnectedness.

Most likely sport: Football

Personality-wise, Eisenhower was tough, methodical in his approach, and a very good strategist. Eisenhower's tactical approach with his X's and O's were always well thought out thanks to the meticulous planning he implored as a general. He would have been best suited for football thanks to his game planning and penchant for play calling.

You don't become the United States' army general without being able to lead others. Though Eisenhower was quiet, he inspired confidence and commanded respect from others through both his words and actions. He was intelligent, able to stay calm in emergencies, and took responsibility for his decisions. The 34th president was a true leader and would have been a natural quarterback.

Best Comparison: Steve Bartkowski

Well before the Atlanta Falcons were seemingly shrouded in permanent misfortune, they were just a bad team. However, optimism began to swell with Bartkowski's arrival in 1975.

The California quarterback brought life to what had been a lifeless franchise. The Falcons had only experienced two winning seasons, both without a playoff appearance, in their nine years of existence prior to Bartkowski.

The Blond Bomber rose steadily while at Cal. Bartkowski didn't play as a freshman, but moved into a timeshare of the quarterback position during his sophomore and junior seasons. By Bartkowski's senior season, he had taken the reins and was selected as a consensus All-American.

Convinced of the potential they saw, the Falcons traded up to the number one overall pick in the 1975 draft to select Bartkowski. He spent 11 of his 12 NFL seasons playing for the Falcons. Bartkowski led the Dirty Birds to their first three playoff appearances despite a 59-68 record overall while he quarterbacked them.

Although the records weren't stellar, neither was his surrounding cast. Bartkowski proved to be pretty productive on his own, though. He amassed 24,124 passing yards and 156 passing touchdowns, while being selected to the Pro Bowl twice.

Expectations are always high for a number one pick and Bartkowski was no different. Though he took them to heights they had never before experienced, Bartkowski couldn't quite reach the lofty goal of winning his team, and his city, a Super Bowl. One major, contributing factor in falling just short of expectation was a series of debilitating knee injuries. In just his second season, Bartkowski suffered a knee injury that required surgery. He ultimately underwent 10 more knee operations, sapping some of the athleticism he once had.

Prior to Eisenhower's military success, he was also a star football player, shining as West Point's running back before a knee injury derailed his career. Once Eisenhower's knee injury ruined his athletics career, he coached for a bit before deciding to fully focus on his military training. Like Bartkowski, Eisenhower also came into office with unbelievably high expectations based on his success in the Army and in WWII. Although the effect of his enacted policies never allowed him to reach that lofty status, a solid resume combined with presidential comportment and good PR kept him in overall good standing.

With similar athletic success in their backgrounds, and similar injuries to boot, it comes as little surprise that both men found solace in the sport of golf. It is reported that both Bartkowski and Eisenhower were once scratch golfers. Bartkowski even helped create a $3 million made-for-TV tournament that ran for a few years. Eisenhower was so infatuated by the game that he had a putting green installed on the White House lawn, near the Rose Garden, though it was inundated by squirrels. Eisenhower spent as much as 150 days a year on the golf course during his administration.

They both conducted themselves as professionals and brought increased respectability to their roles. Bartkowski did this by fighting through injuries and making a listless franchise relevant. Eisenhower did this by fighting the spread of Communism and helping advance the civil rights movement. While each man performed well during his career, neither was Hall of Fame worthy.

Trading Card Stats

Dwight Eisenhower	Name	Steve Bartkowski
•Ike	**Nickname**	•Bart
•1953-1961	**Experience**	•1975-1986
•62	**Age Entering the League**	•23
•5'10"/171	**HT/WT**	•6'4"/216
•Republican	**Team**	•Atlanta Falcons •Los Angeles Rams
•Cold War •Eisenhower Doctrine •Fall of McCarthyism •Civil Rights	**Stats**	•24,124 passing yards •156 touchdowns •144 interceptions •2-time Pro Bowl selection
•Golfing •Dry-fly fishing •Hunting •Landscape painting •Poker •Bridge •Canasta •Cooking •Reading westerns •Smoking •Football	**Hobbies**	•Golfing •Fishing •Hunting •Construction
•"I just won't get into a pissing contest with that skunk." -Referring to Sen. Joe McCarthy	**Quote**	•"I was young and stupid. There were no cell phones and cameras and I had my fun and it just went unrecorded." -On being a young player in the NFL
•So dependent on others to take care of him as president that he had his valet, John Moaney, put on his watch and pull up his boxers	**Interesting**	•Had seven knee operations while playing and has entered double digits since retiring
•No	**Hall of Fame**	•No

35

John Kennedy (1961-1963)

Kennedy seemingly had it all.

He was charming, handsome, intelligent, and largely viewed as a war hero. Oh, and it didn't hurt that his family was rich and powerful.

The Kennedy family's wealth and influence would certainly be an asset throughout his life. He was able to lean heavily on his inherited fortune and some strong sway from his father, Joe, all the way up to his presidential nomination. His father's role as a prominent politician, a leader in the democratic party and Irish community, all played a large part in crafting a path for his own ascent.

After graduating from Harvard, Kennedy volunteered for the Army but was turned away due to a pre-existing back condition, which ultimately led Kennedy to the Navy where he served four years until a ship in his command was attacked by a Japanese boat. Two U.S. sailors were killed by the destroyer and while Kennedy aggravated his ailing back, he successfully led the rest of his crew in a four-hour swim to a nearby island.

It was a grueling trek which featured Kennedy towing an injured comrade by the life jacket strap with his teeth. They were rescued nearly a week later after encountering ally-friendly natives on the island. For Kennedy's efforts, he received a purple heart and was medically discharged from the service. While Kennedy could easily have been court martialed for numerous grievances he committed leading up to the attack, including replacing a lifeboat with a heavy gun and allowing two members of his crew to sleep when combat appeared imminent, his father's connections and influence helped ensure the story was viewed heroically.

After Kennedy's naval stint came to an end, he briefly became a journalist before transitioning to politics. He spent the next 15 years splitting his time as a U.S. representative and a U.S. senator until 1960 when he ran against Richard Nixon. The polls were neck-and-neck until a series of TV debates helped swing the decision in Kennedy's favor. It was the first time a presidential debate had been viewed nationally and Kennedy's style, substance, and smooth appearance played a significant role in making him appear more presidential.

His tenure got off to a rocky start with the Bay of Pigs Invasion where Kennedy attempted to ignite an uprising meant to overthrow Fidel Castro's Communist Cuban regime. While the idea had been hatched under President Eisenhower, it was enacted after Kennedy took control and the CIA-sponsored rebel group was defeated in a mere three days, ultimately serving as a catastrophic failure.

As a response to the Invasion, the Cuban Missile Crisis occurred when Cuba linked up with the Soviet Union and had the Soviets agree to place nuclear missiles on the island in order to prevent a future invasion. Ultimately, after several intense negotiations, a potential nuclear war was averted when the Soviets agreed to dismantle their weaponry in exchange for a public declaration by the United States that it would not invade Cuba again.

Despite the initial hardships with Cuba, Kennedy remained an extremely popular figure. Preventing a cataclysmic nuclear war certainly helped, but Kennedy was also responsible for the creation of the Peace Corps and was a strong civil rights advocate, viewing civil rights as a moral and constitutional crisis. Though some historians view Kennedy as not acting swiftly or strongly enough in the defense of civil rights, Kennedy devised a Civil Rights Act aimed at ensuring full, legal equality for black Americans that was ultimately passed in 1964, one year after his assassination.

The assassination took place on November 22, 1963, during a presidential motorcade through Dallas, TX. The shooter, Lee Harvey Oswald, worked at the Texas School Book Depository and used it to set up his sniper's nest where he hit Kennedy twice. There have long been conspiracy theories about whether or not Oswald acted alone, but he was the lone person charged with a crime. Oswald wound up being shot to death by Jack Ruby before he could be prosecuted, leaving potential details or motives for Kennedy's death unanswerable.

Most likely sport: Baseball

JFK did not have the genetic build or durability to be successful at some of the more physically-taxing sports. He was a bit fragile and needed the help of his famous Doctor Feelgood-shot-concoctions that were mixed with vitamins, amphetamines, steroids, and other substances in order to help his back make it through the day. Baseball would have been the ideal sport for him.

As Kennedy's health was a bit of a question mark, he would have been unlikely to be available to play every day. But he was a gamer—someone who was charismatic, inspired confidence, and was ready to take the big stage when needed. With these traits in mind, Kennedy would have been a starting pitcher.

Best Comparison: Jose Fernandez

A big smile, a golden arm, and newfound freedom—Fernandez had overcome a lot early in his life to reach success.

Born into Castro's Cuba, Fernandez grew up dreaming of baseball. He often walked to a nearby field and, using wooden sticks and rocks, simulated playing games. By the time he was nine, Fernandez was one of the youngest players on the Cuban national youth team.

His life began to change dramatically as a teenager when he and his family began trying to escape Cuba. They failed on three separate occasions, resulting in Fernandez having to spend time in jail. On their fourth attempt, they narrowly evaded gunfire from Cuban soldiers as their boat left the shore. Choppy seas then sent Fernandez's mother overboard, prompting him to dive into the water before safely pulling his mother back into the boat. What had started as a calamity of an escape wound up with them arriving in Mexico before making their way across the border.

Fernandez attended high school in Tampa, FL, where he dominated baseball. As a senior, he went 13-1 with a 1.35 ERA, and saw the Florida Marlins draft him 14th overall that year. His domination continued in the minor leagues, and by the time he was 20, Fernandez was pitching in the majors.

Through four seasons, Fernandez managed to win Rookie of the Year honors and be selected twice as an All-Star. During his final season, Fernandez was striking out an absurd 12.5 batters per nine innings. But with less than a week left in the season, it all came to a crashing halt.

In the early hours of September 25, 2016, Fernandez and two other men, Jesus Macias and Eduardo Rivero, were on a boat that slammed into a jetty off of Miami's South Beach. All three men were killed in the accident. Fernandez was found to have been operating the boat with a blood alcohol content nearly twice the legal limit and with traces of cocaine in his system.

Much like Kennedy, it was a devastatingly unexpected end to a promising career. Just as the nation mourned in stunned silence for Kennedy, much of the nation did the same for Fernandez. From Cubans to Latin Americans, from Floridians to baseball fans, the sudden finality of a young man's life with insane potential sent shockwaves across the country.

Both Kennedy and Fernandez had very charismatic personalities. They were charming and personable, but also understood the need to be serious when it was time to work. They were graceful, with a knack for gathering information and using it to their advantage. Kennedy knew how to take in information about an audience and use it to his advantage to garner support for an issue. Fernandez knew how to take information about another ballplayer's tendencies and use it against them.

They shared some similar difficulties with injuries; JFK with his back and Fernandez with his arm that required Tommy John surgery and resulted in two shortened seasons where he wasn't selected as an All-Star. But both were fighters who managed to bounce back from their ailments and perform at a high level.

Unfortunately, both of their lives ended too soon. Kennedy at the hands of a gun and Fernandez from behind the wheel of a boat. Both men had the early look and feel of Hall of Famers. Sadly, the overall impact both men could have made was cut short by their unexpected deaths, and neither man fulfilled their Hall of Fame potential.

Trading Card Stats

John Kennedy	Name	Jose Fernandez
•Jack •JFK	**Nickname**	•Niño
•1961-1963	**Experience**	•2013-2016
•43	**Age Entering the League**	•20
•6’1”/173	**HT/WT**	•6’3”/240
•Democrat	**Team**	•Miami Marlins
•Civil Rights •Bay of Pigs Invasion •Cuban Missile Crisis •Created Peace Corps •Alliance for Progress	**Stats**	•38-17 record •2.58 ERA •NL Rookie of the Year •2-time All-Star
•Sailing •Swimming •Golf •Touch-football •Movies •Theater •Reading newspapers •Smoking cigars	**Hobbies**	•Raising pigeons •Fishing •Boating •Dominoes •Cycling
•“Forgive your enemies, but never forget their names.”	**Quote**	•“I’ve been in jail, I’ve been shot at, I’ve been in the water. I’m not scared to face David Wright. What’s he going to do?”
•Won a Pulitzer in 1957 for Profiles in Courage, which was largely ghostwritten	**Interesting**	•The Marlins set up a trust fund for Fernandez’s daughter, Penelope, after his death
•No	**Hall of Fame**	•No

36

Lyndon Johnson (1963-1969)

Johnson may have held comparable political views to his fallen predecessor, but that's about as far as the similarities extended. Kennedy was Ivy-League educated from a popular and powerful family, known for his charm and cool demeanor. Johnson was a hissing radiator who once urinated on a secret service agent's leg for the hell of it as Johnson relieved himself outside.

Johnson was foul mouthed, prone to scratching himself in public, and enjoyed a good insult. And that was just his public persona. He reveled in being a bit of a renegade whose tongue could not be kept in check.

As a child, Johnson had initially decided to forgo college after graduating from high school, choosing odd jobs—clerking, fruit picking, dishwashing, and elevator operating—as a means of survival instead. However, college began to look more appealing to Johnson, who ultimately enrolled in 1927, after finding himself broke and lacking steady employment.

He worked his way through college as a trash collector, assistant janitor, and assistant secretary to the college president. Following graduation, Johnson briefly studied law before becoming the Director of National Youth Administration in Texas. He then moved on to three decades worth of political roles as a U.S. representative, senator, and vice president. Johnson also had a brief pitstop in the military, serving as a lieutenant commander in the Navy during WWII.

Kennedy's assassination left Vice President Johnson undeterred when it came to fulfilling his new, presidential duties. Johnson may not have been initially voted in as president, but he possessed the confidence of someone who had. The success of his presidency, however, was a different matter. For Johnson, his presidency was a tale of two halves. One, a successful domestic policy. The other, a dreaded foreign policy.

Domestically, Johnson wasted little time enacting change. He initiated his Great Society program, which covered a myriad of issues such as poverty, Medicare, Medicaid, environmental protection, and consumerism. He also took on agism in the workplace, worked to protect religious freedom, encouraged peaceful protests, and fought for increased education resulting in the public schooling system receiving its largest aid package up to that point.

Johnson's greatest achievement, though, was his championing of civil rights. He signed multiple civil rights acts that legally barred discrimination in public facilities, made it easier (aka fairer) for black people to vote, and fought against housing discrimination while stiffening the penalties for civil rights violators. Without question, Johnson's push for civil rights and black equality helped move the country forward in a way that is unparalleled by most other U.S. presidents.

Internationally, his dealings largely centered around Vietnam. Though Kennedy had sent troops to the area during his tenure, it was Johnson (and his advisors) who stirred the cauldron into an all-out war. The U.S. had become involved in the Vietnam War as a means to stop the spread of Communism as a battle broke out between the Communist-led North Vietnam and the anti-Communist South Vietnam. Despite rising tensions, Johnson promised that the U.S. would avoid a war in Vietnam but his actions differed from his words as just a month after making that declaration, he began requesting (and receiving) open-ended resources to devote to Vietnam.

American troops began showing up to fight in a war that proved much more difficult than the Johnson administration had anticipated. Coupled with an inability to convince the North Vietnamese to enter into peace talks on several occasions and a growing dissidence to war within America's borders, Johnson found himself in an unenviable position.

Johnson had viewed North Vietnam's invasion of South Vietnam as a means to expand Communism rather than as a Civil War between two neighboring nations. Not fully understanding the roots of the aggression, Johnson intervened and wound up costing America money, global esteem, and the lives of thousands of soldiers for a war that the U.S. brazenly miscalculated and lost.

Most likely sport: Baseball

As evidenced by some of his foreign policy decisions, Johnson was fiercely competitive and relished power. That competitive spirit would have translated nicely into the world of athletics.

I already mentioned his proclivity for public scratching and adjusting himself. What additional evidence is needed to peg him as a baseball player?

Being a pitcher would not have worked well for Johnson as he was extremely energetic and became restless if not actively doing something. He would need to play every day and avoid long periods of downtime. However, he lacked the ability to be delicate or nimble and, as a result, he would have played as a corner outfielder.

Best Comparison: Albert Belle

It is well known that Belle's teammates were a bit scared of his violent, and unpredictable, outbursts. How scared? Scared enough that when Belle was about to be caught for cheating during a baseball game, he made a teammate crawl through the stadium ductwork and into the umpire's dressing room in order to retrieve a bat that had been illegally infused with cork.

Yeah, you didn't want to get on Belle's bad side.

Belle always possessed a feisty side that bordered on erratic. Growing up, athletics came easily to Belle who starred as a baseball and football player in high school. He chose to attend LSU and play baseball. While there, he had his first run in with anger issues that would stay with him throughout his career.

During a 1987 conference tournament, Belle attempted to run down a fan who had been hurling racial slurs at him. Two of his teammates managed to tackle Belle before he reached the fan, but it led to Belle being suspended for the College World Series. While his personal makeup was questioned, his ability to hit was not, and he was drafted by the Cleveland Indians.

Belle spent the first eight years of his 12-year career in Cleveland, splitting the last four between the Chicago White Sox and Baltimore Orioles. In total, he amassed 381 home runs and an exceptional .933 OPS. He was a five-time All-Star, and his performance was the main reason teams were willing to live with the episodes that continued to follow him.

He missed much of the 1990 season while in rehab battling alcohol. Once clean, Belle continued to run into trouble with heckling fans. One taunted him about having a keg party, leading to Belle firing a baseball at him from 15 feet away. Another chanted "Joey" to him at a club, which had been the name Belle went by prior to his stay in rehab when he changed it to his birth name, Albert. For that chant, Belle gave the guy two ping-pong paddle smacks to the face.

Belle's short fuse carried over to the clubhouse where he became known as a prickly personality among teammates, staffers, and the media. There is an interesting dichotomy at play for fans who view Belle as both an amazingly talented player, but also a bit of an asshole.

On the one hand, Belle was one of the most feared batsmen of his era with some of the best raw power in the game. He helped lead Cleveland to their first World Series appearance in 41 years. But he wasn't very well-liked in and around the game of baseball. Belle has admitted that he was often guarded with fans and media for fear of being taken advantage of while in the spotlight, but the stigma created in his playing days persists.

Likewise, Johnson also often fell into extremes when it came to committing good and bad deeds. Johnson helped the country progress in many ways—financially, educationally, racially—but his foreign policy failures were pretty damning.

On top of that, he possessed similar characteristics that made him very rough around the edges personality-wise like being blunt and crude. He was also stubborn, boisterous, and vulgar. And he was willing to enlist others in his own shady behavior when necessary. Johnson so commonly had affairs outside of his marriage that he devised a plan for his White House staff to alert him any time his wife was approaching. In order to pull this off successfully, Johnson had a buzzer system installed that would have made the 2017 Houston Astros proud.

While both Johnson and Belle had very productive careers and performed at Hall of Fame levels in various areas of their fields, their overall bodies of work fall short of making the Hall of Fame cut.

Trading Card Stats

Lyndon Johnson	Name	Albert Belle
•LBJ •Big Daddy	**Nickname**	•Joey
•1963-1969	**Experience**	•1989-2000
•55	**Age Entering the League**	•22
•6'3"/200	**HT/WT**	•6'1"/190
•Democrat	**Team**	•Cleveland Indians •Chicago White Sox •Baltimore Orioles
•Vietnam War •Civil Rights •Medicare and Medicaid •Environmental protection	**Stats**	•381 home runs •1,239 RBI •.933 OPS •5-time All-Star
•Dominoes •Reading •Golf •Poker •Swimming •Writing	**Hobbies**	•Ping-pong •Golf •Chess •Reading •Crosswords
•"If you've got 'em by the balls, their hearts and minds will follow."	**Quote**	•"Some people are saying it's a slap in the face for me to go to a competitor, but it also was a slap in my face that they would trade for Matt Williams."
•Johnson would take guests on joyrides in his amphibious car, pretending to have faulty brakes, and careen toward a lake as his passengers freaked out; after hitting water, Johnson would laugh hysterically	**Interesting**	•He was often referred to as the "Charles Barkley of baseball" for his short temper and bad behavior
•No	**Hall of Fame**	•No

37

Richard Nixon (1969-1974)

As the old adage goes: "If you ain't cheatin', you ain't tryin'." Well, by that credo, Nixon tried harder than just about anybody outside the sport of cycling.

The man was sensitive, narcissistic, mean-spirited, and impersonal. But, hey, he was president. And Nixon made sure everyone knew it. He required all

White House members to address him as "Mr. President" and even signed his communications with his wife and daughters by that same moniker.

Nixon didn't exactly ooze charisma. In fact, it was what cost him his first attempt for the presidency against Kennedy. But he certainly never lacked ambition.

Nixon studied law briefly before practicing at a firm for a few years. He had a cup of coffee in the Office of Price Administration before serving four years in the Navy and then transitioned to politics after leaving the military. He became a member of the House of Representatives, then a senator, and then vice president. In between his stints as the second in charge and the commander in chief, he returned to law for five years.

Though few people remember many positives from Nixon's administration, he did find occasional success with his best work coming in foreign affairs where he played a role in guiding the Vietnam War to its conclusion. Some praise for Nixon is merited since the war wound down during his regime, although a lack of success on the battlefield and unprecedented anti-war protests at home also deserve an assist. He helped open the door to a relationship with China by creating dialogue with a country where formal diplomatic relations previously had not existed. Nixon also helped reduce the number of nuclear and chemical weapons in existence through separate deals with the Soviet Union. Let us not forget that his administration also oversaw the first ever man on the moon.

Unfortunately for Nixon (and all Americans), the bad outweighed the good, the sketchy outweighed the bad, and the illegal outweighed the sketchy. Nixon was plagued by his own inconsistency as much as anything during his tenure. While his foreign policy had some direction to it, his domestic goals were ever-changing and lacked a long-term vision. He was bored by economists and didn't stick to a set policy, which led to inflation that soared and unemployment numbers that rose, as well. Nixon also had a mixed track record when it came to helping out minorities and the impoverished as he had pursued different plans and legislative actions that would have improved the livelihoods of those groups but then either gave up on the pursuit (the Family Assistance welfare program) or thwarted his own progress with counterproductive policies (slowing down school desegregation).

Oh, yeah. There was also the whole Watergate scandal. Five people working for the Nixon re-election campaign committee broke into the Democratic National Headquarters to place wiretaps and recover information that would have been useful in Nixon's re-election bid. Though Nixon himself was never found to have been in on the initial scheme, he was smack-dab in the middle of the attempted cover-up that soon took place. To make matters worse for Nixon, most of the evidence that incriminated him came from his own White House recordings. Few administrative officials knew Nixon kept secret recordings of all White House conversations. After the Supreme Court ruled that Nixon turn in his tapes as part of an impeachment trial, Nixon quickly resigned.

Most likely sport: Baseball

Nixon is synonymous with cheating, scandal, and disgrace. What sport has done better at those things over the last century than baseball? Nixon was made for baseball.

His rage and fiery personality always kept life around him heated and contentious. But when Watergate broke, nothing provoked as much heat and contention, this side of Art Briles, than Nixon's actions. That's why third base (the hot corner!) makes the most sense for Nixon.

Best Comparison: Fred McMullin

McMullin may not have a familiar name, but he was infamously involved in a familiar scandal.

He was considered by many to be the "eighth man out" in the Black Sox scandal that saw eight players banned for life from MLB after participating in the intentional throwing of games during the 1919 World Series.

McMullin was not a star and, ultimately, had very little impact on the outcome of the series. Although he played in one game for the Detroit Tigers in 1914, McMullin spent the better part of six years toiling around in the minor leagues. He latched on with the White Sox in 1916, which is where he played for the next five seasons, largely as a utility reserve.

Considered a strong defender, McMullin showed glimpses of potential with the bat but never found sustained success in his limited role. He entered the 1919 campaign in a holdout. Unhappy with his salary, he asked for a trade to the West Coast to be closer to his family, which was ignored. McMullin finally settled on a $2,750 contract and reported to the team where his .743 OPS easily eclipsed his career .635 OPS.

When the 1919 World Series rolled around, McMullin happened to overhear one of his teammates, Swede Risberg, discussing a fix before the series began and demanded to be let in on the deal. He was given a $5,000 bribe by gamblers to help his Chicago White Sox lose the World Series. Ultimately, the Sox did lose to the Cincinnati Reds, although McMullin did very little to actually lose the series as he went 1-2 in his only two plate appearances.

It is believed that in 1920, McMullin took over as the point man, or liaison, for games that were likely thrown during that season. Near the end of the season, a grand jury was put together to further investigate McMullin and his seven teammates. In light of testimony made, the players were suspended by the league and indicted for their role in attempting to commit an illegal act.

The trial took place the following summer. The jury failed to convict any of the men due to flimsy evidence and some prosecutorial bumbling. However, the day after the not guilty verdict was reached, MLB commissioner, Kennesaw (Judge) Landis, banned all eight players for life.

Both McMullin and Nixon paid a hefty price for the illegal acts they committed at the height of their professions. McMullin was kicked out of baseball for life, while Nixon became the only president to resign from office because he saw his impeachment writing on the wall.

It still remains unclear how much either man knew about the illegal dealings of their teammates. Rather, it is more likely that both men were simply brought into the fold after the fact. But instead of outing their teammates or avoiding the situation all together, they became willing co-conspirators. McMullin stepped into the middle of the gambling circle looking for some action. Nixon also jumped into the fray, becoming complicit in the cover-up.

Their failings in the public spotlight made their remaining existence a bit more scrutinized. But in a strange way, it made them both more memorable to history when they otherwise would not have been. Neither man was great at their job relative to their competition. Without the scandals, their names would have largely, if not completely, disintegrated to the sands of time.

Because of the improprieties, though, both men were viewed in a more villainous light. And if the *Sandlot* taught us anything (and who am I kidding, it taught us *everything*), it was that heroes get remembered, but legends never die. If that's true for what's good, isn't it also true for what's bad? That means jerks get remembered, but villains never die.

Neither Nixon nor McMullin were scared to involve themselves in corruption when the opportunity came their way. In that sense, both men have been able to continue living in scandalous lore, long after the memories of their talent have faded away. While they might live on in that regard, neither man will live on in the Hall of Fame.

Trading Card Stats

Richard Nixon	Name	Fred McMullin
•Tricky Dick	**Nickname**	•Lucky Man
•1969-1974	**Experience**	•1914-1920
•56	**Age Entering the League**	•22
•5'11"/175	**HT/WT**	•5'11"/170
•Republican	**Team**	•Chicago White Sox
•Watergate •Vietnam War •New China policy •Wage-price controls •Environmental protection	**Stats**	•.256 batting average •.635 OPS •1 home run •31 stolen bases
•Golf •Bowling •Football •Reading about history •Playing poker •Swimming	**Hobbies**	•Carpentry •Blacksmithing
•"When the president does it, that means that it is not illegal."	**Quote**	•"The only chance I would have against (Eddie) Collins at second base would be for Eddie to drop dead."
•Once gave the middle finger to a protesting student at the Lincoln Memorial and then laughed about it saying the student would go the rest of his life trying to tell people the president gave him the finger, but nobody would believe him	**Interesting**	•His only career home run was an inside-the-parker
•No	**Hall of Fame**	•No

38

Gerald Ford (1974-1977)

Ford didn't ask for any of this. Literally.

He never ran for president. He never even ran for vice president. And, yet, he ended up occupying both of those roles within one year's time.

However, being president was never Ford's dream. His interests were more varied.

Ford turned down professional contract offers from the NFL because he wanted to pursue the study of law instead. He held a number of different jobs throughout the years such as a park ranger at Yellowstone National Park, a male model, and a boxing and football coach while studying law at Yale.

He enlisted in the navy during 1942 and spent nearly four years fighting during WWII, accumulating 10 battle stars. Ford was then elected to Congress and spent 24 years as a representative. His ultimate dream was to become the speaker of the House. That plan changed in 1973 when Spiro Agnew, Nixon's vice president, resigned in disgrace after being indicted for accepting bribes. Nixon selected Ford to take over as vice president due to his moderate beliefs and unlikeliness to upset the applecart. Little did they know that it would soon be Nixon who completely upended the applecart with the Watergate debacle, which led directly to Ford's ascension.

Ford was ushered into the White House with a hero's welcome. He was open, friendly, and considerate. Most of all, though, he was *not* Nixon. Ford, however, soon sabotaged his own honeymoon period by taking the most notable action of his entire presidency—he pardoned Nixon.

By forgiving Nixon of his wrongdoings, Ford wanted to move past that era and let go of the shock and outrage the country had been experiencing. What it actually did was lay a groundwork of mistrust, both publicly and politically. Policy making became more difficult in general as a result of his decision.

One area where Ford did receive praise was with the Vietnam War, which officially ended during his tenure. Also, on the international stage, after an American merchant ship was seized by a Cambodian naval vessel, Ford ordered it to be taken back by force. Despite the loss of several American lives, the ship was taken back and Ford was largely commended for his decisive action in the face of an international threat.

At home, Ford inherited an economy in flux. He enacted four different bills that targeted consumerism in an effort to light an economic spark. Ford even introduced a program called Whip Inflation Now to slow down the rising inflation rates. Unfortunately for Ford, the economic woes got worse before they got better. The economy began to improve right before the general election in 1976, but it wasn't enough to carry him to re-election.

Most likely sport: Football

Ford was not the best leader, but he was tough, honest, and had a good spirit about him. Ford was once offered NFL contracts from the Detroit Lions and Green Bay Packers, so without debate, his best sport would have been football.

Ford was not a great public speaker, lacking the charm and charisma that often comes with the more glamorous roles. In fact, he was known as a bit of a klutz, so he certainly wouldn't be playing at one of the skill positions. Ford would have been best suited as a lineman. Oh, yeah, he also played offensive line during college. So there's that.

Best Comparison: Steve McKinney

Offensive linemen are known for their ability and desire to blend in and go largely unnoticed, even if they are the biggest creatures on a field full of other freakishly big creatures. McKinney was no exception.

McKinney is not well known and largely unheralded by even the most ardent sports fans. By linemen standards, though, that's a fairly favorable designation. Typically, if a lineman is being noticed during their playing days it's largely due to poor performance. Either their quarterback is constantly finding themselves under duress or the offense's plays are being immediately blown up in the backfield.

Although McKinney rarely stood out for individual poor play, he was on one of the worst offensive line groups in the history of the sport, which has undoubtedly diminished his football reputation. Prior to that, however, McKinney had enjoyed successful stints in college and the pros.

He played four years at Texas A&M University and was selected to the second-team All-Big 12 team in 1997. McKinney was selected by the Indianapolis Colts in the 4th round of the 1998 draft, spending his first four seasons successfully protecting Peyton Manning in the pocket. When McKinney became a free agent following the 2001 season, he chose to sign with the Houston Texans who were entering the league as an expansion team for the 2002 season.

As an expansion team, the Texans were bad. Like, really bad. Like 2019 *Cats* movie-level bad.

This was largely due to having a rookie quarterback and an overwhelmed offensive line. David Carr had been drafted number one overall in the 2002 draft and was expected to be the franchise's foundation. But with a swiss cheese-like protection in front of him, Carr endured a beating unlike any other in the history of the NFL.

Carr was sacked a league-record 76 times in his rookie season. In total, he was the most sacked quarterback in three of his first four NFL seasons. McKinney was a key cog in that misshaped wheel each of those years. However, he was not the main reason for their struggle as his Football Reference Hall of Fame Monitor Score and Career Approximate Value figures grade him out as a top-100 player at the Center position all-time; that being said, he wasn't good enough to single-handedly keep Carr standing upright, let alone save the team.

McKinney did provide additional value by being able to play three different positions on the offensive line. Similarly, Ford proved his own level of adaptability by moving from representative to vice president to president in such a short span of time.

Ultimately, though, both men would be considered replacement level (aka average) players who appeared worse because of some bad circumstances and teammates around them. McKinney found success when surrounded by a good Colts team but fell into a historically bad situation that brought down his effectiveness.

Ford also found initial success in being his authentic self during the early days of his presidency, but after pardoning Nixon and losing the trust of his fellow politicians, he found himself devoid of any real support system. This led to a generally ineffective term as president. Neither Ford nor McKinney were great at what they did, but both men are viewed in a worse light than they should be due to their environments. Regardless, neither of them is Hall of Fame bound.

Trading Card Stats

Gerald Ford	Name	Stephen McKinney
•Jerry	**Nickname**	•Steve
•1974-1977	**Experience**	•1998-2007
•61	**Age Entering the League**	•23
•6'0"/190	**HT/WT**	•6'4"/302
•Republican	**Team**	•Indianapolis Colts •Houston Texans
•Nixon pardon •Clemency for draft evaders and deserters •Communist victory in Southeast Asia •1975 Helsinki Agreement	**Stats**	•143 games played •133 games started •7 career holding penalties •8 career false start penalties
•Swimming •Golf •Tennis •Skiing •Working out •Watching football •Smoking a pipe	**Hobbies**	•Hunting •Consulting •Fishing •Radio
•"There is no Soviet domination in Eastern Europe, and there never will be during a Ford administration." -(Actually, there was)	**Quote**	•"I often wonder: is the stuff I'm doing now what I want to be doing, or is there something more?"
•Well known for loudly farting and then blaming a secret service member	**Interesting**	•He has been an owner of several McDonald's franchises since 2010
•No	**Hall of Fame**	•No

39

Jimmy Carter (1977-1981)

Carter was such a political outsider that when he decided to run for president in 1976, his confused mother blankly asked: "president of what?"

It was a fair question. Carter wasn't exactly a born-and-bred politician. He wasn't even a very well-known or relevant figure at the time.

Carter served in the Navy following his graduation from Annapolis, which is what he assumed his career path would be. That all changed when his father died, leaving the family peanut business behind. Following his father's death, Carter decided to return home and began manning the family peanut farm for the next 10 years.

Eventually, Carter decided to give politics a go and was elected as a Georgia state senator which he followed up with a term as Georgia's governor. Carter had little experience relative to many of his peers, but that lack of political background turned out to be just what Americans were looking for at the time. Despite his extreme intelligence, he was more or less a normal person to whom the average citizen felt they could relate. Carter decided to go national and run for president after having success at the state level, defeating Ford in the 1976 election.

Carter's presidency was largely defined by his quest for humanity and peaceful resolutions. Or, to his detractors, his lack of willingness to fight on behalf of Americans. His most notable action, or inaction, while occupying the Oval Office occurred when Iranian militants stormed the U.S. embassy in Tehran, captured 66 hostages and demanded the return of their Shah, Mohammad Reza, who had ruled Iran for nearly four decades and was in the U.S. receiving medical treatment.

Carter's attempts to negotiate with Iran were unproductive, and a rescue attempt via helicopter failed spectacularly due to a malfunction in the helicopters. Upon aborting the mission, two of the helicopters collided, killing eight servicemen in the process. It took 444 days and a brokered deal before Iran agreed to release the U.S. hostages.

Although viewed as a weakness among many Americans, Carter's resolve for peaceful conflict resolution contributed to an improved view of the U.S. from abroad. He helped facilitate a peace treaty between Egypt and Israel. He withdrew U.S. forces from Taiwan and opened up diplomatic relations with China. He adamantly opposed the Soviet Union's invasion of Afghanistan even after a U.S. ambassador had been killed there. Carter threatened the Soviets with military force if they looked to take advantage of ongoing unrest in Iran as a vehicle to obtain power in the Persian Gulf.

At home, while Carter's presidency saw the economy improve from where it had been under Ford, inflation continued to rise. Carter's most dedicated cause was toward environmental protection as he constantly sought new, alternative energy sources. He also cared deeply about advocating for public education and supporting economically-poor citizens by reforming the tax and welfare systems.

Ultimately, however, his ideals lacked strong execution thanks to a reticent Congress and a stubborn economy that wouldn't bounce all the way back from its recession.

Most likely sport: Basketball

Carter had a brilliant mind and worked well with others, seeking to be actively involved with almost everything during his days in the White House. He would have been a good fit for basketball where he could stay engaged and be directly involved in the outcome of the game at all times.

Carter didn't just *want* to control the outcomes of policies and decisions; he *needed* to control them. He was an extreme micromanager who could only operate with the ball in his hands. Unequivocally, Carter needed to control the rock as a point guard.

Best Comparison: Jeremy Lin

Talk about getting yourself 15 minutes of fame.

But Lin's 15 minutes weren't the usual quick dose of fame from appearing on a local news broadcast and having your neighbors recognize you. We're talking about an unadulterated, international, whirlwind-type fame. Lin sat right alongside the likes of YOLO, *Gangnam Style*, and the Kardashians in terms of 2012 fame.

At his peak, Lin had a two-week onslaught, dubbed "Linsanity," which saw him lead an awful New York Knicks team to eight wins in nine games as he averaged 25 points, 9.2 assists, 3.8 rebounds, and 2.2 steals per game. That was after not playing in 13 of the team's first 24 games and averaging just six minutes in the games he did step onto the court.

Lin simply hadn't performed well enough to earn a spot in the rotation at that time. When a number of Knicks players were simultaneously hit by the injury bug, Lin was given extended playing time and took full advantage of it. His performances were certainly elevated by the New York media, but his performances truly were insane.

Prior to the breakout, Lin existed in relative obscurity as far as most of the world was concerned. Culturally, Lin had gained some reverence as an Asian player from Harvard who had made it to the NBA. In terms of basketball notoriety, however, he toiled between the end of an NBA bench and the NBA's Development League during his rookie season.

Lin's second season in the NBA was when his magical run took place. He was signed by the Knicks and had very little outside expectations placed on him. Lin's season went from bench warmer to superstar in seconds. Then just as quickly as it happened, it was over. Lin's star began to fade as he went from demigod to solid player before he was forced to end his season early due to knee surgery.

While Lin managed to stick around as a relevant player, he never recaptured the glory of the Linsanity days. In nine seasons, Lin played with eight different teams. He was largely a back-up, averaging 11.6 points and 4.3 assists per game for his career.

While Linsanity put him squarely on the map, he forged his way into the map's vicinity with undeterred hard work. Being an outsider made his accomplishment all the more impressive. He is one of only four players to make it to the NBA from Harvard and the list of players from Asian descent isn't a whole lot longer. It's fair to say the odds were certainly stacked against Lin.

Carter also grew up as an outsider. He lived in a largely black community where he witnessed America's racial inequalities first hand. His parents were unable to provide electricity or running water, and at five-years-old, Carter began selling boiled peanuts on the street to help make money. Those early years helped shape Carter's ideology as he became older and took the plunge into politics. It provided him with a vastly different outlook on the world than most politicians had at that time.

What Carter lacked in traditional political wherewithal, he made up for with intelligence and an unpretentious disposition. Carter was well regarded in-and-out of school for his ability to read and dissect information very quickly with an incredibly high retention rate. He used introspection, religion, and compassion to gain a better understanding of himself and of others.

Similarly, Lin used his intelligence, and his faith, to help him reach the NBA. He went to Harvard and obtained an economics degree. The high IQ has proven beneficial in being able to read and dissect his opponents. Lin also relied on a strong sense of composure to handle the pressure of being a professional basketball player, being a global icon, and having to largely shoulder the representation of an entire race.

Both Carter and Lin draw parallels in their personalities and their performances. They both made it to the pinnacle of their careers despite long odds and unconventional backgrounds. They both had their moments where they dominated and won the hearts of fans all over the globe; they also had their moments where they fell back down to Earth and struggled to find consistent success. In the end, both Carter and Lin performed solidly, but neither man is reaching the Hall of Fame.

Trading Card Stats

Jimmy Carter	Name	Jeremy Lin
•The Peanut Farmer	**Nickname**	•Linsanity
•1977-1981	**Experience**	•2010-2019
•52	**Age Entering the League**	•22
•5’10”/160	**HT/WT**	•6’3”/200
•Democrat	**Team**	•Golden State Warriors •New York Knicks •Houston Rockets •Los Angeles Lakers •Charlotte Hornets •Brooklyn Nets •Atlanta Hawks •Toronto Raptors
•Human rights •American hostages in Iran •Camp David Accords •Deregulation •Social welfare	**Stats**	•11.6 points, 4.3 assists and 2.8 rebounds per game
•Jogging •Hiking •Bicycling •Tennis •Cross-country skiing •Bowling •Fishing •Reading •Movies	**Hobbies**	•Piano •Golf •Shopping •Video games
•“In a very Christian way, as far as I’m concerned, he can go to hell.” -Referring to Rev. Jerry Falwell	**Quote**	•“Stuff about me dating Kim Kardashian, I mean, I have no idea where that came from...I don’t think I’m that type.”
•Sold boiled peanuts on the street at age five	**Interesting**	•Only player from Harvard in the NBA since 1954
•No	**Hall of Fame**	•No

40

Ronald Reagan (1981-1989)

Reagan was a star.

It was the ~~only~~ first time an actor and real Hollywood celebrity occupied the White House. Okay, a B-list celebrity, but still.

Working in the media and entertainment industry was how Reagan made a living for more than three decades. He began his post-college career as a sports-radio broadcaster. This included play-by-play of Chicago Cubs games that he re-created based on telegraph descriptions sent into the station.

During a trip to California where Reagan was travelling with the Cubs for spring training, he took a screen test to be a Hollywood actor which ultimately resulted in a contract with Warner Bros., spurring his acting career. Reagan went on to appear in more than 50 movies throughout his time in film.

The 1960s saw Reagan begin his transition into politics. He originally identified with the Democratic party, but by the time he became more politically active, Reagan morphed into a staunch conservative. His speech in support of presidential nominee Barry Goldwater in 1964 caught the eye of the Republican base, propelling him to prominence.

Reagan was elected California's governor in 1966. He served eight years in that role before transitioning back to media, writing newspaper columns and giving lectures. In 1980, his platform, and charm, helped him win the presidential election battle against Carter.

His presidency offered a mixed bag of success. Reaganomics was the most noteworthy of policies during his administration. Often referred to as free-market economics, or trickle-down economics, Reagan advocated for reduced government regulation, a reduction in taxes, and a tightening of the money supply in an attempt to curb inflation. Despite an initial recession after Reagan took over, the country's economic fortunes began to improve.

His ultimate economic success, however, is still debated. The GDP grew stronger, inflation rates came down, and unemployment numbers eventually followed suit, as well. On the flip side, the income gap widened, tax cuts often favored the wealthy, and the national debt grew more under Reagan's watch than it did during all of the previous presidential administrations combined.

Internationally, Reagan's biggest policy was one that was never meant to be revealed. It was discovered that the U.S. was secretly selling weapons to Iran in exchange for their help getting American hostages released from Lebanon. The money received from the weapon sales were then used to help fund Contras in Nicaragua, which were right-wing backed anti-Communist rebels. Both of these actions were illegal, and several U.S. officials were relieved of their duties for taking part in the scandal. Initially, impeachment was mentioned as a possibility for Reagan, but no evidence existed to tie him directly to the affair. His old age, charm, and generally aloof nature prevented any of the dirtier parts of the scandal from sticking to him.

Most likely sport: Football

Reagan was almost always affable and even-tempered. While he was a relatively private person, he was also completely comfortable working and living in the public spotlight. His congenial nature meshed well with those around him. Reagan struggled to grapple with issues head-on as president, regardless of their size, and needed a lot of support staff around so that he could delegate tasks. The more teammates the better for Reagan, offering football as his most likely sport.

Reagan was not the team's most talented player. He was, however, the most likable and most popular player, making him ripe for quarterback.

Best Comparison: Tim Tebow

Among certain segments of the sports fan population, Tebow quickly became a deity. I think he even had Chuck Norris 'Tebowing', the act of going to one knee and praying, for extra strength and guidance.

Such are the stories that get generated when you find miraculous ways to win games as a quarterback despite clearly lacking essential quarterbacking talents like throwing accuracy, a quick release, or the ability to read defenses. Having a body chiseled out of rock doesn't hurt, either.

For all of Tebow's misgivings as an NFL quarterback, his pre-NFL resume can't be questioned. The guy dominated college football. He won two national championships, a Heisman Trophy, and two SEC Player of the Year awards. Ask any fan or ~~gasbag~~ pundit, and they'll tell you Tebow was one of the greatest college quarterbacks of all time.

That greatness, however, was widely panned as unlikely to succeed in the NFL. But that didn't stop the Denver Broncos from selecting him with their first-round pick in 2010. They figured Tebow's leadership, character, and intangibles were worth the potential risk.

Tebow received some spot duty during his rookie season. Midway through his sophomore season, Tebow was given the chance to start for a fledgling 1-4 team. He led the Broncos to a 7-4 record and a playoff berth to end the season, which included five, fourth quarter comebacks and game-winning drives as Tebow-mania began to ensue.

The insanity reached a fever pitch in the 2011 AFC Wild Card game when the game went to overtime. The very first play from scrimmage saw Tebow connect on an 80-yard touchdown pass that officially cemented him as a cult hero, despite his passing flaws.

Unfortunately for Tebow, the magic wore off as quickly as it had arrived. The Broncos would lose in the next round, and Tebow was subsequently traded that off-season to the New York Jets where he would play just one uninspiring season before falling out of the NFL.

In total, Tebow lasted just three seasons in the NFL as a quarterback due to his lackluster passing skills. He finished with an 8-6 record as a starter, an ungodly 47.9% completion rate, 17 passing touchdowns, and nine interceptions.

Tebow's cult-like following has long remained in his corner, though. For as many detractors as Tebow had about his prowess as a passer, he had just as many supporters who have maintained that he wasn't given enough of an opportunity as a starter to live up to his full potential.

Most Americans tended to either love Tebow or hate Tebow due to the media attention and adoration he received. Although Tebow often became the butt of a good quarterback joke, his image has remained pristine, winning over a lot of the haters in his post-playing career due to his likable TV persona. Likewise, most Americans tended to love Reagan or hate Reagan. He is one of the more polarizing presidents in history; but his cheery sense of humor and old-man, doddering persona built a likeable-enough image to largely stand the test of time.

Tebow and Reagan both developed devoted followings in spite of their less-than-stellar professional careers. Their previous resumes, and their oozing charisma, made this possible. They each handled themselves with grace and dignity, acting as their own best PR managers.

Both Tebow and Reagan had their moments as professionals but were unable to find sustained success. They peaked prior to arriving on the big stage. As a result, neither man makes the Hall of Fame.

Trading Card Stats

Ronald Reagan	Name	Tim Tebow
•Dutch •The Gipper •The Great Communicator	**Nickname**	•Mile-High Messiah
•1981-1989	**Experience**	•2010-2012
•69	**Age Entering the League**	•23
•6'1"/185	**HT/WT**	•6'2"/236
•Republican	**Team**	•Denver Broncos •New York Jets
•Reaganomics •Social Security •Grenada invasion •U.S.-Canadian trade pact	**Stats**	•2,422 passing yards •17 passing touchdowns •47.9% completion rate
•Collecting bird eggs and butterflies •Raising pigeons and rabbits •Reading newspapers •Football •Swimming •Cheerleading	**Hobbies**	•Baseball •Broadcasting •Practicing religion •Community outreach •Providing charitable support
•"It's true hard work never killed anybody, but I figure, why take the chance?"	**Quote**	•"I got traded to the Jets. That didn't work. When's the last time a Jets trade worked out?"
•Chief of Staff James Baker once showed up at the White House to find that Reagan hadn't looked at the important briefing given to him the day before. Reagan responded, "Well, Jim, *The Sound of Music* was on last night."	**Interesting**	•Tebow played minor league baseball from 2016-2019
•No	**Hall of Fame**	•No

41

George H.W. Bush (1989-1993)

Bush wasn't necessarily the smartest, most gifted, or most interesting politician, but he did have something no one else possessed: Reagan's blessing.

Having Reagan's support was like having a golden ticket. Imagine the *Willy Wonka* scene where Charlie Bucket and his delirious Grandpa Joe are dancing around the living room. You have Bush, enthusiastic but naïve and feeling a bit overwhelmed. Then you have Reagan, experienced and likable but whose lucidity was starting to come into question. With Reagan backing Bush, the two cashed in their golden ticket and went soaring into the sky on their Reaganomics-Wonkavator.

Bush's rise began in the military as the youngest pilot to serve in the Navy during WWII where he would rise to lieutenant. After the war, Bush studied economics at Yale, became an oilman for the better part of two decades following graduation before his transition to politics. His political career featured pit stops as a U.S. representative, an ambassador to the UN, a chief U.S. liaison to China, the CIA director and, finally, vice president.

Bush's presidency is most notably defined by the Persian Gulf War. When Iraq invaded Kuwait in 1990, the United Nations, at the behest of the United States, formally announced a plan that would require Iraq to withdraw its troops or face the use of force. Bush helped coordinate troops from multiple nations and began to strike when Iraq refused to budge. Iraqi forces were expelled in less than a week, representing a big win for the U.S., tactically and symbolically.

While it was a short-term success for Bush, he received criticism for not dismantling the Iraqi army. Instead, Bush gave them the ability to remain intact, allowing Saddam Hussein to stay in power and essentially put targets on the backs of the Kurds and Shiites, who had supported the U.S., but were then left to fend for themselves against a vengeful Iraqi government.

Under Bush's watch, the U.S. also invaded Panama to capture their leader at the time, Gen. Manuel Noriega, who was wanted in Florida on drug trafficking charges. In what was a blatant violation of international law, hundreds of civilians were killed in the effort to detain Noriega. The UN condemned the U.S. but there were no major repercussions from the incident.

At home, Bush had taken over an economy in disarray despite the fact that many had credited Reagan's policies for bolstering the market. Bush walked into an unfavorable economic situation left behind by Reagan. Unemployment and national debt were rising as conditions deteriorated for the lower- and middle-class citizens. The foundation began falling apart at the seams during the savings and loan crisis of 1989, forcing Bush to sign a bill bailing out hundreds of savings and loans institutions that had failed due to banking deregulation rules implemented nearly a decade earlier.

Bush tried to reverse the course of the economy by introducing tax hikes after swearing up and down that taxes wouldn't increase. Other domestic policies of note during Bush's time included the Americans with Disabilities Act and the Clean Air Act. The former was the most comprehensive legislation aimed at antidiscrimination since the 1964 Civil Rights Act, while the latter helped strengthen anti-pollution standards.

Most likely sport: Baseball

Bush had an easy-going personality. He was not very aggressive or spot-light driven and didn't feel the need to stand out in the crowd. He was good with blending in as part of a team dynamic, and his personality fit well with the sport he played in college—baseball.

Bush played first base on his Yale baseball team so we won't overthink this one—his position is first base.

Best Comparison: Dick Siebert

Some people preach their religious gospels. John Wycliffe. Martin Luther. Kirk Cameron.

Some people preach their own personal gospels. Russell Brand on the importance of yoga. Snoop Dogg on the importance of marijuana. Kanye West on the importance of himself.

Siebert was ready to fall into the religious category until sports intervened. Siebert's father had been a minister, so preaching was in his blood. But so was baseball.

Siebert played baseball at Concordia College until a scout for the St. Louis Cardinals offered him a contract to play minor league ball. After one year in the minors, Siebert was released by the Cardinals when he tore a muscle from his collarbone. His career was seemingly at its end.

He enrolled in the seminary and fully planned on becoming a minister during the Great Depression. The Lutheran Church, though, had been ravaged by the Depression just as everything else. Few clergy positions were available in the church, and many studying at the seminary were asked to take a year off before resuming their studies.

Siebert spent his down time playing baseball locally in the spring of 1932 when he was noticed by a New York Yankees scout who wanted him to play first base. Siebert signed, but his contract was soon sold to the Brooklyn Dodgers, and Siebert received a cup of coffee with the big-league team to end the 1932 season, appearing in six games. He had gone from jobless preacher to major league baseball player in the span of one summer.

It would be many years, however, before Siebert managed to stick around the professional ranks. After years of toiling in the minor leagues for various teams, Siebert arrived back in the Cardinals organization. The Cardinals already had a first baseman and preferred to stash Siebert in their minor league system rather than give him a chance at the big-league level or trade him to a team that would give him a chance. Siebert pleaded to then-Commissioner Kenesaw Landis to investigate what he believed to be an injustice. The Cardinals had been placing Siebert on waivers only to pull him back and raise their price each time another team claimed him. During the investigation, the Cardinals decided to rid themselves of the issue by flipping Siebert to the Philadelphia Athletics in a four-player deal.

With the change in scenery came an increased opportunity to play. In all, Siebert wound up playing in 11 professional seasons. He notched a .710 OPS, a career 7.0 WAR, and even made one All-Star appearance in 1943.

Siebert helped forge his own path by questioning the Cardinals' handling of him. In protesting to the commissioner, he stuck up for himself and what he believed in despite his quiet, restrained nature. Similarly, Bush had a reputation for being reserved and deferential to others prior to his presidency. However, he proved during the Persian Gulf War that he had the resolve to lead when necessary.

It was this mixture that made both men likeable to many. They were generally informal, warm, and unpretentious but were able to take charge and lead when necessary. Bush's style called for impromptu meetings, relaxed press gatherings, and even personal relationships with foreign leaders who appreciated his down-to-earth nature. Siebert, meanwhile, also preferred to keep his team's atmosphere loose and relaxed. As a manager, Siebert became known and respected for giving his college players the freedom to largely do as they wanted off-the-field, empowering them to make their own choices and decisions—something that was largely uncommon at the collegiate level during that time.

Both Bush and Siebert had their moments in the sun. Bush walked away from the Persian Gulf War largely receiving praise, even if he could have done more to squash the reign of Hussein. Siebert has an All-Star game on his resume even though he only had a below average .619 OPS before the 1943 All-Star break. Although both men found some success in the big leagues, neither will be making their way toward the Hall of Fame.

Trading Card Stats

George H.W. Bush	Name	Dick Siebert
•Poppy	**Nickname**	•Chief
•1989-1993	**Experience**	•1932-1945
•64	**Age Entering the League**	•20
•6'2"/196	**HT/WT**	•6'0"/170
•Republican	**Team**	•Brooklyn Dodgers •St. Louis Cardinals •Philadelphia Athletics
•Persian Gulf War •Official end to Cold War •Savings and Loans Crisis •1990 Americans with Disabilities Act	**Stats**	•1,035 games played •.710 OPS •32 home runs •7.0 WAR •1-time All-Star
•Tennis •Golfing •Racquetball •Horseshoes •Hunting •Fishing •Baseball	**Hobbies**	•Coaching •Physical education •Broadcasting
•"I have opinions of my own, strong opinions, but I don't always agree with them."	**Quote**	•"After playing 17 years of professional baseball I thought I knew all there was to know about the game...Well, I was wrong."
•Bush vomited in the lap of Japanese Prime Minister Kiichi Miyazawa during a visit in 1992	**Interesting**	•Authored seven different instructional books on baseball
•No	**Hall of Fame**	•No

42

Bill Clinton (1993-2001)

It's pretty amazing that a man could serve as president for eight years, accomplish all that he accomplished, and still be almost single-handedly remembered for something apolitical.

Then, again, if we've learned anything in the tabloid and social media eras, it's that nothing mixes quite like celebrities and sex. Sprinkle in some reckless and scandalous behavior and the situation becomes highly combustible. Clinton is widely considered one of the most intellectually-gifted presidents, but emotions outweighed rationale when it came to relationships.

Clinton had no problems forming relationships with others while growing up. He was always personable, outgoing, and charming. He graduated from Georgetown University with a degree in international affairs before studying at Oxford as a Rhodes Scholar. He then obtained a law degree from Yale and shortly thereafter became a law professor at the University of Arkansas.

He stayed in his home state and became the attorney general of Arkansas, followed quickly by a brief stint as the governor. After raising some state taxes and fees to help pay for road work and increased spending on education, he was ousted from his gubernatorial role in 1981. Clinton returned to practicing law, but he didn't give up on politics. Just two years later, Clinton found himself back in office as the governor, which he would hold onto until he was elected president nearly a decade later.

Clinton's presidency was, of course, stained by scandals. Extramarital affairs. The Paula Jones sexual harassment lawsuit. Whitewater. Filegate. Chinagate. Travelgate. There were so many immoral and legally-questionable activities that gave Americans pause. Ultimately, though, most citizens gave Clinton a pass because if you could look beyond all the personal indignities, you saw an economy that was booming.

When Clinton entered office in 1993, there was a $327.3 billion deficit. By 1998, the U.S. had a budget surplus for the first time since 1969. Meanwhile, unemployment was the lowest it had been in two decades.

Clinton's other domestic initiatives included invoking a "don't ask, don't tell" policy in the armed forces that prevented superiors from inquiring about a person's sexual orientation ("don't ask") but also barred service men and women from disclosing their homosexuality ("don't tell"). He also sought to implement universal health care but was unable to receive the necessary support. Clinton fought hard for educational reform that placed an emphasis on providing more funding to public schools. He also had a track record for successfully fighting for racial justice in Arkansas though he had fewer accomplishments in those areas during his actual presidency.

Globally, Clinton had a lot of tense encounters with foreign countries. Clinton had the U.S. invade Haiti and restore the elected president's power after a military coup had briefly ousted him. He ordered airstrikes on suspected Iraqi manufacturing sites for chemical and biological weapons. He also had U.S. forces intervene in Somalia to reduce violence and help with widespread famine taking place, but they were unable to institute government stability in the country. Bombings in Afghanistan and Sudan were carried out in response to bombings of U.S. embassies, though many viewed this as an overreaction.

Clinton also helped form the North American Free Trade Agreement (NAFTA), which worked to reduce or eliminate any barriers to trade or investment throughout North America. While it is debatable as to whether this agreement helped farmers economically, the agreement is generally heralded as a success.

Most likely sport: Baseball

Clinton's intelligence was such that he could come up with hundreds of different methods for reaching a singular goal. He would need a game that requires a lot of strategy. His easy-going, gentle demeanor would help push him into baseball.

Clinton loved to analyze the opposition and dissect the task at hand. As someone who likes to think through the game, study his opponent, and then attack strategically, Clinton's best position would be as a starting pitcher.

Best Comparison: Denny Neagle

If the average fan remembers Neagle, chances are it isn't because of what he did on the field.

The man morphed from baseball player to TMZ-style sports fodder quickly. He is like the Charlie Sheen or Britney Spears of baseball who had legitimate success in their profession before outside factors brought down how the general public now remembers them.

Before Neagle's personal and professional life began to unravel on the public stage, he was a well-regarded pitching prospect at the University of Minnesota. He helped lead the Gophers to a Big Ten title in 1988 and was an All-Big Ten selection the following year when he was drafted in the third round by the Minnesota Twins.

His career spanned across 13 years with six different teams. He compiled 124 wins, a 4.24 ERA, and a 22.4 WAR in his 392 games pitched, most of which came as a starter. Neagle was considered one of the better pitchers in the game throughout the mid-to-late '90s. He was a two-time All-Star and pitched in one of the most notorious starting rotations of all time with the Atlanta Braves next to Greg Maddux, Tom Glavine, and John Smoltz.

The tail end of Neagle's career, however, would not be so kind. Neagle signed a five-year, $51 million contract to play for the Colorado Rockies. His first couple of seasons in Colorado were ineffective at best and awful when considering the expectations going into the deal. In 2003, Neagle's season ended after an elbow injury required surgery. It would be the last time he appeared in the major leagues.

As Neagle was recovering, he would be charged with driving while intoxicated. Not long after that, Neagle was charged with patronizing a prostitute. He pled guilty on both accounts. Additionally, Neagle was identified as one of the many players who illegally used human growth hormone (HGH), according to the MLB's famous Mitchell Report. The report was a nearly-two-year investigation that detailed who was known to be using anabolic steroids or HGH in the MLB. Neagle was one of 89 names to appear in the report, having used them from 2000-2004, which resulted in Neagle's contract being voided due to a morals clause violation.

Neagle had gone from well-respected pitcher to humiliated outcast. The spotlight only became brighter each time his name was associated with the next batch of bad news. Not even Neagle's loosey-goosey persona could stem the tide of public perception. Before his troubles began to mount, Neagle was known for being very personable, getting enjoyment from playing practical jokes and doing impressions. At one point, it became popular for media members to ask Neagle for his impression of a train whistle that was so good the Pittsburgh Pirates used it on the public address system whenever they began to mount a rally.

Likewise, Clinton was as personable as they come. He has a folksy way of speaking that makes him seem more down-to-Earth. Clinton combined good interpersonal skills, an outgoing demeanor, and a strong desire to peacefully deal with all walks of life in a way that enhanced his likability. But it could only help Clinton so much once the Lewinsky scandal blew up, and he was impeached for obstruction of justice after having illegally lied about, and covered up, his relationship with the intern.

Clinton's enduring legacy in the eyes of the lay person will always be tied to his impeachment trial. Similarly, Neagle's will be tied to his fall from grace that led him out of the big leagues. Fair or not, they won't be remembered for the work they did during their careers. The misconduct may have given their reputations a hit, but scandals or no scandals, they weren't good enough to merit entry in the Hall of Fame.

Trading Card Stats

Bill Clinton	Name	Dennis Neagle
•Bubba •Slick Willie •Comeback Kid	**Nickname**	•Denny
•1993-2001	**Experience**	•1991-2003
•46	**Age Entering the League**	•22
•6'2"/223	**HT/WT**	•6'4"/200
•Democrat	**Team**	•Minnesota Twins •Pittsburgh Pirates •Atlanta Braves •Cincinnati Reds •New York Yankees •Colorado Rockies
•NAFTA •Family and Medical Leave Act •Air attacks on Iraq •U.S. involvement in Somalia	**Stats**	•124-92 record •4.24 ERA •1,415 strikeouts •2-time All-Star
•Swimming •Golf •Basketball •Playing cards •Trivial pursuit •Crossword puzzles •Reading •Collecting porcelain objects	**Hobbies**	•Movies •Charity work •Golf
•"I want you to listen to me...I did not have sexual relations with that woman, Miss Lewinsky."	**Quote**	•"There's no way I'd put up with all that Nazi crap."
•Received many musical scholarship offers from colleges thanks to his saxophone abilities	**Interesting**	•His favorite actor is Nicolas Cage
•No	**Hall of Fame**	•No

43

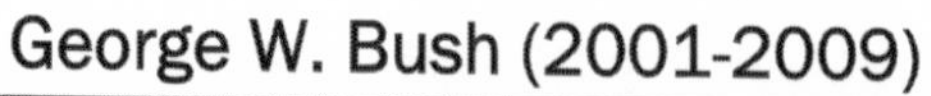

As comedian Steve Martin once said, "Some people have a way with words, and other people…oh, uh, not have way."

So it can be said about Bush.

Perhaps it was because he took command when internet accessibility began to explode and interesting video clips were starting to spread before they were commonly dubbed *viral videos*. Perhaps it was because of the copious amounts of alcohol he consumed as a younger man.

Whatever the case, Bush didn't always get along well with the English language. Supporters found it endearing, while detractors found it to be eye-roll inducing. There was an element of comedy and head-scratching astonishment, though, regardless of what side of the aisle you sat on.

The astonishment around Bush's tenure, however, existed well before his quotes began making headlines. It stretched back to election night when he competed in one of the craziest elections in American history.

Bush ran against Democratic challenger, Al Gore. The election swung back-and-forth, too close to call on election night thanks to a series of voting-related concerns in the state of Florida. A number of lawsuits and counter lawsuits emerged as the potential recount efforts grew more partisan depending on who got involved. The Supreme Court, consisting of a majority of conservatives, ultimately sided with Bush in quashing the recount by hand. They declared Bush the winner, more than a month after the initial election-night confusion.

As president, Bush got off to a hot start as he dealt with the fallout from the terrorist attacks that saw airplanes fly into the World Trade Center buildings, the Pentagon, and a Pennsylvania field on September 11, 2001. The attacks, carried out by Al-Qaeda, killed nearly 3,000 people and served as a rallying cry for Bush. In a time of despair, he used it to galvanize the nation, and he showed resolve to the world in the face of evil. He even threw out the single most clutch first pitch in the history of opening baseball ceremonies before game three of the World Series at Yankee Stadium.

Bush's War on Terror began with hunting for the leader of the 9/11 attacks, Osama Bin Laden, whom intelligence agents believed was hiding in Afghanistan. Unable to find Bin Laden, Bush decided to turn his attention to Iraq and Saddam Hussein, despite their lack of involvement in the 9/11 plot. Bush cited false intelligence reports that declared Iraq was storing weapons of mass destruction and used it as the impetus to invade, resulting in thousands of unnecessary and innocent casualties. Not surprisingly, they didn't unearth any weapons of mass destruction because, well, there were none to be found.

From there, Bush's tenure and legacy began to unravel. As part of the War on Terror, Bush established Guantanamo Bay as a U.S. military prison off the coast of Cuba. It held a number of alleged terrorists, though it was later discovered to also be holding a number of innocent foreigners. The detention center was widely criticized for torturing individuals and violating human rights. While

Guantanamo's inmate population has been downsized considerably since the War on Terror, it is still operating as of 2021.

On the home front, the economy was the central focus of Bush's administration. After inheriting a $230 million budget surplus from Clinton, Bush initiated a series of tax cuts, which largely benefited the wealthy and corporations. Combined with the spending on wars in Afghanistan and Iraq, the budget had flipped to the other side of the ledger, creating a $413 million deficit.

The economy only worsened by the end of Bush's tenure. In 2008, the housing market collapsed, leading to a crash on Wall Street. It was the most severe recession since the Great Depression of the 1930s, resulting in nearly $1 trillion being spent to bailout the banking industry.

Bush also had to deal with the aftermath of Hurricane Katrina in 2005, which ravaged New Orleans and the Gulf Coast. Nearly 2,000 people lost their lives as a result of the hurricane and subsequent flooding. Bush was widely criticized for the slow and unprepared federal response to the natural disaster. Many New Orleans natives argue that their city still hasn't fully recovered from the devastation caused by Katrina as some lower income areas have seemingly been left behind in the rebuilding efforts.

Most likely sport: Baseball

Despite some tumultuous events, Bush has generally been regarded as having a lively personality. He is known for being able to connect on a personal level with everyone he encounters. He has a quick wit, competitive nature, and has always been interested in athletics.

Bush is a baseball man through-and-through when it comes to sports. From watching to playing to owning, Bush has a love for America's pastime that has existed in his life since he was a child. Additionally, he had the easy-going demeanor of a baseball player, which he played as a freshman at Yale.

Bush tended to act decisively on issues and then disconnect from the world that disagreed with him or suggested alternatives. In other words, he focused on the days and moments where his action was needed, or when he was starting, and tuned out everything else in between. Bush remained unfettered by outside noise and would fit in as a starting pitcher.

Best Comparison: Jason Bere

Sometimes a movie franchise is developed, and it seemingly gets better with its subsequent movies. Movies like *Toy Story* and *Mission Impossible*, for example.

Sometimes, though, they get worse. Much worse. There have to be some franchises like *Transformers* and *Pirates of the Caribbean* to keep the world on an even axis.

Enter Bere.

The original version of Bere was really good. He was drafted in the 36th round from a small community college in Massachusetts in 1990. By 1993, he had worked his way into being one of the game's top prospects for the Chicago White Sox. Bere compiled a 24-7 record across 48 starts in his first two seasons. He finished as a runner-up for the Rookie of the Year award in his first season and was selected as an All-Start in his second.

The following year, however, Bere began to stumble. Combined with an injury that culminated in elbow surgery, Bere's once promising career went careening into a ditch. Bere wound up pitching for five different teams across 11 seasons. He finished with a record still above .500 at 71-65 but an ERA of 5.14 and a career 3.3 WAR.

Bere was never able to recapture that initial success. Like Bush, who started off amid strong success and fanfare, Bere had the same adoration. He was the youngest White Sox pitcher to ever appear in an All-Star game. Executives, scouts, and fans all largely agreed that Bere's future was promising.

That bright future was derailed, however, as other factors began to snowball. Bere first hurt his arm in 1995 but ultimately pitched through the discomfort. After resting it in the offseason, he tried doing the same in 1996 until he had no option left but to have Tommy John surgery. Bere then rushed back in the summer of 1997, returning before his body was ready.

Bere's wounds were a mix of bad luck and self-infliction. Had Bere listened to his body more closely and not attempted to pitch through the pain, perhaps his career would have turned out differently. Instead, his elbow only worsened and the issue was compounded by the fact that he and the White Sox decided to ignore doctors who recommended surgery a year before he elected to have it. By the time Bere returned, he had lost some of his velocity and the ability to fully finish his throwing motion, which led to him performing like a shell of the player he once was.

Bush's fall from grace was also due to a confluence of unfortunate missteps. When 9/11 occurred, Bush showed initial resolve and helped unify Americans. The attacks left a terrible, but fertile, ground for Bush to cultivate and build an impenetrable legacy as the leader who guided America through dark times and stood up against terrorism.

Instead, Bush squandered the opportunity by tying the U.S. invasion of Iraq to the 9/11 attacks when, in fact, Iraq had nothing to do with them. He decided to go after another country in the Middle East for any number of reasons—to re-assert U.S. power, to show other nations that the U.S. would not be messed with, to finish the task his father had started a decade prior in attempting to remove Hussein from power, or to possibly find weapons of mass destruction as is most commonly believed.

Bush received plenty of faulty information from advisors about Iraq's supposed weapons of mass destruction and used this as his public justification for the invasion. Had Bush listened more closely to the FBI and CIA intel provided to him, the war would have either ended much sooner or may never have started in the first place.

If Bush's and Bere's career were film franchises, it would be easy to say they both started with a blockbuster. They were initial hits with the public. Unfortunately, their initial success was met with deep disappointment in subsequent versions that ultimately led to them being box-office flops, resulting in neither man making it to the Hall of Fame.

Trading Card Stats

George W. Bush	Name	Jason Bere
•Junior •Dubya	**Nickname**	•JB
•2001-2009	**Experience**	•1993-2003
•54	**Age Entering the League**	•22
•5'11"/191	**HT/WT**	•6'3"/185
•Republican	**Team**	•Chicago White Sox •Cincinnati Reds •Milwaukee Brewers •Cleveland Indians •Chicago Cubs
•9/11 •Invasion of Afghanistan •Iraq War •Hurricane Katrina •Recession and financial bailout	**Stats**	•71-65 record •5.14 ERA •1,111 innings pitched •920 strikeouts •1-time All-Star
•Baseball •Golf •Painting	**Hobbies**	•Billiards •Golf
•"They misunderestimated me."	**Quote**	•"...when I got to the mound and Ron Karkovice squatted behind the plate, suddenly I couldn't feel my legs!"
•Arrested for disorderly conduct at Yale for stealing a Christmas wreath	**Interesting**	•He was once ranked as a better prospect than Derek Jeter, Manny Ramirez and Mike Piazza, among others
•No	**Hall of Fame**	•No

44

Barack Obama (2009-2017)

The first black president. The first social media president. The first illegal president?

Okay, the first two statements are true. The third was simply a conspiracy theory with pretty clear racial undertones that offer a glimpse into some of the difficulties Obama had to endure as president. The "birther movement" as it was often referred, sought to question Obama's legal legitimacy as president of the United States by claiming he was not a natural-born citizen; rather, he was alleged to have been born in Kenya where his father's side of the family hails.

This was propagated by a number of media outlets, politicians, and citizens. Chief among them was some guy named Donald Trump. The accusations continued for a number of years until Obama released his actual birth certificate to prove where he was born. This largely, though not entirely, put the issue to rest.

So, where was he actually born? Hawaii. It doesn't sound as cool as being able to say he was the first illegal president but, hey, at least he can now be considered the first Hawaiian president.

Obama's journey to the presidency began in Hawaii but eventually led him to the mainland. He graduated from Columbia University in 1983 with a political science degree. Obama then spent some time as a community organizer in Chicago before entering Harvard's law school. Later, Obama taught law at the University of Chicago after graduating from Harvard in 1991.

He served as an associate for a civil-rights law firm and served on various company boards for a few years before transitioning to politics. He was elected as an Illinois state senator in 1996 which he followed up with a seat in the U.S. Senate.

Obama emerged as a longshot candidate when he began campaigning for the Democratic nomination in 2007. His ability to resonate with young people and first-time voters through his campaign's skilled use of the internet catapulted him from unlikely Democratic nominee to winning the presidential election with general ease.

As president, Obama ended the Iraq war, though he kept troops deployed in Afghanistan indefinitely to deal with a deteriorating political situation in the country. Obama scored what many consider to be the biggest win of his presidency when he killed Osama Bin Laden, al-Qaeda's leader and orchestrator of the 9/11 attacks. Okay, Obama didn't personally kill him, but he did have a unit of Navy SEALs conduct a nighttime raid on Bin Laden's compound in Pakistan that led to his death in 2011. It was one of the few moments of bi-partisan joy and unity during his term.

The situation was a bit more tenuous on American soil. Obama's biggest difficulty entering office was navigating the financial crisis inherited from the Bush tenure. The stimulus package passed in early 2009 saved the auto industry from collapse, provided tax cuts, and included money for various domestic entities designed to spur economic revitalization. Though the recession was officially declared over in the U.S. by the summer of 2009 thanks to positive GDP growth, it took much longer for the average American to regain their economic footing.

Obama passed the Affordable Health Care for America Act, which simply became known as Obamacare. Key inclusions in the act were: mandating almost all Americans to have health insurance, assessing a penalty fee to those who weren't enrolled, prohibiting denial of coverage based on pre-existing conditions, covering preventative care, and expanding coverage rights for women. The act was extremely controversial and constituted one of the more bitterly contested issues during his administration. Opponents of Obamacare thought the law imposed too many costs on businesses and decried the mandates as an affront to individual liberties.

Other areas of focus for Obama were advocating for women's equal rights, the LGBTQ community, and initiatives aimed to combat climate change. Additionally, he placed a strong emphasis on the expansion of science and technology.

Most likely sport: Basketball

Obama is known for being scholarly, laid back, and charismatic. Obama was great at calculating the moves of his political opponents and worked well within a team construct. He grew up loving and playing basketball, so Obama would have naturally been best suited for that sport.

Obama's intelligence and ability to stay calm in big moments were qualities indicative of why you wanted him to have the ball in his hands as often as possible. He was an incredibly skilled orator in office, so you know he could communicate effectively with his team. He also had a unique ability to be assured in his decisions and comfortable with how the results played out, which inspired confidence in others. As a result, Obama would have been a point guard.

Best Comparison: Mike Conley

Conley is like the dude at your gym who isn't flashy and doesn't possess any one particular skill that makes your eyes widen and silently mutter, "Shit…we've got to play that guy?"

He's completely unassuming. Then you start to play and he just systematically caves your skull in with a fluidity and precision that leaves you somewhat confused and thoroughly impressed.

That's what Conley has been doing at the professional ranks for over a decade now. Conley played one season of college basketball at Ohio State

University before turning pro. In that one season, he was named a first-team All-Big Ten player and helped lead his team to the national championship game.

Conley was drafted fourth overall by the Memphis Grizzlies, where he spent the first 12 years of his career. He moved on to the Utah Jazz prior to 2019-20, where he has played the last two seasons. And while his current career averages of 14.9 points, 5.7 assists, and 1.4 steals per game scream "good" rather than "great," his ability to consistently perform at a high level for more than a decade, shouldn't be overlooked.

Conley's accomplishments and steadiness don't receive the same type of media attention as some of his flashier contemporaries, which leaves him flying under the radar. His performance is largely underrated and requires a closer examination, and some analytics, to grasp how impressive his career has been.

Win shares is a statistic designed to divide credit for a team's success by mathematically evaluating how many wins an individual contributed based on both their offensive and defensive performances. Conley's career total win shares is 80.1, and he has never recorded a win shares total of less than four in any season in which he played at least 55 games.

That's great and all, but what the hell does that actually mean?

It means that you can better assign a value to a player, or measure just how strong of a correlation they have on team success, in a way that utilizes your basic statistics (points, rebounds, assists, etc.) but contextualizes them in a way that accounts for factors outside that player's control (how much of their success is because of the teammates around them, what pace their team plays at, etc.). When you calculate individual win shares on a team, the total will come out to roughly the same number of wins garnered by the team as a whole.

Conley's career win shares total puts him inside the top-160 all time. It's well behind the greatest players of all-time (Kareem Abdul-Jabbar leads that list at 273.4), but it's also ahead of some players who have made it into the Hall of Fame.

Conley's Player Efficiency Rating, a stat that attempts to account for all of a player's positive and negative contributions, indicates the same belief—he has been really good for a long time. At 17.6, he again cracks the top-200 all-time, ahead of several Hall of Famers. Of course, there are many factors that can contribute to someone making the basketball hall of fame like were they on championship winning teams, potential coaching resumes, general contributions to the game, etc.; but it gives you a better idea of how consistently good Conley has been to this point in his career.

Similar to Conley, Obama's accomplishments are often underrated because of traditional and social media platforms that have led to increased mudslinging and placed a brighter spotlight on the vast ideological differences that exist in America. Obama is responsible for authorizing the operation that took out one of the most dangerous terrorists in the world and did so without any American, or Pakistani civilian, casualties. He helped lead the nation out of the 2008 recession and provided economic stability. He also was a pioneer for a number of minority and underrepresented groups during his tenure.

In those efforts, Obama became known for his support of all people—regardless of their race, gender, religion, ethnicity, sexual orientation, citizenship, etc. Obama was awarded the 2009 Nobel Peace Prize as a result of his efforts. While Conley may not be able to boast about a Nobel Peace Prize, he does have the respect of his peers. Conley is a three-time recipient of the NBA's sportsmanship award and was also voted as the NBA's teammate of the year in 2019. Both Obama and Conley are heavily invested in charity work, using their elevated platforms to further their causes.

There are no questions about Obama or Conley when it comes to their humanitarianism. The difficult question that exists for both of these guys is: how do you properly assess someone's time in office, or on the court, when their legacy hasn't been fully shaped?

We tend to try and do that with public figures, regardless of their profession. We don't always evaluate someone's successes, or their failures, properly in real time because we're blinded by recency bias and lacking a complete contextual framework. We need the passage of time to assess their accomplishments and their failures. We need to see how those who come after them either expand upon, or tear down, what had been built. We need to see how our cultural beliefs evolve as a society. The direction of the country is guided by the president but formed by its people.

Abraham Lincoln was a very polarizing figure when he was alive. It wasn't until after his death, as the nation began to move forward, that his legacy was actualized. Joe Namath would be an example of someone who used a Super Bowl guarantee and the New York media to catapult himself into the conversation of greatest quarterbacks of all time. Only years after the fact did football fans begin to include his career 62-63-4 record, 220 interceptions, and 50.1% completion rate into a proper contextualization to show Namath as a pretty good quarterback with some historic moments.

The same could be said of movies. *The Wizard of Oz* and *The Shawshank Redemption* were considered flops originally. It took a while before they caught on as widely respected cult classics. Regardless of what's being examined, we realistically need a period of time to place the successes and failures into their rightful context. This is the case for both Obama and Conley.

At the moment, both guys are known for being very good performers. Underrated, even. While the sands of time are likely to continue to alter our opinions of them professionally, at the moment, neither Obama nor Conley are first ballot Hall of Famers.

Trading Card Stats

Barack Obama	Name	Mike Conley Jr.
•Barry •King Obama •No Drama Obama	**Nickname**	•Money Mike
•2009-2017	**Experience**	•2007-present
•47	**Age Entering the League**	•20
•6'2"/175	**HT/WT**	•6'1"/175
•Democrat	**Team**	•Memphis Grizzlies •Utah Jazz
•Affordable Healthcare Act •2009 American Recovery and Reinvestment Act •Auto bailout •Ending of Iraq War •Osama Bin Laden assassination	**Stats**	•14.9 points, 5.7 assists and 3.0 rebounds per game •80.1 win shares •17.6 PER •1-time NBA All-Defensive Second Team
•Basketball •Cooking •Writing •Reading •Body surfing •Golf	**Hobbies**	•Golf •Bowling •Video games •Monopoly •Community service
•"If I had to name my greatest strength, I guess it would be my humility. My greatest weakness, it's possible that I'm a little too awesome."	**Quote**	•"I come from playing in Indiana, where we don't care who's scoring, or how many shots you get."
•He admitted to using cocaine, marijuana and alcohol as a teenager	**Interesting**	•His five-year, $153 million deal in 2016 was the biggest contract in NBA history at the time
•No	**Hall of Fame**	•No

45

Donald Trump (2017-2021)

The man. The myth. The…president?

Holy shit. Nobody predicted that. Well, okay, maybe *The Simpsons* did. But nobody outside of that.

Well, at least it was a quiet presidency without any turmoil where Americans banded together as one in harmony and unity, right? Or maybe it was one where partisan rancor nationally dissolved into bitter, sometimes violent, divisiveness across the country. I guess it depends on which version of facts you ascribe to.

Whether you loved him or hated him, Trump evoked strong emotions and strong ratings in an insatiable, content-craved society. The American population was fed by an endless number of content-producing networks and platforms that have emerged, designed to lure readers and viewers in with click-bait headlines. This has been aided by human attention spans that have increasingly shrunk, grown desensitized in recent years to the ongoing political tumult, and now seek news only to affirm their preconceived notions. When mixed together, these ingredients create a potent cocktail of chaos.

But one man's chaos is another man's order, and Trump figured out how to capitalize on this country's chaos about as well as anyone. He shook up American politics by tapping into a base of supporters who didn't just tolerate the disruptions; they embraced Trump's "political incorrectness" and upheaving of norms established by lifelong politicians.

Trump challenged the political and societal status quo in a system that has been fraught with economic insecurity, a growing class disparity, and increasingly volatile racial tensions. He learned how to galvanize his followers through fear mongering, developing a cult-like following along the way as evidenced by a wave of hats, shirts, and flags all in the name of supporting Trump. Earned or not, Trump has developed a brand over the last few decades as a businessman, TV entrepreneur, and now as a political force.

Trump's path to the presidency was paved in gold. He grew up in New York, the son of a real estate tycoon. He initially attended a military academy but avoided serving in the Vietnam War after a controversial medical deferment, allegedly given as a favor to Trump's father, classified him as having bone spurs and disqualified him from service.

Trump then went to the University of Pennsylvania and graduated with an Economics degree before returning home where he was given a $1 million loan by his father as part of his first foray into the business world. Trump ultimately took over the family real estate business after his father died in 1999, and he expanded the business branding and holding power despite his businesses filing for bankruptcy on six separate occasions.

While he garnered some national attention as the owner of the Miss Universe, Miss USA and Miss Teen USA pageants, he gained true pop-culture relevance through a reality television show called *The Apprentice*, where contestants competed for a year of employment at the Trump organization. Trump's catchphrase, "You're fired," which he used when eliminating contestants, became an integral part of the pop-culture lexicon.

After several years of teasing a run for presidency, Trump announced his candidacy in 2015 using the slogan "Make America Great Again." Trump wound up winning the primary and the general election in a stunning upset despite what poll numbers suggested and what the political establishment wanted. In doing so, he became the first president to never have held an elected position in office or have served in the military.

Trump's tenure was known far less for its actions than its words, but he did implement a number of policy changes worth noting. He signed legislation making widespread changes to the existing tax code, slashing corporate tax rates from 35% to 21%. Trump pulled America out of the Paris climate accord since one of his chief areas of concern was rolling back a number of Obama-led environmental regulations. He ignored climate scientists at every turn, loosening restrictions to oil companies and curbing auto emission efficiency improvement standards. Trump's longest lasting political impact will be his appointment of federal judges. He installed three supreme justices and 226 judges overall at the federal level, all of whom have lifetime appointments and will carry out judicial decisions that shape the country long after Trump's reign.

What Trump's time in office is most likely to be remembered for, though, is the litany of controversies, lies, and vitriol that can only be adequately covered in the form of a full-on dissertation. Just know that *The Washington Post* reported Trump made 30,573 false or misleading claims as president. His most damaging lies and failures came from his administration's handling of COVID-19, a strain of influenza that birthed a global pandemic and has inflicted more than four million deaths worldwide and more than 600,000 deaths in the U.S. as of July 2021.

There were a number of astonishing missteps in handling COVID-19 that likely caused him to lose his bid for re-election. Some of those include: initially saying there was nothing to worry about, significantly downplaying its existence, being late to the party on touting the importance of face masks and social distancing, insisting it would vanish by the way of a miracle, calling it the "Kung Flu" and sparking violence toward the Asian community, suggesting bleach injections as a potential cure, saying the U.S. was handling the response well, and then also refusing to fully acknowledge or accept the growing death toll that resulted from COVID-19.

Oh yeah, he also was impeached twice, lied about his loss in the 2020 election while pressing officials to "find" the additional votes he needed in order to win, incited a violent insurrection on Capitol Hill that killed five people after losing the election, and was banned from some high-profile social media platforms for continually spreading misinformation. And that is just the tip of a Titanic-like iceberg that engulfed the nation during his time in office.

Most likely sport: Golf

It's no secret that one of the activities Trump loves most in this world is golfing. He reportedly golfed more than 300 times during his term, meaning he spent nearly a quarter of his time in office out on the course. Given his lone-wolf nature when it comes to looking out for his own best interest, golf couldn't be a more fitting sport. Trump's penchant for alienating teammates would not be a concern. Golf would not require Trump to expend a lot of energy and would allow him to work at a leisurely pace.

Best Comparison: Robert Allenby

Where do we begin with Allenby? Is it the feuds with fellow competitors? Perhaps it's the nearly two dozen caddies he has cycled through while developing a reputation as "The Beast"? What about reporting his own kidnapping that never actually occurred?

Yeah, and you thought golf was boring.

Allenby's cliff notes read more like a drama script than a professional golf resume. In fact, we're a "back-from-the-dead" moment away from official soap opera status. Despite being a professional golfer for more than three decades, if the casual fan is familiar with Allenby, it's almost assuredly because of something other than his play.

He grew up playing as an amateur in Australia. Allenby has four career victories as part of the PGA Tour, all coming within a 17-month stretch spanning 2000 and 2001. He has played in more than 500 PGA-sanctioned events, making the cut in 62% of them while finishing top-10 in 13% of his tournaments

Additionally, Allenby has notched 18 career international victories outside the PGA Tour. His career PGA earnings have accumulated more than $27 million. Not a bad gig if you can get it. However, for better or for worse, Allenby's newsworthiness has usually been determined by events other than his golf scores.

On the tamer side of his indiscretions, Allenby has occasionally gotten into spats with his competitors. He once accused Anthony Kim of being out all night partying before the final day of the Presidents Cup, a team-based golf tournament pitting U.S. golfers against international golfers. Kim had soundly beaten Allenby, likely resulting in the frustration that fueled his comments. Kim denied the allegation, which made Allenby look like a reckless, sore loser. Allenby also mixed it up with Geoff Ogilvy two years later at another Presidents Cup event, arguing over who was responsible for their team's loss.

Trump is also no stranger to contentious moments with political foes. You would have to unfurl a scroll to the ground to properly recite all of his disputes. Trump has most often gone after clear political opponents like Joe Biden, Barack Obama, and Hillary Clinton, but he was not afraid to go after opponents who would eventually become allies like Ted Cruz, Marco Rubio, and Mitch McConnell.

Trump's willingness to light into others even extended into full-fledged teammates. His cabinet had an extremely high turnover rate as Trump found it difficult to maintain a good working relationship with his underlings. By the time Trump left office, 12 of his Senate-confirmed Cabinet members had either resigned or been fired by the president. Only six survived the duration of his term. He laid into his subordinates for any number of reasons, but chief among them was a refusal to support and defend the president at all times.

Two of the more notable fallouts occurred with James Comey and William Barr. Comey, serving as the FBI director, was sacked for investigating the alleged connection between the Trump campaign and Russian interference in the 2016 presidential election. Trump had expected complete loyalty from his FBI leader and insinuated that Comey needed to drop the investigation. When Comey continued to pursue it, he was dismissed by Trump. The second instance came when U.S. Attorney General Barr was unwilling to support Trump's presidential election lawsuits claiming widespread voter fraud had taken place, resulting in Trump's 2020 election loss. The backlash and pressure applied by Trump to help find evidence of Democratic wrongdoing led to Barr's resignation.

Similarly, Allenby often has found it difficult to work with the people closest to him. He has gone through at least two dozen different caddies during his career and stated back in 2015 that only three of them were any good. Allenby has earned the nickname "The Beast " thanks to his reputation for being so mean and vulgar with his caddies, blaming them when he performs poorly. His most contentious run-in with a caddie occurred with Mick Middlemo. After playing four holes at the 2015 RBC Canadian Open, Middlemo walked off the course after Allenby had been verbally abusive. Allenby shot back that he had actually fired Middlemo mid-round for being the one with the abusive language, though another caddie in Allenby's group backed up Middlemo's version of events.

One of the reasons for the heated disagreement stemmed from a bizarre incident early in 2015 when Allenby reported that he had been kidnapped, beaten, and robbed while out at a bar in Hawaii. He was allegedly drugged and then dumped several miles away from the bar in a harrowing experience. Except, it wasn't.

Police inspection uncovered no evidence to suggest a kidnapping or beating had taken place, though Allenby had been robbed. A suspect was eventually arrested for identity theft but police made it clear there was no ongoing investigation into a kidnapping. Allenby maintained his version of what happened, though some around golf, including Middlemo, believe Allenby more than likely got blackout drunk, hurt himself in a fall, and was then pick-pocketed while he was passed out.

Although Trump has never dealt with an incident like this, he is no stranger to stories in which the truth is stretched, distorted, or all out ignored. Trump and Allenby are both known to have tempers and have shown a general disdain throughout their careers in accepting responsibility for their actions. Regardless of any perceived personality foibles, their professional resumes are not Hall of Fame worthy.

Trading Card Stats

Donald Trump	Name	Robert Allenby
•The Don •The Donald •Drumpf	Nickname	•The Beast
•2017-2021	Experience	•1991-present
•70	Age Entering the League	•20
•6'3"/244	HT/WT	•6'2"/185
•Republican	Team	•Independent
•Tax codes •Environmental deregulation •Federal judge appointments •Covid-19 •Impeached twice	Stats	•4 PGA tournament victories •70 top-10 finishes •18 international tournament wins
•Golf •Social media	Hobbies	•Fishing •Boating
•"We have it totally under control. It's one person coming in from China. It's going to be just fine." -On the coronavirus	Quote	•"It's kind of that thing in Vegas—what happens in Vegas stays in Vegas. Well, what happens on Tour stays on Tour."
•Trump was a registered democrat from 2001-2009	Interesting	•The lowest round of his career was a 62, shot at the Air Canada Championship in 2002
•No	Hall of Fame	•No

Bibliography

Anderson, Curt. 2006. *Ocala.* June 2. https://www.ocala.com/news/20060602/redskins-safety-taylor-to-avoid-jail-in-assault-charge.

Arpi, Rich. n.d. *SABR.* https://sabr.org/bioproj/person/9aee41e7.

n.d. *ATP Tour.* https://www.atptour.com/en/players/kyle-edmund/e831/overview.

Auerbach, Nicole. 2012. *USA Today.* December 18. https://www.usatoday.com/story/sports/ncaab/2012/12/18/college-basketball-xavier-cincinnati-crosstown/1774975/.

Baker, Ken, Holly Passalaqua, and Corinne Heller. 2015. *E Online.* October 18. https://www.eonline.com/news/707694/lamar-odom-slowly-making-progress-after-waking-up-from-coma-what-we-know-so-far.

Bartsch, Tom. 2016. *Sports Collectors Digest.* July 26. https://www.sportscollectorsdigest.com/interview-theismann-played-in-a-tough-era-with-the-injuries-to-prove-it/.

n.d. *Baseball Almanac.* https://www.baseball-almanac.com/quotes/albert_belle_quotes.shtml.

1993. *Baseball America.* https://www.baseballamerica.com/rankings/1993-top-100-prospects/.

Baseball Reference. https://www.baseball-reference.com/players

Basketball Reference. https://www.basketball-reference.com/players

2020. *BBC News.* March 1. Accessed May 10, 2021. https://www.bbc.com/news/world-us-canada-35318432.

Beasley, Adam. 2017. *Miami Herald.* August 6. https://www.miamiherald.com/sports/nfl/miami-dolphins/article165756707.html.

Benjamin, Ross. n.d. *Interbasket.* https://www.interbasket.net/news/21984/2017/05/how-basketball-players-relieve-stress-after-game-offseason/.

Benton, Emmanual. 2012. *Pro Player Insiders.* November 28. http://archive.proplayerinsiders.com/nfl-player-team-news-features/the-meast-sean-taylor/.

BewareofDog. 2014. *SBNation.* April 17. https://www.canalstreetchronicles.com/2014/4/17/5623840/nfl-draft-saints-ricky-williams-mike-ditka-trade.

2017. *Biography.* April 27. https://www.biography.com/athlete/tim-tebow.

Bishop, Greg. 2016. *Sports Illustrated.* https://www.si.com/longform/2016/ricky-williams-weed/index.html.

2012. *Bleacher Report.* January 21. https://bleacherreport.com/articles/1032978-the-greatest-university-of-west-alabama-football-players-of-all-time#slide48.

Bohn, Terry. n.d. *SABR.* http://sabr.org/bioproj/person/a4848647.

Brent, Harry. 2021. *The Irish Post.* January 20. Accessed May 11, 2021. https://www.irishpost.com/life-style/donald-trumps-craziest-quotes-as-us-president-201911.

Bricker, Charles. 1990. *South Florida Sun Sentinel.* November 4. http://articles.sun-sentinel.com/1990-11-04/sports/9002230541_1_david-griggs-tough-guy-virginia.

—. 1990. *South Florida Sun Sentinel.* August 22. http://articles.sun-sentinel.com/1990-08-22/sports/9002100037_1_tight-end-david-griggs-billy-griggs.

—. 1990. *South Florida Sun Sentinel.* December 31. http://articles.sun-sentinel.com/1990-12-31/sports/9003050559_1_todd-mcnair-david-griggs-dolphins.

Brinson, Will. 2016. *CBS Sports.* August 11. https://www.cbssports.com/nfl/news/ricky-williams-once-smoked-under-the-bus-by-willie-nelson-and-his-case-for-hof/.

Bumbaca, Chris. 2019. *USA Today.* September 13. https://www.usatoday.com/story/sports/college/2019/09/13/college-athletes-tim-tebow-speaks-out-against-paying-players/2312200001/.
n.d. *Calbears.* https://web.archive.org/web/20151203204416/http://www.calbears.com/ViewArticle.dbml?DB_LANG=C&DB_OEM_ID=30100&ATCLID=208198774.
Capozzi, Joe. 2013. *Palm Beach Post.* April 6. https://www.palmbeachpost.com/sports/baseball/miami-marlins-phenom-jose-fernandez-makes-debut-sunday-already-has-gone-through-lot/ynEMD6Rgy6vwNcQEPqL3yL/.
Castillo, Jorge. 2016. *The Washington Post.* January 21. https://www.washingtonpost.com/sports/wizards/the-big-shorts-an-era-in-basketball-fashion-is-coming-to-an-end/2016/01/21/70d97d12-bf84-11e5-9443-7074c3645405_story.html?noredirect=on&utm_term=.b7a146546ba2.
2016. *Chicago Tribune.* January 11. Accessed May 12, 2021. https://www.chicagotribune.com/sports/ct-robert-allenby-hawaii-robbery-20160111-story.html.
2014. *Clemson Tigers.* June 2. https://clemsontigers.com/clemson-vault-william-the-refrigerator-perry/.
2020. *CNN.* April 5. http://www.cnn.com/2013/04/29/us/kobe-bryant-fast-facts/index.html.
Coffer, Jim. 2009. *Jim Coffer.* October 29. https://jimcofer.com/2009/10/29/righting-the-wrongs-joe-theismann/.
Cottrell, Jay. 2013. *WBAL.* August 12. https://www.wbal.com/article/102014/3/local-product-denny-neagle-talks-about-peds-and-charity-golf-tournament.
Crowe, Jerry. 2007. *Los Angeles Times.* April 16. http://articles.latimes.com/2007/apr/16/sports/sp-crowe16.
Cunliffe, Marcus. 1960. *George Washington: Man and Monument.* Signet.
1996. *Daily Bruin.* November 5. http://dailybruin.com/1996/11/05/jim-harrick-resigns-as-head-co/.
Dater, Adrian. 2016. *Bleacher Report.* November 18. http://bleacherreport.com/articles/2676844-ranking-the-most-quotable-players-in-nhl-history.
Davis, Nate. 2014. *USA Today.* September 26. https://www.usatoday.com/story/sports/nfl/2014/09/26/lavar-arrington-sean-taylor-washington-redskins-a-football-life-nfl-network/16261669/.
DeGregorio, William A. 1989. *The Complete Book of U.S. Presidents.* New York: Dembner Books.
Dent, Jim. 1985. *Los Angeles Times.* September 7. https://www.latimes.com/archives/la-xpm-1985-09-07-sp-6784-story.html.
Depew, Bryan. n.d. *Sports Kings.* http://sports-kings.com/baseball-news/jose-fernandez-picks-new-hobby-stay-shape.
Do, Jimmy. n.d. *OKC Thunder.* https://www.nba.com/thunder/community/felton-festival-181216.
Dodson, Aaron. 2018. *The Undefeated.* January 31. https://theundefeated.com/features/jamarcus-russell-went-from-top-overall-pick-to-nfl-bust-in-a-hurry/.
Domonoske, Carmila. 2018. *NPR.* May 24. https://www.npr.org/sections/thetwo-way/2018/05/24/614114966/legendary-boxer-jack-johnson-gets-pardon-105-years-after-baseless-conviction.
Downey, Mike. 1997. *Los Angeles Times.* October 12. https://www.latimes.com/archives/la-xpm-1997-oct-12-sp-42170-story.html.
n.d. *Draft Express.* http://www.draftexpress.com/profile/Raymond-Felton-5/awards/.
Dudley, Christian. 2015. *Fansided.* May 15. https://bealestreetbears.com/2015/06/15/memphis-grizzlies-mike-conley-takes-up-golfing/.
Editors, History.com. 2017. *History.* December 4. https://www.history.com/topics/21st-century/great-recession-timeline.
n.d. *Encyclopedia.* https://www.encyclopedia.com/people/sports-and-games/sports-biographies/albert-belle.

2006. *ESPN.* April 25. http://www.espn.com/nfl/news/story?id=2421774.
2016. *ESPN.* April 26. http://www.espn.com/nfl/story/_/id/15384038/jamarcus-russell-says-play-free-just-wants-another-chance.
2010. *ESPN.* July 5. http://www.espn.com/nfl/news/story?id=5356585.
n.d. *ESPN.* http://www.espn.com/tennis/player/_/id/1858/kyle-edmund.
2017. *ESPN.* June 1. https://www.espn.com/mlb/story/_/id/19509152/miami-marlins-create-trust-fund-family-jose-fernandez.
2004. *ESPN.* June 5. https://www.espn.com/espn/news/story?id=1816460.
n.d. *ESPN.* https://www.espn.com/page2/s/questions/neagle.html.
2016. *EXNBA.* May 17. http://exnba.com/miscellaneous/manute-bol-vs-william-refrigerator-perry-video/.
Faber, Charles and Richard. 2000. *The American Presidents Ranked by Performance.* Jefferson, N.C.: McFarland & Company, Inc.
2018. *Facts Five.* January 23. https://factsfive.com/kyle-edmund-net-worth/.
Falk, Aaron. 2020. *NBA.* April 17. https://www.nba.com/jazz/news/qa-horse-champion-mike-conley-trick-shots-covid-19-and-how-hes-staying-possible-playoff-push.
n.d. *Fandom.* https://survivor.fandom.com/wiki/John_Rocker.
n.d. *Fangraphs.* https://www.fangraphs.com/leaders.aspx?pos=np&stats=bat&lg=all&qual=500&type=8&season=2019&month=0&season1=1871&ind=0&team=0&rost=0&age=0&filter=&players=0&startdate=1871-01-01&enddate=2019-12-31&sort=10,d.
Farber, Michael. 1997. *Sports Illustrated Vault.* September 15. https://vault.si.com/vault/1997/09/15/matinee-idol-movie-buff-mimic-and-20-game-winner-the-braves-denny-neagle-makes-quite-an-impression.
Fields, Mike. 2016. *KHSAA.* March 4. https://khsaa.org/recalling-tim-couchs-basketball-glory-days/.
Flatter, Ron. n.d. *ESPN.* https://www.espn.com/sportscentury/features/00014275.html.
Flessa, Maria-Elpida. 2016. *Useless Daily.* October 16. https://www.uselessdaily.com/sports/lamar-odom-trivia-47-amazing-facts-about-the-basketball-star/#.XPPrzYhKiUk.
Football Reference. https://www.pro-football-reference.com/players
Fowler, Michael. 2017. *Fox Sports Radio.* May 8. https://foxsportsradio.iheart.com/featured/the-herd-with-colin-cowherd/content/2017-05-08-jay-cutler-en-route-to-a-bear-hunt-calls-into-the-herd/.
Fuhr, Ernie. n.d. *SABR.* http://sabr.org/bioproj/person/b9c3739f.
Genessy, Jody. 2019. *Desert News.* June 19. https://www.deseret.com/2019/6/19/20676013/11-things-utah-jazz-fans-should-know-about-new-point-guard-mike-conley-jr.
Gillin, Joshua. 2015. *Politifact.* August 24. Accessed May 11, 2021. https://www.politifact.com/factchecks/2015/aug/24/jeb-bush/bush-says-trump-was-democrat-longer-republican-las/.
n.d. *Good Reads.* Accessed June 7, 2020. https://www.goodreads.com/quotes/10870-i-can-accept-failure-everyone-fails-at-something-but-i.
Goodwill, Vincent. 2016. *Slam Online.* October 25. https://www.slamonline.com/nba/rajon-rondo-interview-chicago-bulls/.
n.d. *Gophersports.* https://gophersports.com/news/2001/2/5/NEAGLE_ENDOWS_BASEBALL_SCHOLARSHIP_IN_HIS_NAME_AT_UNIVERSITY_OF_MINNESOTA.aspx.
Greene, Jerry. 2010. *ESPN.* May 6. http://www.espn.com/espn/page2/story/_/id/5166442.
Greenfield, Jimmy. 2000. *Chicago Tribune.* January 13. https://www.chicagotribune.com/news/ct-xpm-2000-01-13-0001130353-story.html.
Grossi, Tony. 2018. *ESPN.* July 30. http://www.espn.com/blog/cleveland/post/_/id/5190/tim-couchs-returns-to-browns-as-a-broadcaster-17-years-after-he-led-the-expansion-franchise-to-its-only-playoff-appearance.

Haigh, Marilyn. 2018. *CNBC.* October 23. https://www.cnbc.com/2018/10/23/kobe-bryant-once-took-up-tap-dancing-to-improve-his-game--heres-why-.html.

Haltiwanger, John. 2021. *Business Insider.* January 20. Accessed May 10, 2021. https://www.businessinsider.com/trump-biggest-accomplishments-and-failures-heading-into-2020-2019-12#failure-replacing-the-affordable-care-act-aka-obamacare-10.

Harper, Zach. 2013. *CBS Sports.* July 12. https://www.cbssports.com/nba/news/baron-davis-says-he-was-abducted-by-aliens-about-two-weeks-ago/.

Harry, Chris. 1996. *South Florida Sun Sentinel.* November 17. https://www.sun-sentinel.com/news/fl-xpm-1996-11-17-9611170145-story.html.

Hissner, Ken. 2017. *Boxing Insider.* April 23. https://www.boxinginsider.com/columns/just-good-heavyweight-champion-jack-johnson/.

Hlava, Chuck. 2002. *Chron.* July 2. https://www.chron.com/neighborhood/article/McKinney-at-home-with-NFL-s-Texans-9900155.php.

n.d. *Hockey Reference.* https://www.hockey-reference.com/players/w/williti01.html.

Hoffman, Roy. 2010. *AL.* January 31. http://blog.al.com/entertainment-press-register/2010/01/mardi_gras_mamga_king_elexis_i.html.

n.d. *Home of the Leafs.* http://www.homeoftheleafs.com/players/williams.php.

2017. *Hoopshype.* March 19. https://hoopshype.com/2017/03/19/11-things-you-may-not-know-about-jeremy-lin/.

Horning, Clay. 2019. *The Norman Transcript.* April 12. https://www.normantranscript.com/sports/national_sports/thunder-given-a-chance-raymond-felton-has-thrived/article_5e7486a2-7811-58e9-b4d8-22b7ef7f9e5a.html.

2009. *Houston Texans.* February 11. https://www.houstontexans.com/news/where-are-they-now-steve-mckinney-2672969.

2014. *Hudson Reporter.* May 9. https://archive.hudsonreporter.com/2014/05/09/sports-corner-blp-joe-borowskis-incredible-journey/.

Hummer, Steve. 2019. *Atlanta Journal Constitution.* July 12. https://www.ajc.com/sports/falcons-ring-honor-bartkowski-resets-very-good-life-montana/brfAxs7JWIC1qR7ZTlTh5N/.

n.d. *IMDB.* https://www.imdb.com/name/nm2325442/bio?ref_=nm_dyk_trv_sm#trivia.

Ingle, Sean. 2018. *The Guardian.* January 23. https://www.theguardian.com/sport/2018/jan/23/kyle-edmund-steel-quietness-tennis-australian-open.

n.d. *Inspiring Quotes.* https://www.inspiringquotes.us/author/9981-sean-taylor.

Jenkins, Lee. 2015. *Sports Illustrated.* October 15. https://www.si.com/nba/2015/10/15/lamar-odom-lakers-clippers-rhode-island-new-york.

Joanou, Brian. 2017. *Yahoo.* November 2. https://sports.yahoo.com/interview-rams-great-henry-ellard-023945088.html.

n.d. *JockBio.* https://www.jockbio.com/Bios/Nomar/Nomar_facts.html.

Johnson, Dalton. 2018. *NBC Sports.* November 4. https://www.nbcsports.com/bayarea/raiders/jamarcus-russell-clearly-didnt-watch-film-heres-hilarious-story .

Johnson, Kirk. 2004. *The New York Times.* September 2. http://www.nytimes.com/2004/09/02/us/prosecutors-drop-kobe-bryant-rape-case.html.

Kamka, Chris. 2020. *NBC Sports.* April 21. https://www.nbcsports.com/chicago/white-sox/remember-guy-white-sox-pitcher-jason-bere.

Kawakami, Tim. 1999. *Los Angeles Times.* February 10. http://articles.latimes.com/1999/feb/10/sports/sp-6796.

n.d. *Kedders.* https://www.kedders.co.uk/.

Keim, John. 2020. *ESPN.* April 1. http://www.espn.com/nfl/story/_/id/20848497/remembering-sean-taylor-washington-redskins-oral-history-breakout-game-10-years-death.

Kessler, Glenn. 2021. *The Washington Post.* January 23. Accessed May 11, 2021. https://www.washingtonpost.com/politics/how-fact-checker-tracked-trump-claims/2021/01/23/ad04b69a-5c1d-11eb-a976-bad6431e03e2_story.html.

Key, Andre. 2017. *Clutch Points.* August 24. https://clutchpoints.com/jeremy-lin-excited-part-dota-2-championship-action/.
2006. *Kidzworld.* December 27. http://www.kidzworld.com/article/3819-nomar-garciaparra-biography.
Lammers, Craig. n.d. *SABR.* http://sabr.org/bioproj/person/1ad84d3d.
Langenkamp, Jake. 2009. *SBNation.* April 23. https://www.battleredblog.com/2009/4/23/851064/an-interview-with-an-original.
Lantz, Brandon. 2011. *Bleacher Report.* October 19. http://bleacherreport.com/articles/902528-bears-news-cutler-unapologetic-for-comments-to-martz.
Laurila, David. 2005. *Baseball Almanac.* https://www.baseball-almanac.com/players/jason_bere_interview.shtml.
n.d. *Laver Cup.* https://lavercup.com/player/kyle-edmund.
Lawson, Victor. 2019. *Sports&Study.* November 1. https://sportandstudy.org/jeremy-linbasketball-player-with-a-degree-in-economics/.
Lee, Michael. 2016. *The Washington Post.* September 26. Accessed May 11, 2021. https://www.washingtonpost.com/politics/2016/live-updates/general-election/real-time-fact-checking-and-analysis-of-the-first-presidential-debate/fact-check-has-trump-declared-bankruptcy-four-or-six-times/.
Leerhsen, Charles. 2015. *Sports Illustrated.* May 8. https://www.si.com/mlb/2015/05/08/book-excerpt-ty-cobb-babe-ruth-detroit-tigers-charles-leerhsen.
Lerner, Keven. 2016. *South Florida Sun Sentinel.* October 18. https://www.sun-sentinel.com/sports/miami-marlins/sfl-giancarlo-stanton-pays-tribute-to-jose-fernandez-with-graffiti-art-in-brazil-20161018-htmlstory.html.
Letourneau, Connor. 2019. *San Francisco Chronicle.* February 11. https://www.sfchronicle.com/warriors/article/How-Warriors-great-Baron-Davis-went-from-hardwood-13609075.php.
Lin, Jeremy. 2013. *JLin7.* April 2. https://www.jlin7.com/blogs/journal/7616135-playoff-push.
n.d. *Linkedin.* https://www.linkedin.com/in/steve-mckinney-9152248.
Locker, Melissa. n.d. *Southern Living.* https://www.southernliving.com/culture/celebrities/tim-tebow.
1985. *Los Angeles Times.* April 1. http://articles.latimes.com/1985-04-01/sports/sp-28342_1_tiger-williams.
Lowe, Zach. 2014. *Grantland.* March 6. https://grantland.com/the-triangle/qa-mike-conley-on-being-tricky-and-the-why-not-us-grizzlies/.
MacMahon, Tim. 2019. *ESPN.* November 15. https://www.espn.com/nba/story/_/id/28059997/mike-conley-quest-technical-perfection-how-almost-ended.
Mandell, Nina. 2012. *New York Daily News.* February 21. https://www.nydailynews.com/entertainment/gossip/jeremy-lin-dating-kim-kardashian-knicks-phenom-denies-report-dating-reality-star-article-1.1026246.
—. 2015. *USA Today.* January 2. https://ftw.usatoday.com/2015/01/rajon-rondo-i-havent-played-defense-in-a-couple-of-years.
Manfred, Tony. 2013. *Business Insider.* March 5. http://www.businessinsider.com/kobe-bryant-woke-up-at-4-am-to-practice-before-olympics-2013-3.
Matthews, Alex. 2018. *Daily Mail.* January 22. https://www.dailymail.co.uk/news/article-5297043/Edmund-got-tennis-annoying-mother.html.
Maxey, Wendell. 2012. *The Comeback.* April 5. http://thecomeback.com/crossoverchronicles/2012-articles/feltons-fight-in-portland-turns-personal-with-media-fans.html.
n.d. *Mayo Clinic.* https://www.mayoclinic.org/diseases-conditions/guillain-barre-syndrome/symptoms-causes/syc-20362793.
McKinley Jr., James. 2014. *The New York Times.* June 23. https://www.nytimes.com/2014/06/24/sports/basketball/knicks-raymond-felton-avoids-jail-in-gun-possession-case.html.

Melas, Chloe. 2019. *CNN.* May 31. https://www.cnn.com/2019/05/30/entertainment/lamar-odom-interview-khloe-kardashian/index.html.

Mitchell, George. 2007. *MLB.* December 13. http://files.mlb.com/mitchrpt.pdf.

Murphy, Chris and Sweetman, Tom. 2015. *CNN.* February 13. Accessed May 12, 2021. https://www.cnn.com/2015/02/13/golf/golf-robert-allenby-kidnapping-hawaii/index.html.

Nación, One. 2016. *ESPN.* April 12. http://www.espn.com/blog/onenacion/post/_/id/3559/kobe-bryant-en-espaol.

2015. *Newsweek.* October 17. https://www.newsweek.com/missing-cut-382954.

Nocera, Joe. 2016. *The New York Times.* February 19. Accessed May 11, 2021. https://www.nytimes.com/2016/02/20/sports/football/donald-trumps-less-than-artful-failure-in-pro-football.html.

Normandin, Marc. 2016. *SBNation.* January 7. https://www.overthemonster.com/2016/1/7/10729478/nomar-garciaparra-red-sox-hall-of-fame.

Nusbaum, Eric. 2011. *Deadspin.* July 13. https://deadspin.com/the-100-worst-baseball-players-of-all-time-a-celebrati-5820716.

O'Brien, Cormac. 2004. *Secret Lives of the U.S. Presidents.* Philadelphia: Quirk Books.

O'Malley, Nick. 2020. *MSN.* April 15. https://www.msn.com/en-us/Sports/nfl/tim-tebow-roasts-jets-in-easter-sermon-e2-80-98i-got-traded-to-the-jets-when-e2-80-99s-the-last-time-a-jets-trade-worked-out-e2-80-99/ar-BB12G7eX?ocid=a2hs.

Ovalle, David. 2017. *Miami Herald.* March 16. https://www.miamiherald.com/news/local/community/miami-dade/article138834953.html.

Paige, Woody. 2007. *Denver Post.* December 13. https://www.denverpost.com/2007/12/13/rockies-dont-escape-role-in-steroid-report/.

n.d. *PBS.* https://www.pbs.org/kenburns/unforgivable-blackness/johnsons-arrest.

Pearlman, Jeff. 1999. *Sports Illustrated Vault.* December 27. https://www.si.com/vault/1999/12/27/271860/at-full-blast-shooting-outrageously-from-the-lip-braves-closer-john-rocker-bangs-away-at-his-favorite-targets-the-mets-their-fans-their-city-and-just-about-everyone-in-it .

Petchesky, Barry. 2012. *Deadspin.* January 4. https://deadspin.com/5873047/nomar-garciaparra-tried-to-convince-astronauts-the-moon-landing-was-fake-and-other-stories-from-six-years-in-red-sox-pr.

Peter, Josh. 2015. *USA Today.* October 1. Accessed May 12, 2021. https://www.usatoday.com/story/sports/golf/pga/2015/10/01/life-robert-allenbys-caddie-can-hell/73142742/.

n.d. *PGA Tour.* Accessed May 12, 2021. https://www.pgatour.com/players/player.10885.robert-allenby.html.

Pluto, Terry. 2019. *Cleveland.* February 22. https://www.cleveland.com/pluto/2019/02/faith-you-as-life-nears-the-end-and-none-of-the-choices-are-good-terry-pluto.html.

Polin, Mitch. 1987. *Los Angeles Times.* May 28. https://www.latimes.com/archives/la-xpm-1987-05-28-ga-3282-story.html.

2021. *Politico.* January 18. Accessed May 11, 2021. https://www.politico.com/news/magazine/2021/01/18/trump-presidency-administration-biggest-impact-policy-analysis-451479.

Pomrenke, Jacob. n.d. *SABR.* https://sabr.org/bioproj/person/7d8be958.

Pote, Jamie. 2015. *Tewksbury Town Crier.* August 29. http://homenewshere.com/tewksbury_town_crier/sports/article_9b8be23e-4d83-11e5-8901-47bf17448a20.html.

Press, Associated. 2000. *CBS News.* December 12. https://www.cbsnews.com/news/unlv-fires-coach-put-on-probation/.

—. 2020. *ESPN*. May 15. https://www.espn.com/nba/story/_/id/29180785/kobe-bryant-helicopter-pilot-had-no-drugs-alcohol-system-autopsy-shows.

—. 2009. *ESPN*. June 2. http://www.espn.com/nba/playoffs/2009/news/story?id=4225789.

—. 2004. *ESPN*. December 14. https://www.espn.com/mlb/news/story?id=1946300.

—. 2015. *FOX59*. October 14. https://fox59.com/2015/10/14/lamar-odom-on-life-support-khloe-kardashian-to-make-medical-decisions/.

—. 1995. *Los Angeles Times*. June 21. http://articles.latimes.com/1995-06-21/sports/sp-15374_1_david-griggs.

Price, Dwain. 2015. *Fort Worth Star Telegram*. September 30. http://www.star-telegram.com/sports/nba/dallas-mavericks/article37105638.html.

Price, Satchel. 2015. *SBNation*. April 29. https://www.sbnation.com/2015/4/29/8515411/rajon-rondo-playoff-share-fake-injury-mavericks-rockets-free-agency-2015.

n.d. *Project Gutenberg Self-Publishing Press*. Accessed March 18, 2020. http://www.self.gutenberg.org/articles/eng/Gus_Weyhing?View=embedded%27%27.

Puit, Glenn. 1997. *Review Journal*. August 19. https://web.archive.org/web/20040227045741/http://www.reviewjournal.com/lvrj_home/1997/Aug-19-Tue-1997/news/5912511.html.

Resnick, Steven. 2009. *Bleacher Report*. July 24. https://bleacherreport.com/articles/223212-is-albert-belle-a-hall-of-famer.

Robertson, Linda, and Michelle Kaufman. 2016. *Miami Herald*. September 28. https://www.miamiherald.com/sports/mlb/miami-marlins/article104814596.html.

Roling, Chris. 2016. *Bleacher Report*. October 28. https://bleacherreport.com/articles/2672203-10-stars-with-awesome-out-of-sport-hobbies#slide2.

Rollins, Khadrice. 2018. *Sports Illustrated*. March 18. https://www.si.com/nba/2018/03/18/rajon-rondo-ray-allen-book-celtics.

Rosenberg, I.J. 2014. *Atlanta Journal Constitution*. October 3. https://www.ajc.com/sports/whatever-happened-steve-bartkowski/8i35TolfAbemggFLhznXLK/.

Rosenthal, Gregg. 2009. *Pro Football Talk*. July 20. https://profootballtalk.nbcsports.com/2009/07/20/former-nfl-linebacker-darren-hambrick-behind-bars/.

Rubino, Michael. 2015. *Indianapolis Monthly*. December 24. https://www.indianapolismonthly.com/longform/larry-birds-greatest-shot-one-didnt-take#:~:text=Twenty%2Dfour%20days%20into%20his,Bird%20left%20the%20Bloomington%20campus.&text=%E2%80%9CLarry%20was%20pressured%20into%20going,'%20%E2%80%9D.

Rubinstein, Julian. n.d. *Sports Illustrated Vault*. https://vault.si.com/vault/1995/09/18/henry-ellard-aerial-pursuits.

n.d. *SABR*. http://sabr.org/bioproj/person/310d6270.

Sallee, Paul, and Eric Salle. n.d. *SABR*. https://sabr.org/bioproj/person/c6889260.

Schaefer, Matt. 2011. *Bleacher Report*. January 25. http://bleacherreport.com/articles/584342-jay-cutler-deserves-the-criticism-after-quitting-during-the-nfc-championship.

Schmitz, Brian. 1985. *Orlando Sentinel*. November 7. https://www.orlandosentinel.com/news/os-xpm-1985-11-07-0340260195-story.html.

Schrader, Ann. 2006. *Denver Post*. January 25. https://www.denverpost.com/2006/01/25/neagle-reaches-plea-in-vice-case-2/.

Schudel, Jeff. 2002. *The Morning Journal*. August 13. https://www.morningjournal.com/news/hambrick-just-wants-to-play-football/article_b9acb2f4-d4e1-50f0-bcad-86810d00f296.html.

Serby, Steve. 2012. *New York Post*. November 18. https://nypost.com/2012/11/18/serbys-sunday-q-a-with-raymond-felton-2/.

Smith, Marcel. 2009. *Bleacher Report*. February 28. https://bleacherreport.com/articles/131997-mjs-1st-retirement-was-it-a-secret-suspension.

Spears, Marc. 2016. *The Undefeated.* December 9. https://theundefeated.com/features/baron-davis-adds-a-bit-of-color-to-christmas-with-the-black-santa-company/.
Springer, Shira. 2011. *Boston.* August 21. http://archive.boston.com/sports/baseball/redsox/articles/2011/08/21/nomar_garciaparra_goes_from_tight_lipped_player_to_talkative_tv_personality/.
—. 2009. *Boston.* May 17. http://archive.boston.com/sports/basketball/celtics/articles/2009/05/17/no_catching_rondo/?page=full.
Staff, Slam. 2011. *Slam Online.* February 25. https://www.slamonline.com/archives/byron-scott-promises-to-get-along-with-baron-davis/.
Steinberg, Dan. 2011. *The Washington Post.* June 6. https://www.washingtonpost.com/blogs/dc-sports-bog/post/joe-theismanns-nickname-was-captain-bubbly/2011/06/06/AGsyqIKH_blog.html?noredirect=on&utm_term=.b0178645ad0e.
Stites, Adam. 2018. *SBNation.* June 12. https://www.sbnation.com/2018/6/12/17451348/cincinnati-bengals-trade-saints-ricky-williams-akili-smith.
Stone, Ken. 2016. *Masterstrack.* August 9. http://masterstrack.com/meet-henry-ellard-from-nfl-to-m55-triple-jump-record-man/.
Swain, Susan, and Brian Lamb. 2005. *The Presidents: Noted Historians Rank America's Best--and Worst--Chief Executives.* PublicAffairs.
TalkOfFame. 2016. *Sports Illustrated.* October 24. http://www.talkoffamenetwork.com/henry-ellard-interview/.
Telander, Rick. 2016. *Sports Illustrated.* June 27. https://www.si.com/nfl/2016/06/27/william-perry-refrigerator-weight-where-are-they-now.
n.d. *The Baseball Cube.* http://www.thebaseballcube.com/players/profile.asp?ID=16590.
n.d. *The Famous People.* https://www.thefamouspeople.com/profiles/jack-johnson-boxer-5275.php.
2006. *The Gainesville Sun.* March 26. https://www.gainesville.com/news/20060326/ex-gator-hambrick-trying-to-make-a-comeback-to-pros.
Thompson, Phil. 2017. *Chicago Tribune.* March 13. http://www.chicagotribune.com/sports/chicagoinc/ct-jay-cutler-chicago-inc-spt-0314-20170313-story.html.
n.d. *Totally History.* http://totallyhistory.com/jack-johnson/.
Tredinnick, Andrew. 2012. *Business Insider.* November 19. https://www.businessinsider.com/raymond-feltons-workout-habits-2012-11.
n.d. *Ultimate Albert Belle.* http://www.albertbelle.net/bio.php.
n.d. *University of Miami Sports Hall of Fame.* http://www.umsportshalloffame.com/sean-taylor.html.
Villamarzo, Andy. 2017. *Tampa Bay Times.* July 12. https://www.tampabay.com/sports/footballpreps/darren-hambrick-offers-skills-camp-in-lacoochee-this-weekend/2330004.
Walks, Matt. 2015. *ESPN.* July 18. http://www.espn.com/espn/story/_/page/instantawesome-KobeQuotes/wit-wisdom-words-kobe.
Wancho, Tom. n.d. *SABR.* https://sabr.org/bioproj/person/1d993b9b.
Waugh, Joan. n.d. *Miller Center.* https://millercenter.org/president/grant/domestic-affairs.
2019. *WDRB.* May 28. https://www.wdrb.com/news/education/rajon-rondo-donates-books-reading-space-to-academy-shawnee/article_8161e69a-818e-11e9-8e16-131797e1e8da.html.
White, Lonnie. 1988. *Los Angeles Times.* May 2. https://www.latimes.com/archives/la-xpm-1987-05-28-ga-3282-story.html.
Winton, Richard, and Katie Mather. 2013. *Los Angeles Times.* August 30. https://www.latimes.com/local/lanow/la-me-ln-lamar-odom-to-lose-driviers-license-after-dui-arrest-chp-says-20130830-story.html.
Wood, Allan. n.d. *SABR.* https://sabr.org/bioproj/person/9dcdd01c.

Wyshynski, Greg. 2018. *ESPN*. February 9. https://www.espn.com/nhl/story/_/id/22384286/former-nhl-player-dave-tiger-williams-charged-sexual-assault.

Zgoda, Jerry. 2018. *Star Tribune*. April 12. http://www.startribune.com/eighth-seeded-nba-playoff-teams-who-knocked-off-the-top-seed/479589273/.

Made in the USA
Middletown, DE
19 April 2022

64522094R00151